THE PSYCHOLOGY OF
COURAGE

JULIA YANG, ALAN MILLIREN, AND MARK BLAGEN

THE PSYCHOLOGY OF
COURAGE

An Adlerian
Handbook
for Healthy
Social Living

Routledge
Taylor & Francis Group
New York   London

On the Cover

The water lily is universally known as a symbol for courage, resilience, and tenacity. The pure and simple blossom, with a will of its own, unfolds in the mystic early morning. Taking root in muddy water, its stem is straight, easy to bend but difficult to break. The sacred meaning of the water lily does not stop in its beauty and humble upbringing. All parts of water lily are edible, giving back to life. Petals, roots, and seeds of the water lily are believed to have a soothing and cleansing effect when used either for cooking or medicine. Spiritually, the water lily represents cosmic harmony.

Routledge
Taylor & Francis Group
711 Third Avenue,
New York, NY 10017

Routledge
Taylor & Francis Group
27 Church Road,
Hove, East Sussex BN3 2FA, UK

First issued in paperback 2014

Routledge is an imprint of the Taylor and Francis Group, an informa business

© 2010 by Taylor and Francis Group, LLC

ISBN 978-0-415-96519-4 (hbk)
ISBN 978-1-138-88439-7 (pbk)

For permission to photocopy or use material electronically from this work, please access www.copyright.com (http://www.copyright.com/) or contact the Copyright Clearance Center, Inc. (CCC), 222 Rosewood Drive, Danvers, MA 01923, 978-750-8400. CCC is a not-for-profit organization that provides licenses and registration for a variety of users. For organizations that have been granted a photocopy license by the CCC, a separate system of payment has been arranged.

Trademark Notice: Product or corporate names may be trademarks or registered trademarks, and are used only for identification and explanation without intent to infringe.

Library of Congress Cataloging-in-Publication Data

Yang, Julia.
    The psychology of courage : an adlerian handbook for healthy social living / Julia Yang, Alan P. Milliren, Mark T. Blagen.
    p. cm.
  Includes bibliographical references and index.
  ISBN 978-0-415-96519-4 (hardcover : alk. paper)
    1. Courage. I. Milliren, Alan P. II. Blagen, Mark T. III. Title.

BF575.C8Y36 2009
150.19'53--dc22
                                                                                      2009001382

Visit the Taylor & Francis Web site at
http://www.taylorandfrancis.com

and the Routledge Web site at
http://www.routledgementalhealth.com

Contents

List of Figures	ix
List of Tables	xi
List of Socratic Dialogue Boxes	xiii
Foreword	xv
Preface	xvii
Acknowledgments	xxiii

Part I Foundation

1 What Is Courage?	3
The Psychology of Courage	4
InFEARority	5
Inferiority	6
Compensation	8
Corequisites of Courage	10
Courage as a Spiritual Concept	12
Courage Defined	14
Closing Thoughts	14
2 Community Feeling and Mental Health	17
What Is Social Interest?	17
Cooperation	19
Contribution	20
A Measure of Mental Health	21
The Horizontal Axis	22
The Vertical Axis	23

The Courage of Community Feeling	25
Closing Thoughts	26

3 Tasks of Life — 27
- Work, Love, and Social Relations: The Basic Tasks — 27
- Being and Belonging: The Existential Tasks — 28
- The Normative Ideal — 29
- The Evasion of Life Tasks — 31
- Closing Thoughts — 33

Part II The Courage of Social Living

4 The Courage to Work — 37
- What Is Work? — 37
- Individual Inferiority — 39
- Collective Inferiority — 41
- New Fear: Protean Career — 42
- Career Construction in Style — 44
- The Encouraged Worker — 46
- Work Is Sacred — 48
- Closing Thoughts — 51

5 The Courage to Love — 53
- What Is Love? — 53
- The Use and Misuses of Sex — 54
- The Myth of Romance — 55
- Problems of Love and Marriage — 57
- Same-Gender and Transgender Love — 59
- Training for the Love Task — 62
- The Perfect Love: *Agape* — 64
- Closing Thoughts — 65

6 The Courage for Friendship and Family — 67
- Understanding Friendship — 67
- Making Friends — 69
- Birth Order and Family Constellation — 70
- The Use of Children's Goal-Seeking Behaviors — 73
- Lifestyle Goal Seeking for Teens and Adults — 77
- Thoughts on Parenting — 78
- Closing Thoughts — 81

7 The Courage to Belong — 83
- Problems of Belonging — 83
- The Courage of Social Equality — 86
- Harmony: The Human Best and the Ideal Society — 89

Community Feeling at Work: The Courage of Recovery	92
Closing Thoughts	94

8 The Courage to Be 95
   The "No" Attitudes 95
   CHARACTERistics with the "Yes" Attitude 98
   The Use of Emotions 101
   The Use of the Neurotic Symptoms 104
   Living in Harmony with Oneself 107
   Affirmation and Ambivalence 109
   Closing Thoughts 111

9 The Courage to Spiritual Well-Being 113
   Spirituality as a Life Task 113
   Striving: The Courage to Overcome 115
   Pain and Suffering 116
   The Courage to Heal 118
   Courage and the Allied Spiritual Attitudes 121
   The Courage to Agape Love 123
   Closing Thoughts 125

Part III Implications

10 The Art of Facilitating Courage 129
   The Courage of the Facilitator 129
   Socratic Questioning 130
   The Use of Encouragement 131
   Facilitating Processes 134
      Relationship 135
      Psychological Investigation 135
      Psychological Disclosure 136
      Reorientation 137
   About the Tools for Facilitating Courage 138
   Tool #1: A Conversation Guide: Socratic Questioning 139
   Tool #2: Attitude Modification 142
   Tool #3: Birth Order 143
   Tool #4: Change in Harmony 145
   Tool #5: CHARACTERistics: Directed Reflection 147
   Tool #6: Constructive Ambivalence 149
   Tool #7: Courage Assessment 152
   Tool #8: Consultation With Parents and Teachers 154
   Tool #9: E-5 Group Session Guide 156
   Tool #10: En-COURAGE-ment 163
   Tool #11: Family Constellation in the Workplace 165

Tool #12: Goal Disclosure: The "Could It Be's" 166
Tool #13: Home Page 169
Tool #14: Hope Is a Choice 173
Tool #15: In Store: Eleven Seven 175
Tool #16: Lifestyle Interview: Variations 180
Tool #17: Lost or Stuck? 183
Tool #18: Most Memorable Moment 187
Tool #19: Recollecting Early Memories 189
Tool #20: Trust Only the Movement 192
Tool #21: Ups, Downs, and Side by Sides: Relationships of Equals 194
Tool #22: Walk the Line 196
Appendix 199

Epilogue 215

Notes 217
References 237
The Authors 247
Author Index 249
Subject Index 253

List of Figures

1.1	The Individual Psychology model of courage.	5
1.2	Felt minus to perceived plus.	7
2.1	Social interest as a measure of mental health.	21
3.1	Life task map.	30
6.1	Rachel's family constellation.	72
6.2	Active, passive, socially useless, and socially useful goals and behaviors.	78
7.1	Training for social equality.	87
8.1	Measuring social interest by cooperation and contribution.	100
8.2	Disjunctive emotions, rejection movement.	103
8.3	Conjunctive emotions, "move forward" words, encouraging movement.	103
9.1	The processes of healing.	120
10.1	Life movement and attitudes.	133
10.2	Components of facilitating change.	135
10.3	Balancing eight directions of change.	146
10.4	Affirmation coupon.	161
10.5	Nontangible gift certificate.	162
10.6	"Home" page.	171
10.7	Motivation scale.	194
10.8	Circle of courage.	197

List of Tables

5.1	Effects of Eros versus Agape on Love	57
5.2	Effects of Eros and Agape on Marriage	59
6.1	Effects of Eros Love and Agape Love on Friendship	70
6.2	Children's Goals and Misbehaviors	74
6.3	Parents' Efficient and Mistaken Methods of Training	76
6.4	Effects of Eros and Agape on Family	81
6.5	Autocratic and Democratic Methods of Parenting	82
8.1	CHARACTERistics: The "Yes" Attitudes	101
8.2	Patterns of Neurotic Traits	107
9.1	Causes and Elimination of Suffering	117
9.2	Characteristics of Agape Love in Social Relationships	124
10.1	Sample Socratic Questions by Life Tasks	132
10.2	Psychological Investigation Tools	136
10.3	Life Goal, Direction of Change, and Balance Worksheet	147
10.4	Aspects of Courage Worksheet	153
10.5	Strength and Stress Responses of Pooh Bear and Friends	166
10.6	Hope Worksheet #1-2	174

10.7 Summary of Early Recollections and School Days	192
10.8 From Felt Minus to Perceived Plus	193
10.9 Stages of Relationships	195
10.10 Problems as Opportunities	198
A10.1 Replacing Negative Attitudes with Positive Attitudes	199
A10.2 Components of Character and Examples of Directed Reflections	203
A10.3 Twelve Roadblocks to Communication	210
A10.4 Hope Worksheet #2-2	213

List of Socratic Dialogue Boxes

Socratic Dialogue 4.1	38
Socratic Dialogue 4.2	40
Socratic Dialogue 4.3	42
Socratic Dialogue 4.4	43
Socratic Dialogue 4.5	45
Socratic Dialogue 4.6	46
Socratic Dialogue 4.7	48
Socratic Dialogue 4.8	50
Socratic Dialogue 5.1	55
Socratic Dialogue 5.2	56
Socratic Dialogue 5.3	60
Socratic Dialogue 5.4	62
Socratic Dialogue 5.5	63
Socratic Dialogue 6.1	70
Socratic Dialogue 6.2	73
Socratic Dialogue 6.3	73
Socratic Dialogue 6.4	77

Socratic Dialogue 6.5	78
Socratic Dialogue 7.1	85
Socratic Dialogue 7.2	88
Socratic Dialogue 7.3	89
Socratic Dialogue 8.1	100
Socratic Dialogue 8.2	104
Socratic Dialogue 8.3	109
Socratic Dialogue 9.1	114
Socratic Dialogue 9.2	121

Foreword

It is easier to fight for one's principles than to live up to them.

—**Alfred Adler**

I once heard that "truly courageous people choose to endure the fearful for the sake of the good." I thought of this passage while traveling in Asia with Drs. Julia Yang and Al Milliren. I recall being among the featured speakers at a conference being held at the National Hsinchu University of Education in Taiwan. There was a panel consisting of professionals from the United States and Taiwan including Julia, Al, and myself. I was listening to Julia talk fluently in English and then in Chinese, holding the audience's total attention. I thought of how she was raised in this culture before receiving her graduate education in the United States. She lectures with great effectiveness and provides social justice in both cultures. I thought about her level of courage at leaving the security of her home culture (as well as the financial security of a tenured professorship) and journeying to a new country as a single mother with two young children.

Al was in the chair next to her. He had just made the long flight from the United States followed by a round-trip train to the southern end of the island. It was only a few days prior that Al received medical clearance to make this trip. He was fully alive; the wheelchair that accompanied him was seldom unfolded. Al was once a tenured full professor with a comfortable lifestyle. Al gave up comfort in the pursuit of helping others to learn the gifts that Adler provided. Al has the courage to pursue his calling and not comfort. He chooses to live his life by his values in spite of the "temptations, sideshows, and shortcuts" that trap many of us.

There is a direct connection between courage and acting in a socially responsible fashion. This is what the Adlerians refer to as *social interest*. Those with courage cooperate with others and are committed to social justice. Those lacking courage (or discouraged) are engaged in dysfunctional living. Having courage leads to the ability to address the life tasks of work, love, and friendship.

In this book, Julia and Al along with Mark Blagen write about courage or what has been referred to as "psychological muscle." This is material that they know firsthand. This book is about what the title states—courage. The authors provide a clear theoretical foundation via Adlerian or Individual Psychology. This approach stresses the "indivisible" nature of the human character and the holistic nature of life. The authors highlight how to master the five life tasks needed to create a good life and provide 22 tools for the facilitation of courage. I especially like the Socratic questions placed throughout the text. In truth, this is less of a book and more of a manual on healthy living. I hope readers have the courage to read this book and the courage to use the "tools" to create a satisfying life. I remind the reader of Adler's statement: "Mistakes in business and science are costly and deplorable, but mistakes in the way we live our lives may endanger life itself." Paraphrasing *Star Wars*, "May courage be with you!"

Jon Carlson, PsyD, EdD
Distinguished Professor of Psychology & Counseling
Governors State University

Preface

> We must understand that courage is a social function, because only the person who considers himself [or herself] as part of the whole can have courage. We find courage when a person feels at home, when he [or she] does not consider merely the acceptable part of life as belonging to him [or her], but also the unacceptable things; who accepts the difficulties in our culture as a task on which he [or she] has to work to improve the situation for all.
>
> —**Alfred Adler (1870–1937)**[1]

Why a book on courage? Why write another book about better living when so many have already been written? What do we know about a good life? Is it attainable? How do we get there? What is courage? How do we acquire and give courage? How can psychology help us along our quest for courage while we face the many demands of living?

From Apathy to Hostility

Existentialist philosophers and psychologists have called the problems of the 20th century *apathy*. People who were overwhelmed by fears and anxiety escaped into a state of feelinglessness (*affectless*) space and were unable to *affect* the world around them. These themes of attitudes of "mind your own business" and "it doesn't matter" have endured into the 21st century when the quiet, depressive apathy has turned into *hostility* toward self and others. Many decades ago, Rudolf Dreikurs described a rather gloomy picture of how people live:

Man, who has learned so much, still does not know some of the fundamental requirements of social living. He cannot live at peace within his family; nor does he know how to raise his children. He cannot enjoy his life without intoxication, without rushing madly to acquire, to accomplish, to get somewhere. Unselfish love has become a lost art; faith in anything, an outdated notion; relation, an idle dream.[2]

Problems of living today seem worse now than ever as fears dictate our thoughts, feelings, and actions at home, school, and work, and in our society. At the turn of the new millennium, the outburst of public offenses and acts of destruction locally and globally have us convinced that we are no way prepared to live in a world where we no longer feel safe. Needless to say, the goal of living a happy life seems unattainable to us.

Furthermore, we now live in an individualistic and materialistic society where there is much ambiguity and ambivalence in how we respond to established ethics and values. We also live in an era when we have lost the access to a communal support system for our development and adjustment.[3] We have to do it all alone. In emotional and social isolation, we operate from fear.

Our need for predictability and control in our social relationships is stripping away our natural ability to accept life as it is. Individuals who strive for a good life with all good intentions fall prey to the need to compete and compare. Competing and comparing harbors destructive feelings as we realize that life is not perfect. The assumption and assertion of our right for happiness is directly related to the prevalent cultural phenomenon of me-centeredness.

From Fear to Courage

The discussion of courage of social living is necessary as we face the challenges of fostering individual well-being and creating a better world that encourages a sense of belonging and significance for all. Courage has generally been overlooked in the psychological literature. The 20th century was also designated as the *century of fear* and as the *century of psychology* following the previous centuries of science.[4] Birthed in a confusing time where the premodern communal values were replaced by values in science, psychology did not escape the dominance of materialism and individualism in the last century. It had hoped but failed to promote *care*. On the contrary, psychology has taken much more interest in the analysis of fear rather than cultivating its counterpart, courage.

Mental health is not the absence of mental illness. It is not enough for psychology to point only to the presence or absence of disease. We are more resilient than most of the psychological theories are willing to describe. Health is best expressed by our optimal coping and development even in the face of adverse living conditions. Individual health and public health may be better looked at as a construct for happiness or characteristics that empower the individual to pursue happiness. Psychology, therefore, must recognize and embrace the values that promote and prepare the individual to undertake the problems of living. In the 21st century, we are charged with the courage to care. We need a psychology that can help us face fears, overcome our inadequacies, care for one another, endure suffering with courage and hope, and live in harmony with oneself, family, community, and humankind.

Community Feeling: The Cure of Apathy

> Of particular significance in the course of my examinations, was finding the importance extending over the entire lifespan of overcoming, of the onset of difficulties. This seems to lead to an apparent paradox that perhaps great achievements regularly come from courageously overcoming obstacles, and are not a consequence of original aptitude, but rather the absence of aptitude.
>
> —Alfred Adler[5]

To Alfred Adler, the answer to apathy is our innate aptitude and training for community feeling, the core concept of Individual Psychology. The road to happiness (or better put, the meaning of life) is the courage for community feeling. The criterion for the healthy social living, for Adler, was the extent to which the individual experiences belonging via contribution and cooperation. The feeling of community can inspire and prepare us to face life problems with courage and to take responsibility for ourselves and others.[6]

Adler's psychology is often called Individual Psychology. The Greek origin of the term *individual* refers to the unique individuality of the individuals. Adlerian psychology is, however, not the opposite of its name but is a social psychology emphasizing expansion of the individual and the enhancement of community feeling or social interest. Individual Psychology operates from the following principles.

1. We are social beings. The meaning of life is to achieve belonging and significance via cooperation and contribution in the interest of our fellow humankind.
2. All behaviors have a purpose of achieving social significance and belonging.

3. We are whole beings (i.e., thinking, feeling, and acting); all aspects of life are inseparable (i.e., work, love, friendship/family/community, harmony with self and others).
4. We make meaning of our early experiences and act within this framework throughout our lives.
5. Life is movement. We are endowed with creative power to overcome, compensate, and strive toward a guiding goal of perfection.
6. Perfection is fiction. When we strive for perfection we are bound to experience problems of overcompensation or undercompensation.
7. Equality presupposes belongingness. Problems of living stem from the individual inferiority as well as collective inferiority.
8. Courage and social interest are universal values, which are both the ends and means of personal and social well-being.
9. Personal freedoms exist together with social responsibility.
10. Happiness is the goal of global humanity. It is attainable when individuals and societies recognize the strengths from within and without that cultivate the courage of social living.

Global Humanity

Neither courage nor community feeling is a new concept. As virtues, they are permeated in cultural and spiritual traditions of the West as well as the East. When regarded as virtues and ethics of social ideal, community feeling is comparable to agape in Christian spirituality, *ren* in Confucianism, harmony of the Taoist thoughts, and transcendental wisdom of Buddhist Zen. When regarded as character traits in the individual, community feeling is accomplished with courage and its corequisite attitudes that are socially useful for us and others. We share Adler's hope and positivism that these attitudes or character traits are both innate aptitudes and abilities we develop via family, school, and other life settings. Individual Psychology is the only psychology that enables the understanding and development of virtues from the intrapersonal and interpersonal as well as extrapersonal perspectives.

Individual Psychology offers the most amendable framework that is open to a collaborative understanding of what courage is and how we may use courage to enhance our social living. Adler is recognized for his views of social equality for women and children. He is regarded as the father of self-help and self-psychology, and the forerunner for cognitive, existential, humanistic, and positive psychology.[7] Adler has been compared to Confucius in the East and Socrates in the West. Adler's thoughts of community and self-help deeply influenced the cofounder of Alcoholics Anonymous and its practices.[8] Such interconnectedness allows us a wonderful opportunity to develop and compile cross culturally applicable tools by which we can uncover our strengths and train for courage.

Organization of the Book

In this book, we have organized our writings into three parts. Part I, "Foundation," contains three conceptual chapters. In Chapter 1, courage is defined based on the Individual Psychology principles. In Chapter 2, we focus on the definition components of social interest that lead to a measurement model of mental health. Chapter 3, though a continuing conceptual chapter, also serves as the introduction to Part II, "The Courage of Social Living," where we elaborate on each of the life tasks originally postulated by Adler and later added by his followers.

In Chapters 4 to 7 we will discuss the courage to work, love, and participate in social relations that we call basic life tasks for this book. The love task means the task of intimacy between two adults.[9] The topic of the friendship/family/community task (what Adler originally called the "society task") is broad and is arranged into Chapters 6 and 7. We named Chapter 7 "The Courage to Belong" with a focus on the psychosocial aspect of community living. In Chapters 8 and 9 we approach the existential tasks of getting along with oneself and the universe from the existential-spiritual perspective. Chapter 8, "The Courage to Be," covers the task of being in harmony with self. In Chapter 9 we refer to the task of being in harmony with the universe as the task of spiritual well-being that is related to the idea of cosmic social interest or spiritual belonging.

In each chapter of Part II, we explore the meaning of each life task, problems of fear, and compensation or evasion, as well as Adlerian insight on socially useful attitudes of approaching the task under discussion. To better illustrate the challenges of each task, we included many short reflections and narratives from many individuals we interviewed.[10] We also used Socratic dialogue boxes throughout the chapters to encourage interactivity between the text and readers' thought processes.

Part III, "Implications," contains 22 helping tools. Chapter 10, "The Art of Facilitating Courage," pertains mainly to the several overarching concepts about the use of these tools: Socratic questions, encouragement, and components of facilitation. The helping tools are based on Adlerian techniques of psychological investigation, such as early recollection, family constellation, and life style assessment. They are creatively designed for our readers to use for self-exercise or for helping others to uncover or acquire courage. The readers may find that there are many ways of using these materials that are cross-referenced with the readings in Part I and Part II of the book. We believe that courage and community feeling are transcultural concepts that are actually teachable and hope this handbook may also be used in training in academic or practice settings.

To make sure that we correctly convey Individual Psychology and its applicability in our contemporary living, we based our writing mostly on the classical works of Adler and some of his followers, but sought to affirm our ideas in consultation with our fellow Adlerians via literature or personal communication. To make the reading both inviting and sensible, we decided to put all our citations and scholarly speculations in the Notes chapter at the end of the book. We believe that the chapter notes represent further inquiry opportunities for those readers who aspire an in-depth understanding and study of Adler and how his psychology embraces contemporary schools of thoughts in our field.

Closing Thoughts

Adler regarded his psychology as common sense for common people. We wrote this handbook with the conviction that happiness is attainable when we courageously love, work, and achieve harmonious relationships with ourselves, others, and the world.

We hope, in times where hostility and apathy seem to reign, both our fellow professionals and other readers will find the information and tools in this handbook useful in uncovering and facilitating courage. Ultimately, we hope that this handbook provides a convenient roadmap that is capable of guiding us to the goal of healthy social living for all.

Acknowledgments

When we love, we are in God's heart.

—**Kahlil Gibran**

Believe it or not, we experienced many fears while writing this book on courage! This project took on a life of its own, expressing itself in ways that were in contrast with our accustomed academic style of writing, and the more we wrote, the more we realized that we had so much more to learn. We risked it anyway and so we would like to first thank our readers who share with us in the courage of imperfection.

Thanks go to Jon Carlson who saw the value of the subject and was most instrumental in connecting us to our publisher. Georgia, Debra, David H., Mario, Ms. V., and Jon R. provided us with much practical assistance with our interviews, video/audio recording, and transcription. We are also greatly indebted to Dana Bliss (our editor) for his extreme patience and frequent generous affirmations even though our progress and completion was delayed. We must also thank Chris Tominich, also from Routledge, for his hard work on the production.

Many thoughts in this book were not original. We owe thanks to our friends (e.g., West W., Dan E., Richard W., and Erik M.) in the Adlerian circle and the many classical writers from both the West and the East. Special gratitude goes to Michelle A., Shannon D., Gina G., David L., Cinthie C., Georgia S., Donna S., Mary W., and Monica W. who made great contributions with their reflective writings. We especially thank the individuals who taught us the many faces of courage and allowed us to share their true life stories.

This book was truly a community project as the authors traveled far and deep around the world in various space and time. The actual writing began virtually in the shadow of snow-covered Mount Blanca in Colorado. Major concepts and many of the tools of facilitating courage were developed or refined based on the participants' input when we taught and conducted workshops in the United States, Taiwan, China, and Slovakia. Support and encouragement from counseling faculty, students, and staff at Governors State University and National Hing Chu University of Education in Taiwan were invaluable in the completion of this book.

We are forever grateful to our family and friends whose presence inspired us to see the fabric of God's love. Writing in her second language was not without struggle for Julia. She is forever grateful for her son, Alan Lin, who took a summer to correct his mother's Chinese English while fully understanding and respecting her original thoughts. She also holds so close to her heart her daughter, Joy Lin, who managed the last months of her senior year in high school when Mom was an ocean away writing and fulfilling her sabbatical leave responsibilities. Thanks to Lao Lao, a soul mate, who took leave from her graduate studies to be with Joy in Julia's absence. Many hugs go to Max, X, and Sidney who loyally kept Julia in good company at her feet when she was in need of the courage to write.

The book is only made possible by the love that is manifested in the very special relationships the authors have with one another. Julia was a graduate student of Al's at Illinois State University. Many of the books cited were graduation gifts from Al who knew the needs and aspiration of his student. Al often took her along when he drove three hours to visit the Chicago Adlerian Institute (now the Adler Professional School of Psychology in Chicago). Julia remembers then how the noise of the Chicago Transit Authority train outside the window could never compete with the wonder of the open family forum interactions Al and other Adlerians were facilitating. A quarter century later, Julia continues to marvel at Al's ever-renewing art of Socratic questioning, live demonstrations, and scripting. Many of the tools included in the book are actual records of Al's work that would not have been otherwise accessible to our readers.

Mark's discovery of Adler's influence on Bill W., a cofounder of Alcoholics Anonymous, brought to life how community and unconditional love work to transform one's pain and doubts into healing and recovery. In the midst of despair of losing his wife to cancer, Mark chose life and provided a most authentic narrative of hope for the book. As a coauthor, Mark tirelessly offered critique and encouragement that gave Julia much confidence. As we embarked on the process of writing, Julia and Mark began sharing a new adventure. They celebrated their wedding on March 28, 2009. They attribute this union to God who binds them in His majestic love. With courage, the beauty of imagining and living life to its fullest potential is infinite!!

Turn the page with us. Life is good!

PART I
Foundation

CHAPTER 1

What Is Courage?

I think courage is walking into a building that you know could collapse at any minute, to try to save others.

> —A witness to the 2001 World Trade Center towers tragedy
> (From Phillips, 2004)

Henry, the boy with an operable cancer who feels fortunate just to have been alive. He lives every moment as fully as he can. Henry has so much dignity in the face of death.

> —From Phillips, 2004[1]

As a classroom teacher in an urban, poverty-stricken, school district, I encounter courage on a daily basis. Sometimes it is in witnessing a single mother with 3–4 children who is struggling to make ends meet while not allowing her little ones to experience anything but the love she has to offer. Other times courage radiates from the first grader who has trusted her teacher enough to tell her that somebody is beating her at home. Courage is strength from within, but from the outside—observing it, courage is simply awe-inspiring.

> —Gina

Stories of courage exist in the heroes of history as well as in common people in our everyday life. Courage can be a virtue, a state of mind, an attitude, an emotion, a force, or an action. Establishing a psychology of courage is difficult, however.[2] When we encounter obstacles and fears, we do not know whether courage is best manifested in overt overcoming or in covert endurance, in confrontation or in persevering and suffering. Hard work toward self-actualization does not qualify one to be courageous, but hard work toward overcoming pain and fear does.[3] What seems plausible for one gender as courageous behavior may seem inappropriate for the other. Courage certainly means many things for individuals, families, and communities as depicted by various cultural and spiritual traditions.

The Psychology of Courage

Courage, simply put, refers to a willingness for risk taking and movement forward in the presence of difficulties. When we ask a question, such as what is courage, we also ask the questions of courage for what purpose and for and to whom our courage is directed. Courage finds its expressions in our thoughts, feelings, and actions. We cannot help but notice that the acts of courage are characterized by selflessness and other directedness. Courage is an intrinsic life force that allows us to recognize the goal of the common goodness as we seek our own actualization.

In this book, we hope to approach the conceptual understanding and the use of courage from the vantage point of Individual Psychology. Courage, as a psychological construct, is best addressed in Adler's positive, phenomenological, and pragmatic approach of understanding human nature, family influence, and our characteristic approach to meet the life demands of work, love, and society.

Adler was the pioneer to the systems thinking that we are only part of the whole and, thus, life is never perfect for the individual. The discouraged individual operates from the fear of failure, and lacks acceptance and courage for imperfection. The discouraged individual resorts to an exaggerated feeling of inferiority that propels his/her excessive attempts to strive toward success by overcompensation or self-preservation or by undercompensation or evasion in some or all life tasks (see Figure 1.1).

We believe that Adler's mature theory is the psychology of courage that provides us the best roadmap by which the virtue of courage and its corequisite characters become teachable. As illustrated in Figure 1.1, we approach the basic life tasks of work, love, and society (family/friendship), and the existential tasks of being (harmony with self) and belonging (via equality and harmony with the universe) as they are relational and have to do with our attitudes toward living that we acquired in our early social living. Our fear of rejection and failure is the root of all problems. Comparison and competition is our typical coping method in the home, at school, and at work. The answer to these difficulties is courage. Change is possible when we modify our attitude of self-interest to social interest by the courage to cooperate and to contribute.

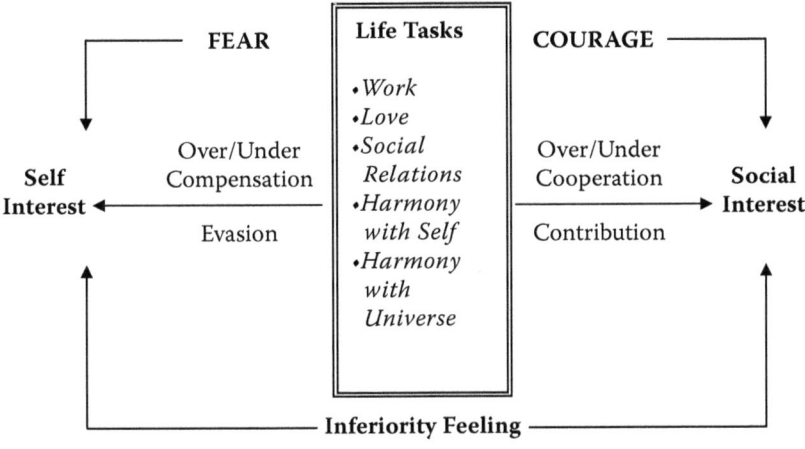

Figure 1.1 The Individual Psychology model of courage. Copyright 2008 by Julia Yang.

InFEARority

Courage is not the absence of despair; it is rather, the capacity to move ahead in spite of despair.[4]

A commonality exists in the various definitions of courage discussed in the philosophic, military, and religious literature. That is, adversarial conditions must be present prior to the occurrence of courage. Courage is a response to danger, despair, or fear. *Fear* is central to courage; it must be present for courage to exist.[5] When we sense danger, fear takes us immediately to the need of self-preservation. As a response to danger, fear functions like an alarm system with the goal of protection. Fear is a gift when it, in working with our intuition, serves as a signal to our survival.[6]

Our fear is heightened when we encounter the world around us, the world with us, and the world within us. We fear rejection, failure, and mistakes. We are afraid of what others may think of us and, therefore, we are afraid to be ourselves. We are afraid of death and, therefore, we live in fear. Fear is finding a lump where there should not be a lump. We are afraid of loss and change. Fear is a device we use to bridge between our past and the unknown future. Fear follows us just like a shadow follows everything under the sun.

Fear is basic, normal, and necessary until it grows larger than our danger. In that case, fear becomes *anxiety*. Fear provoked by tangible situations or unidentifiable reasons is mostly faceless, lurking within us when least expected. Unfounded fear, however, can exercise its power over us and become worry or anxiety. Anxiety strips away our freedom and isolates us from the ironically intimidating world. Unlike fear, anxiety lacks identifiable sources and it arises from being torn between our expectations and the discrepant realities. Existentially, fear is about our ultimate death and its manifestations in our feelings of doubt and meaninglessness in the midst of our everyday living.[7]

In Individual Psychology, fear is more than an emotion. Fear serves a purpose for those who feel inferior and incapable of meeting the demands of the world. Fear can be used as hidden hostility that disguises an individual's choice of negating contribution or not moving forward to his other responsibility for self and others. Adler used fear and anxiety interchangeably. Adler saw anxiety as the apprehension of social living. Anxiety is the manifestation of the striving of those with incomplete feelings (inferiority) to their goal of completion (superiority), although such striving takes them further away from their desire to connect to the society to which they wish to belong.

> The new goal [prevention of a visible or felt defeat] presents a new form of life in sharply delineated features. Since due to fear of failure everything must remain unfinished, all striving and movement turn into pseudo-activity which, at least on balance, takes place on the useless side.[8]

When we operate from fear, we allow fear to dominate our thoughts, feelings, and actions. We often respond to fears with what would lead to a momentary sense of okayness or control within ourselves or with others. Deep down, we know we compromise who we are, and our true desires and needs are not met. When fear outweighs our problem, it makes our development and adjustment challenging as we relate to ourselves and the world. When we are constant captives of fear, we become restricted and blind to the world and what it can offer. It can take away our vitality and vision. Fear can stop our forward movement. Fear can hinder our sense of being and belonging. In our extreme fear, hostility toward self and the other (instead of harmony) becomes the prevalent way of response to conflict. In our inFEARority, living becomes helpless, hopeless, and meaningless. In our fears of defeat or not making it, we feel inferior.

Inferiority

Biologically speaking, we were all born feeling small, dependent, and helpless. Whereas the physical inferiority may be realistic, the psychological feeing of inferiority is acquired as we began to interact with our caretakers, siblings, and, later in our formative years, playmates and peers in home and school. Although true inferiority should exist only in a physical sense, our feeling of inferiority is mostly our subjective and evaluative perceptions that influence our behaviors and feelings. A sense of being "less than" or in a "minus" position may lead the individual to either a universal feeling of inferiority or an exaggerated inferiority complex.[9] The inferiority feeling exists not only individually, but also collectively and spiritually. Our sense of belonging is deeply hindered when the feeling of less than is joined by the presence of social inequalities and an absence of meaning of life or spiritual connection.

Fear and inferiority work to either propel us for socially useful action or lead us to the feeling of inadequacy. Inadequacies are safeguarding devices that deprive us from our freedom and responsibilities of living. Instead of contributing to the *main tent* of community life, fear and inferiority encourages us to create *sideshow* activities that distant ourselves from resolving the problems of love, work, and friendship.

We respond to the inferior feeling with a natural desire to strive from the *felt minus* or our feeling of being less than to our private sense of superiority or *perceived plus* (Figure 1.2). This psychological movement is motivated by our innate creative power that manifests itself in our adoption of behavior strategies and emotions, and safeguards devices for self-preservation. This creative power gives us individual uniqueness while it generates the goal

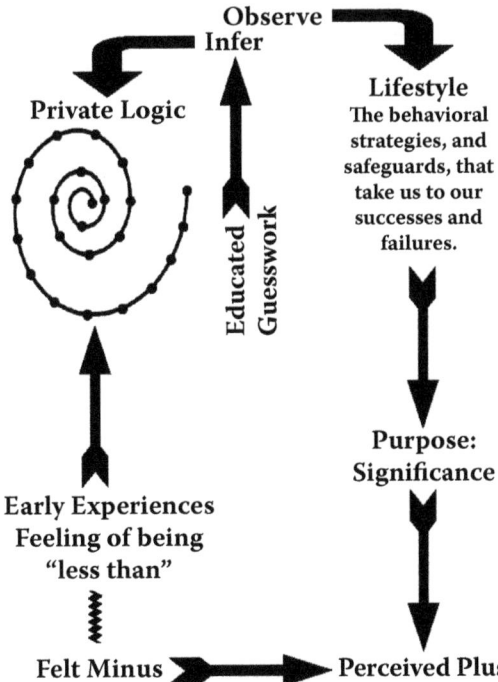

Figure 1.2 Felt minus to perceived plus. Copyright 2005 by Al Milliren.

in response to our environment and, thus, takes us to success or failure. In addition, it privately moves us from the felt imperfection toward perceived perfection or a sense of purpose/significance/belongingness. The creative power of each individual generates movement toward unique life goals that were established early in life. In this movement, our emotions, thoughts, and behaviors are consistent with our private logic as well as our life plan (also see the discussion of striving in Chapter 9).

According to Adler, we live in our mental world in a particular style. Our memory, perception, emotions, imagination, and dreams all convey the individual unity and uniqueness of how we think, feel, and act. He named this unity *life style*. Life style, therefore, is "the totality of the behavioral strategies and safeguards that take us to our successes and failures."[10]

Our life style allows us to use our experiences differently as we assimilate impressions, accept or reject challenges, decide on our subjective understanding, and evaluate how to be the best in our social life. It is "a guide, a limiter, and a predictor."[11] Our fear-driven inferiority (or superiority) is manifested in our life style by which we make use of our circumstances as our creative power creates obstacles as well as options as we cope with life demands.

> The behavior of the entire great life movement ... is a striving from incompletion to completion. Accordingly, the entire individual life line has the tendency to overcoming, a striving for superiority.[12]

Our life style is a cognitive map of how we creatively move from the feelings of being less than to the goal of better than. As fear is manifested in inferiority, courage is present as the creative power that motivates the individual's movement toward the chosen goal. The timid or safeguarding individual often meets challenges with blaming, wishful thinking, self-centering, double mindedness, competition, fictional life goals, and other methods that create a need for undue attention, power struggles, revenge, or depression. On the contrary, the profile of a courageous individual is characterized by the absence of self-serving interest, safeguards, exploitation, and superioritty, and the presence of aesthetics, agape, altruism, courage, hope, empathy, meaning, endurance, movement, stillness, coherence, encouragement, reconciliation, wholeness, regeneration, and social connectedness.

Compensation

The threat to our courage comes largely from our lack of preparedness, which is masked as our fear. The fundamental problem for an individual lacking courage is the fear of making mistakes. Our discouraged or less than feeling becomes worse when it is interlocked with a society that is mistake centered. It seems as though the harder we try to be good, or better than, the worse our problems will become. Our fear is mostly guided by the fictional goal of perfection and the sense of superiority as *compensation* in response to our feeling of inferiority even when we are motivated by the desire to be useful.

There can be positive effects from obstacles if one looks at self-development as a process. Our creative power is the motivating force that helps us gear our inferior feelings into our compensatory self-ideal. The compensation processes are attempts to overcome felt minus. Our compensatory striving is the motivating force that brings our movement toward the self-ideal. As we imagine this ideal differently, our innate striving for perfection may either lead to defeat or a sense of social belonging and significance. Hitler is a classic example of the former, whereas Edison, Helen Keller, and Beethoven are known to have transcended their physical limitations with exceptional gifts.

In the compensating process, our fears of not making it, not being good enough, or rejection often become disguised by our creative goals that guide our thoughts, feelings, and actions. For example, lacking the courage for imperfection, we naturally adopt the compensating desire to be perfect (e.g., being the favorite child seeking recognition and approval with socially praised behaviors). When this ultimate desire is not fulfilled, our striving may change its course by defying authority and power or seeking other immediate goals less approved by society.

Another way to look at compensation is to consider that our basic tasks of living (i.e., work, love, and friendship/family) are not really separable, but we may excel on some areas but not others. Our satisfaction in one task area may be used to compensate for failure in another. In a capitalistic society where work, individual identity, and achievement are stressed, we see more dissatisfaction at home. This imbalance is readily seen with the differential emphasis society exercises on men and women at work and home.

Social usefulness and a sense of balance/harmony are criteria of good and bad compensations.[13] Bad compensation refers to our tendency to overcompensate or undercompensate in one or all life task areas. Overcompensation usually leads to an immediate heightening of the ego feeling such as arrogance and pride, whereas undercompensation allows us to evade responsibilities with feelings of helplessness and hopelessness. Bad compensation devices provide us with a make-believe security and produce an immediate but subjective sense of power that gives away signs of a lack of courage for individuals who sidestep to useless or false compensation based on a fictional goal and psychological camouflage. They are cowardly in a social sense and their life style leads them to a deep sense of isolation.

On the other hand, our choice of socially useful activities defines good compensations that transform our perceived liabilities to assets such as social responsibility, closer contact with humanity, acceptance and conquest of difficulties, and social courage. Activities of good compensation lead, secondarily, to a sense of power, to social esteem, and to security. We can achieve social significance with useful attitudes that reflect the courage of self-affirmation and the courage of participation in spite of difficulties as we meet the life demands of work, love, and social relations. To Adler, courage is a precondition to real cooperation by which we may move from the useless side to the useful side of adjustment to face life tasks, to risk mistakes, and to feel the sense of belonging. A lack of courage, in contrast, breeds feelings of inferiority, pessimism, avoidance, and misbehaviors.

> Only those are able to muster the courage to advance on the useful side who consider themselves a part of the whole, who are at home on this earth and in this mankind.[14]

Our problems are expressions of how we respond to external life situations or our attitudes toward tasks of living. The individual strives to overcome problems either by the commonly useless (neurotic compensation) or the commonly useful (good compensation) methods. When individuals perceive that there is incongruity in their style of living and the demands of society, they are faced with a choice. They must decide whether to safeguard themselves fearing the revelation of inadequacies, or to follow the natural tendency to interconnect with others and consider learning to live in harmony with self and society. The choice is really based on "a question of more or less courage."[15]

Corequisites of Courage

Courage is the answer to fear and, therefore, to inferiority as well. We need courage to meet the demands of life. However, courage does not equate to fearlessness and it does not make fear disappear. Courage also takes a strong sense of who we are and who we want to be when the going gets difficult. Courage is perseverance in the face of fear, requiring intelligence, patience, and endurance. Courage has many allied characters that allow us to evaluate risk, acquire skills, and solve problems.

It is practical wisdom that differentiates true courage from the semblances of courageous acts. What we see in those who fail to recognize danger, possess unrealistic optimism, and make fear-based assessments of the situation are only semblances of courage. Truly courageous people choose to endure the fearful for the sake of the good, but people displaying the semblance of courage are merely focused on the perceived advantage or what they fear to lose the most.[16] In the presence of fear or despair, true courage requires a careful evaluation of the situation and is mutually informed by a person's feeling of compassion and the expression of confidence. Even though the act of courage is reflective of an internal goal, it always results in incommensurable good for others.

An evaluative attitude is therefore necessary for true courage. Cognitively, courage is a construct closely related to confidence. "Confidence is only where there is courage."[17] Our perceived confidence and displayed behaviors are expressions of our courage to strive. This rational aspect of courage can be observed when we ask such questions as to whom our striving is directed and for whom the courageous act will bring advantages.

Courage is an important element to the Confucius' ideal of *ren* (benevolence, compassion toward humankind), which finds its counterpart in Adlerian psychology: *social interest*. The feeling of *ren* applies to all men and women and guides all of our actions. In Confucius' teaching, courage is preceded by benevolence and intelligent awareness. Courage can be despised if practiced without other accompanying strengths such as ritual, love of learning, and a sense of rightness in order to keep it from producing unruliness.

> A gentleman who possessed courage but lacked a sense of rightness would create political disorder, while a common person who possessed courage but lacked a sense of rightness would become a bandit.
>
> What you do not want done to yourself, do not do unto others.
>
> The injuries done to you by an enemy should be returned with a combination of love and justice.[18]

The value of courage depends not only on our evaluated goals and directions, but also on an affectionate sentiment we have toward others. This is seen in the courage stories where individuals choose self-sacrifice with honesty and integrity. The passion aspect of courage parallels the concept of *agape* (unconditional love), which is the common denominator to the world religions as well as humanist psychologies. In Individual Psychology, humans strive after a goal of perfection not only for oneself, but also for the whole mankind.

> One concretization of the idea of perfection, the highest image of greatness and superiority, which has always been very natural for man's thinking and feeling, is the contemplation of a deity. To strive towards God, to be in Him, to follow His call, to be one with Him— from this goal of striving (not of a drive), there follow attitude, thinking, and feeling.[19]

Adler was often regarded as Confucius of the West.[20] His concept of community feeling shares a focus on moral quality with Eastern practical wisdom and passion, portraying the ideal individual ethical behaviors for society. Overall, courage can be seen in the individuals whose characteristic attitudes toward life are optimistic, creative, and prepared to cooperate and contribute for the benefit of other people. Lack of courage and social feeling, on the other hand, accounts for all failures in social life. Courage is often seen in the development of a well-adjusted individual who possesses a sense of social interest. Within this feeling, he/she is affirmed with self-worth and willingness to participate in social living.

Courage as a Spiritual Concept

Courage was recently defined by the positive psychologists as "emotional strengths that involve the exercise of will to accomplish goals in the face of opposition, external or internal."[21] Although still not easily understood, courage can be best observed with additional character strengths such as bravery (valor), perseverance (industriousness), integrity (authenticity, honesty), and vitality (zest, enthusiasm, vigor, energy). Courage, seen as the warrior fortitude, often implies the use of willpower to choose between one's moral belief and physical sacrifice.

This personal willfulness is not to be mistaken as the existential concept of the *will to power* that is mostly concerned about our spiritual affirmation in the cosmos, a topic we will elaborate on in Chapter 9. To Adlerians, all human striving originates from a sense of inferiority that propels our striving for will to power to make belief.[22] Adler discussed Nietzsche's concept of will to power as the root to his theory of the guiding fiction in relation to the striving for superiority as a compensatory response to inferiority. To Adler, the will to power is a process of creative energy or a psychological force desiring to exert one's will in overcoming life problems. It leads us to either normal self-enhancement in the interest of others, or a safeguarding tendency endlessly striving for perfection. This goal of self-ideal is also understood as superiority. Adler also put this willingness to act into a social context: "But only the activity of an individual, who plays the game, cooperates and shares in life can be designated as courageous."[23]

The will to power, as a cosmic inner force that animates our existence, provides the ground for us to speculate that courage is indeed a spiritual concept. Similar to the existential thoughts of the will to power, Herbert Gardiner Lord, a philosopher in the early 20th century, described courage as various kinds of *pushes*. We have an inborn tendency (push) to override difficulties, and when we encounter resistance (without fear), this push becomes more forceful. Especially when obstructions occur and fear or other emotions arise, we push back harder to overcome them. These pushes can be biological mechanisms or social masterfulness.[24]

Higher forms of courage can be found with sentiments for comrades, compassion for justice, and a sense of self-regard. In fact, the ultimate courage is rested on one's belief and faith. In Western philosophy such as that postulated by Aquinas, courage is a virtue that makes the mind competent to endure any danger. The role of courage is the manifestation of the gift of the Holy Spirit by which courage gets the resources of making us confident of escaping each and every danger. In this sense, we are participating in the relationship with God that grants courage as a part of the agape love.[25]

The urge to conquer obstacles or overcome via the creative power in Individual Psychology is part of the life force expressed in the Chinese character of courage (勇氣) that is rooted in 力, "force," and 氣, "spirit" or "energy." Courage means the "vital force" in the individual and the universe. Courage, if defined only as strength and willfulness by contemporary psychology, may find no expression in Eastern cultural traditions such as Confucianism, Taoism, and Buddhism that view courage as *chi* or a psychological force. These age-old traditions of more than 2,500 years often value mellowness, patience, indifference, inaction, pacifism, and harmony that may often border on cowardice. Courage, based on the cumulative understandings of life in the course of cultural development, is the common sense of the common people who believe in the ideal of social harmony and in the movements against competitive beliefs of wealth, fame, power, and success.

These thoughts are similarly expressed in the Rogerian view of *quiet power* and the Taoist view of *soft courage* by which the individual develops character by acting in harmony with The Way, the truth.[26] Embracing simplicity, patience, and compassion as life's greatest treasures is essentially the Taoist concept of harmony, a naturalistic dynamic movement of life or *generation and regeneration* of the nature. Nietzsche's concept of will to power, when interpreted as the will to more life with the idea of eternal recurrence interestingly coincides with the Taoist view of cosmic life movement.

The spiritual goal of courage and human efforts in Eastern thought finds its equivalent in Adler's belief of how we are bound to this earth where our care for our fellow human beings is of supreme importance.[27] Social interest takes on the religious value in Individual Psychology in that our contribution and cooperation for the best interest of ourselves and our community is the ultimate meaning of life.

> Man as an ever-striving being could not be like God. God, who is eternally complete, who directs the stars, who is the master of fates, who elevates man from his lowliness to Himself, who speaks from the cosmos to every single human soul, is to date the most brilliant manifestation of the goal of perfection.[28]

Courage Defined

In this chapter, we have discussed courage as a psychological construct that is related to the creative power that moves us from the felt minus feeling to the perceived plus by good compensation, which can result in socially useful activities. Courage is the mental strength that allows a person to venture forth, to persevere, and to hold one's own in the face of adversity, differing values, difficulties, and temptations. Adler in the same vein would contend that to have courage means the willingness to take a risk even when the outcome is uncertain. It is the "psychological muscle"[29] each of us needs for coping through cooperation and contribution with the exigencies of life and living.

We have also presented courage as a commonly shared virtue in the West as well as in the East. Courage is a necessity for a cognitive/behavioral/emotional/spiritual response in the presence of a perceived difficulty. We recognized that courage, both a self and social ideal, implies the use of reason and passion we possess while overcoming impediments of our living. In addition, courage sometimes takes the form of the spiritual energy when it is guided by a higher communal value of what is good for the whole.

Given the psychological, cultural, and spiritual contexts we have discussed in this chapter, we now can provide a tentative definition of courage as *the creative life force from within and without that moves us forward in the interest of self and the other in the presence of difficulties. Specifically, courage and acts of courage are best expressed by the individual's willingness to contribute and/or cooperate in socially useful ways via the tasks of living (i.e., work, love, friendship/family/community, harmony with self, and harmony with the universe).*

Closing Thoughts

"What is the meaning of courage, Master?" the young traveler asked of his companion. The Teacher seemed to be deep in thought for a quite a while before answering.

"It has no meaning," came the reply. "Courage only exists in action."

The two walked on in silence with only a few birds calling to one another to disturb the quiet of their contemplation. Finally, the young traveler broke the silence. "Can I not possess thoughts of courage?"

"One does not really possess anything," the Teacher answered.

"Oh, but Master," said the youthful companion, "I have done so much in my mind. I have battled demons, achieved fantastic successes, and conquered the many challenges of living. I have the benefit of experiencing great things and know what it is to have courage."

"Be clear, my young friend," replied the Master, "that you separate that which is real from that which is just your wish."

"Do you mean I cannot think of these things?"

"You can dream and imagine all that you desire, but those are not real accomplishments. Those thoughts are only thoughts," responded the wise man. "A thought is but a puff of smoke. It has no substance and, even then, it quickly disappears. Only by what you do can courage become meaningful."

"But Master, am I not to think before I act?"

"Life requires movement. You might have a good intention, but if never realized, you have done nothing," the Teacher responded. "Just as a journey can only be known by taking the first step, courage can only be seen in what is done. You must walk your thoughts of greatness!"

Life is movement. What gives the movement a direction, a goal? In Chapter 2, we will explore the positive mental health theory of Adler that explains how our goal of perfection, striving, and overcoming must bear within the courage for commonweal.

CHAPTER 2
Community Feeling and Mental Health

It is almost impossible to exaggerate the value of an increase in social feeling. The mind improves, for intelligence is a communal function. The feeling of worth and value is heightened, giving courage and an optimistic view, and there is a sense of acquiescence in the common advantages and drawbacks of our lot. The individual feels at home in life and feels his existence to be worthwhile just so far as he is useful to others and is overcoming common instead of private feelings of inferiority. Not only the ethical nature, but the right attitude in aesthetics, the best understanding of the beautiful and the ugly will always be founded upon the truest social feeling.

—Alfred Adler[1]

What Is Social Interest?

For Adler, the criterion for "success" in life is the healthy personality inherent in the extent to which the individual embodies *gemeinschaftsgefühl* in his characteristic approach to life. Gemeinschaftsgefühl is the word that Adler gave us to describe the ideal state of mental health. In the German language, the meaning is perfectly clear; however, gemeinschaftsgefühl represents considerable difficulty in terms of translation into English. There are no available English equivalents that convey the same meaning. This became extremely clear recently while teaching a class in the Slovak Republic. We were asking for the translation of various English words such as empathy, respect, and so on. For the most part, the words we were asking had fairly direct translations and were even recognizable in the Slovak language, that is, *empatie* and *rešpect*. When we came to gemeinschaftsgefühl the group responded with *gemeinschaftsgefühl*. They replied that they did not require a translation; they understood it just as it was. Not so in English.

We have to struggle to understand the meaning of gemeinschaftsgefühl. A number of English terms—social feeling, community feeling, fellow feeling, sense of solidarity, communal intuition, community interest, social sense, and social interest—have been used in attempts to communicate that meaning.[2] It appears from research in the 1950s that Adler seemed to prefer the latter term, *social interest*. However, later writings by Heinz Ansbacher indicate that Heinz, himself, would have preferred to have used the term *community feeling*. Our preference is also to use the term *community feeling*, but out of respect and deference to the majority of writings that have gone before ours, we will use *social interest* interchangeably in our writing here.

Social interest is not an inborn ability, but a potential for us to develop, such as learning to add or subtract, throw a football, or cook a meal. As in any educational process, there are three basic elements: First, we have to assume that social interest exists as an *aptitude* for cooperation and social living that *can be* developed through training. Therefore, we have to believe it is there just waiting to be encouraged and brought forth. Second, we have to acknowledge that this aptitude can be expanded into the objective *abilities* of cooperating and contributing, as well as those of understanding others and empathizing with them. Third, social interest can become the subjective *evaluative attitude* that determines choices and influences the dynamics of the individual. However, when not backed up by the skills and abilities, such an attitude of social interest may not be sufficient to meet all contingencies of living.

> Every human being brings the disposition for social interest with him; but then it must be *developed* through *upbringing*, especially through correct guidance of the *creative power* of the individual.[3]

Assuming that social interest, then, is an innate potential that must be consciously developed, the next step—the function of education and training—is its development, the converting of the aptitude into an ability or skill. Just as one must train a potential for music or numbers or artistic productions, so must social interest be trained. With this training comes the capacity for cooperation and contribution. In brief, these could be described as the ability to accept *what is* (the implication here being one of cooperation) with a view of *what could be* (the implication being contribution).

Adler viewed life as presenting the individual with two, often contradictory, demands. On the one hand, the individual had to be capable of meeting the acute problems of the existing environment; she/he had to have the capacity to cooperate. On the other hand, the individual had to have the capacity to make a contribution to be able to meet the demands for social improvement. The resolution of this dilemma requires that the individual find the balance between present needs and the demands of evolution.[4]

Cooperation

The capacity to cooperate begins to develop almost from birth since the relationship between the child and mother requires cooperation. Thus, Adler saw it to be, initially, the primary responsibility of the mother to begin to train the child in the development of his social interest.[5] In the relationship between mother and child, the potential for social interest begins to take form. However, the mother (primary caretaker) must not restrict this social development by confining it to herself, but must expand the child's circle of human contacts to the father, brothers and sisters, other children, strangers, and so on.

A function of this ability to cooperate in an ever-widening circle of human relationships is the comparable ability of identification. "The ability to identify must be trained, and it can be trained only if one grows up in relation to others and feels a part of the whole. One must sense that not only the comforts of life belong to one, but also the discomforts. One must feel at home on this earth with all its advantages and disadvantages."[6] The social interest dimension described by cooperation is best exemplified by the ability of individuals to give and take. Individuals must not only feel a part of life as a whole, but must also be willing to accept the good and the bad aspects of living. Individuals might be described as being neither optimist nor pessimist, but functioning effectively with the realities of their situation. Individuals operate as a part of life, in conjunction with others.

> Life presents only such problems as require ability to cooperate for their solution. To hear, see, or speak "correctly," means to lose one's self completely in another or in a situation, to become identified with him or with it. The capacity for identification, which alone makes us capable of friendship, love of mankind, sympathy, occupation, and love, is the basis of social interest and can be practiced and exercised only in conjunction with others.[7]

For Adler, the only means for solutions to the immediate problems of life that faced the individual was to develop a high degree of the ability to cooperate. One of the measures, then, of the degree of social interest developed by the individual is expressed by the extent to which the individual is willing to cooperate. Though many individuals may have only a limited capacity to cooperate, life does not always present to them such demanding problems that their cooperation is found to be in short supply. Often, they are never called upon to cooperate to such an extent that they will be found lacking in their ability. It is only under difficult situations and stress that we can truly assess the cooperative ability of the individual.[8]

Contribution

> Life means—to contribute to the whole.[9]

Not only must individuals develop a capacity for cooperation, but they must, in addition, develop a capacity for contribution—a willingness to consider in their own personal striving for overcoming and perfection, the welfare of others. Man does not live an isolated existence; his every action and feeling has some effect and impact on his fellow man. Adler considered it to be a major function of each individual that he becomes his "brother's keeper."[10]

As an additional measure of individuals' social interest, their willingness to contribute must be considered. A major aspect of this dimension is the idea that there is not a one-to-one correspondence between contribution and reward, and individuals must be able to give far more than they receive. This willingness to contribute must take place in the context of a primary concern for others and the general welfare. Concern for personal benefit can only be secondary and must follow solely as a derivative of the primary concern. However, the self-esteem accruing to the individual will follow as surely as day follows night, the feeling of usefulness engenders the individual's feeling of self-worth and value.

In summary, the individual must be able to function on two planes: horizontal and vertical. The horizontal plane consists of the day-to-day demands of social living; it is part of the here and now. This includes a person's immediate relationships to all elements of the environment, incorporating all things and all individuals with which the person comes in contact, either directly or indirectly. Thus, the horizontal plane is not restricted solely to social relationships, as may be implied in the term social interest, but is viewed as the totality of one's environment. This plane might be adequately described as a continuum of cooperation.

The second plane, which is vertical in nature, consists of a type of evolutionary movement that is continuous and upward in direction. This plane can be designated as a continuum of contribution. To remain solely on the horizontal plane would constitute a type of conformity with no element of a futuristic or evolutionary orientation. Devoting sole attention to the vertical would constitute a striving for superiority without a concomitant interest in the immediate environment. A balance or equilibrium must be maintained between the two directions of these planes if the social interest is to exist to any high degree in the individual.

The evaluative attitude, then, consists of an overall guiding set of principles or values that consider the interests of humankind and the development of the human community as the primary objective for the efforts of the individual. This stands as a relative norm describing the normal man's behavior, a man whose goal in life is to be a complete human being. The focus is on courage, initiative, and creativity, and it places the whole of man's existence upon a dynamic foundation of movement and improvement.

A Measure of Mental Health

Social interest is the expression of our capacity for give and take.[11]

Our mental health (or social interest) exists in the balance between present needs and the demands of evolution. In an effort to represent this subjective dimension more graphically, Figure 2.1 represents the process model by which we conceptualize social interest as the interaction between one's abilities of contribution and that of cooperation.[12] Inherent in the model is the assumption that all individuals have the potential or aptitude for social living, and its manifestation is ultimately the result of training. This potential or aptitude is more amenable for training if the appropriate psychological atmosphere is provided wherein it becomes an actual ability.

The diagonal of the model depicts the evaluative attitude—the sum of the expression of the individual's capacity for cooperation and contribution. It includes both attitude and feeling relating to the adequacy of the individual to meet and solve the problems of living. If on each axis one could objectively measure the capacity of the individual for both cooperation

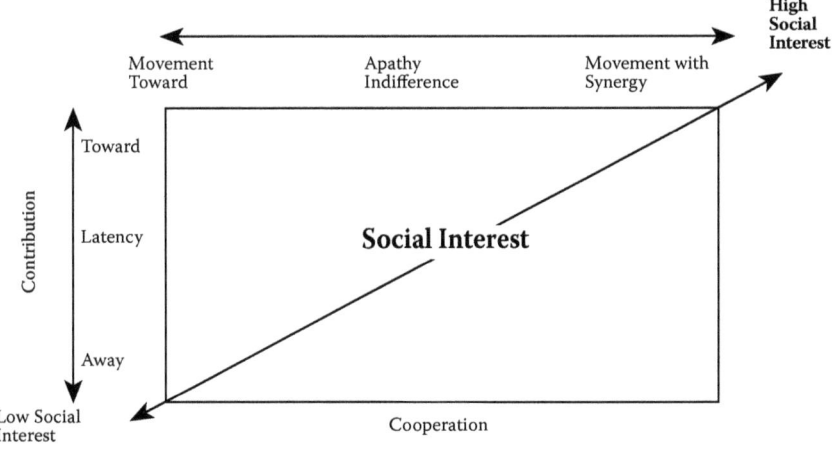

Figure 2.1 Social interest as a measure of mental health.

and contribution, a plot could be made on the diagonal as a representative measure of the extent to which the social interest is developed.

The Horizontal Axis

The horizontal axis of the model constitutes a continuum of cooperation. Here, the term *cooperation* cannot be considered in the traditional sense of mutual agreement of assistance and support, but is conceived in both a positive and a negative sense since cooperation is also necessary for the task of getting along with ourselves when we have the need to be right by proving others wrong, to dominate, to hurt, or to give up. This attitude of cooperation applies not only in the sphere of human relationships, but also in all aspects of the individual's relationships to the elements of the environment.

If, for example, one examines the behavior of any individual who displays a talent or skill, such as an accomplished pianist, it becomes obvious that the individual has not *mastered* the instrument or tool being worked with in the sense of overpowering it, or achieving superiority over it, or defeating it in some type of battle. Instead, one can observe a highly positive cooperative relationship wherein the pianist is working in harmony with the instrument. In the same vein, the skilled mechanic treats tools with appreciation and respect, in effect, maintaining a synergetic relationship with them. Even in the learning of subject matter, one must approach the material with a positive cooperative spirit, for without it, limited learning is inevitable. Arithmetic (or statistics), for example, cannot be learned with a fighting attitude.

In these instances, as well as all others in which a high degree of positive cooperation is evidenced, the individual is in the process of working *with* the other, be it animate or inanimate. The relationship can be described as harmonious, sympathetic (as in physics), and synergetic. Conversely, one can find in situations, where failure more typically occurs, a negatively oriented attitude of cooperation. These situations can be viewed as if neither partner is willing to be defeated or mastered, and the elements seem to work against each other to ensure defeat. The individual, to use the previous example, who does not wish to learn the piano will find it to be highly cooperative in the sense that it will not respond musically, nor will it serve to reinforce the idea that the individual is at all capable of playing. Herein, the movement is *against* the other.

Thus, the horizontal axis in Figure 2.1 can be viewed more broadly in the context of it being an ability to meet the immediate demands of the environment, an environment that must be viewed as being internal as well as external. Sickness and ill health are often the results of one's negative cooperation with his or her own physiology. At a simple level, witness the discomfort that results as a consequence of overeating. At a more complex level, allergies might be considered as a form of negative cooperation with one's environment.

> For many years now it's been known that allergies are essentially a "mistake" of the immune system. When the immune system is functioning well, it identifies truly dangerous substances and responds to them in order to protect your body. This is the way the body protects you from harmful bacteria or viruses. But sometimes a person's immune system makes a mistake and identifies a harmless food, pollen, dust, or a bee sting as being dangerous when it really isn't. If your immune system thinks something like that is dangerous, you end up with an allergy instead of protection.[13]

The extremes of the continuum can be characterized in terms of the kind of cooperative movement displayed by the individual—whether it be *with*, in a synergetic relationship, or *against,* in a hostile, fighting relationship—toward the total spectrum of environmental objects.

The midpoint of this continuum might be characterized by two different sets of behaviors. On the one hand, apathy or indifference might be highly descriptive for the individual who seems to take things for granted. On the other hand, there is the individual who vacillates between working with and working against others. For every step forward, there is, in effect, a step backward. This latter description may be characteristic of our present-day crisis of social conflict and confusion and environmental disruption. Working against the environment often occurs in the same breath as working with it; though in either case, the degree may be only slight. Of both sets of behaviors, however, it can be said that there is an apparent absence of cooperation, a lack that is vividly evidenced from the ecological standpoint, at least.

The Vertical Axis

The vertical axis of the model in Figure 2.1, a continuum of contribution, must be viewed from a dual perspective. This continuum is comprised of two basic elements, which, for purposes of simplification, will be termed *action* and *effect*. In the former, the idea of action is abstracted from the physicist's concept of energy in that it refers to a capacity both for doing work—creating some type of effect—and overcoming resistance. The use of the analogy to energy provides us with a more comprehensive understanding of the action aspect of this continuum since it allows us to view all individuals as making contributory efforts or, at least, as having the potential to do so.

In consideration of action, the form of the activity is of little import, since highly aggressive as well as highly passive observable behaviors may often be equally effective in achieving the comparable ends. One can become extremely disliked, for example, just as easily by being a clinging vine as by being pushy and brash. Hunger strikes and fasting can lead to social reorientation and reform as effectively as militancy. However, one must take care to differentiate physical activity from psychological. In the preceding examples, a high degree of psychological activity is present although the observed physical behaviors are extremely different and may range from complete inactivity to hostile attacks and violence.

Of greater importance, then, is the counterpart of action—effect. Viewed from the context of social development and improvement, effect can range from being highly constructive or useful to being highly destructive or useless. In total, this continuum may be construed as being equated to the idea of creating change, although this is only partially correct and some incompatible aspects do exist. The major difference between the continuum of contribution and the creation of change probably occurs in the area in which *no observable change* takes place or no effect is created. Yet, the individual may be making a considerable contributory effort of either a constructive or destructive nature. For example, the individual who exercises judiciousness waiting for an appropriate opportunity to make a constructive move creates no change *at the moment*, but is still being useful—particularly if this is the most appropriate means to the end.

A case in point for the preceding situation might be drawn from the behavior of a statesman wherein, in the conduct of his affairs, there is more positive effect, for the moment, in the absence of his acting. In fact, it is often the *power of silence* that achieves the greatest gain in the long run. But look at another man who watches an elderly person fall and waits to see who will come to provide assistance. His espoused purpose is to evaluate the behavior of others, which may seem to have some constructive merit, but can only be classified as a useless form of inactivity. He serves no one but himself by not providing his assistance where it is needed. He uses this situation to evaluate the behavior of others and sits in judgment of their efforts.

The midpoint in this range of contribution consists of an absence or lack of effect, which is more often the result of psychological inactivity rather than physical. It describes contentment with the status quo and conformity to the prevailing social norm. The individuals, whose behavior might be described by this midpoint, are neither concerned with the development of mankind as a whole, nor do they work to lead it in any direction, positive or negative, constructive or destructive, useful or useless. They may approach life much as a worm in an apple, only interested in taking advantage of the efforts and contributions of others.

The final form of the evaluation of effect can only be viewed from the standpoint of eternity. That which is constructive will be reflected in a movement toward the creation of values for mankind and will bring us closer to a more perfect form for human living. That which is destructive will prove, in the long run, to be a movement away from improvement and social development.

The Courage of Community Feeling

> Social interest remains throughout life. It becomes differentiated, limited, or expanded and, in favorable cases, extends not only to family members but to the larger group, to the nation, to all of mankind. It can even go further, extending itself to animals, plants, and inanimate objects and finally even to the cosmos.[14]

Gemeinschaft, as Adler used the term, is not restricted solely to the community of individuals, but describes a holistic relationship between the individuals and the cosmos. As one's horizons begin to expand, his/her relationships begin to include more and more of life and, ultimately, there is a feeling of connectedness with the society, nature, and the whole of the universe. Consequently, he or she not only has to develop a set of interlocking relations with family members, but must also develop these relationships with the whole of the environment.

> Such a state of mind and attitude give him more than a feeling of social interest, for he behaves as a part of the whole of mankind, he feels at home in a conception of the world as near as possible to the real world, and he has courage and common sense, social functions which are frustrated among all failures. He is ready to accept the advantages of our social life and is a good loser whenever disadvantages cross his way. He is and wants to be the master of his fate with an effective regard for the welfare of others.[15]

All failures in life stem from individuals striving to attain significance through personal power and status. Herein, they approach life with their own private meaning and view their place in the community from the standpoint of their private logic. They do not benefit anyone but themselves by the achievement of their private goals and any triumphs they do achieve have their major relevance only to themselves. These individuals are highly vulnerable and will only cooperate and contribute as long as personal gain is involved.

Healthy individuals, on the other hand, are affected by society or in the much broader sense, the gemeinschaft, as well as the gemeinschaft being affected by each individual. These individuals not only react to these various environments, but also adopt an individual attitude that changes this real environment to one that appears subjective. Thus, the stance that individuals take toward the gemeinschaft is of their own creation and the extent to which they identify or feel belonging is a product of their own development. Community feeling, the ultimate measure of our mental health, therefore, extends both within and without the individual.

A mentally healthy attitude toward life pertains a feeling of self-worth and a sense of belonging. Through the individual's developed capacities for cooperation and contribution he is able to achieve a measure of significance. The individual develops a feeling of harmony with the universe and he functions in keeping with the demands of his existence in the world. He feels comfortable and "at home" on this earth and works in conjunction with his environment. He has a strong feeling of identification with others and knowledge of his worth and esteem.

> He [who recognizes the goal of the commonweal] will regard all difficulties of life, whether they originate within himself or outside his person, as his task, to be solved by him. He will, so to speak, feel at home on this poor earth crust, "in his father's house." Thus he will regard not only the comforts but also the discomforts of this life, which come to him and to others, as belonging to him, and will cooperate in their solution. He will be a courageous fellow man, a co-worker, without asking for any other recompenses that which he bears within himself. But his work, his contribution to the common weal is immortal; his spirit will never perish.[16]

Closing Thoughts

Social interest is not a thing or trait a person possesses. Rather, it is an ideal that gives our psychological movement goals and directions. It is an ideal we, with our own imperfections, strive toward in the interest of ourselves and the common welfare. Social interest as a construct can be seen in our choices and acts that express courage, confidence, cooperation, contribution, and compassion. Social interest was Adler's criterion for mental health that has had impact on the humanistic psychology and its concept of self-actualization.[17]

Adler's notion of social interest has contemporary purposes. The individual's optimal mental health is expressed by his/her courage to cooperate and contribute, which shapes one's feelings of social usefulness and evolution. To have a view of the totality of the concept of gemeinschaftsgefühl (social interest or ideal state of mental health), we will illustrate in Part II how the ideal community feeling is achieved by how we respond to the basic life tasks of work, love, and friendships, and the existential tasks of getting along with ourselves and to find meaning in life.

CHAPTER 3
Tasks of Life

> True strength can never be derived only from talent but from the courageous struggle with difficulties. Whoever overcomes wins.
>
> —Alfred Adler[1]

To be mentally healthy is to have the courage to follow and develop social interest that establishes an ideal and direction for all our strivings both individually and communally. The courage of our social living is best observed in how we strive to overcome difficulties. Adler originally postulated that there are three major tasks—work, sex, and society—that embrace the whole of human life, which are set for each individual by virtue of his/her very existence. Adler's followers later added two existential tasks that are central to the original tasks: Our ability to be in harmony with (1) ourselves and (2) the universe. With the social interest as our ideal goal, we strive to overcome problems and challenges, and fulfill these tasks by our contribution and cooperation. These tasks are inseparable and it takes both courage and social interest for us to self-educate and influence others as we eventually contribute to the total whole of human community.

Work, Love, and Social Relations: The Basic Tasks

> All human problems can be grouped under there three headings: occupational, social and sexual. It is in their response to these there problems that individuals unfailingly reveal their own personal interpretation of the meaning of life.[2]

Dreikurs defined these three basic life tasks as: "*work* which means contributing to the welfare of others, *friendship* which embraces social relationships with comrades and relatives, and *love* which is the most intimate union and represents the strongest and closest emotional relationship that can exist between two human beings."[3] The love task is sometimes referred to as the intimacy task. The friendship task is inclusive of family and community relationships. These life tasks are the connectors between people and the world to which they belong. These are the objective abilities of cooperating and contributing. To Adler, for a person of courage who can fully cooperate and participate in all these three tasks, life means *being interested in people, being part of the whole,* and *contributing* to the welfare of humankind.

It was Adler's consideration that all other questions of life were secondary to the fulfillment of these major tasks. In fact, it was these three concerns confronting the individual that constantly tested one's degree of social interest. It is through the individual's approach (with or without courage) to these tasks that we know his/her style of cooperation.

Adler indicated that these three problems of living are interwoven and cannot be resolved separately. They are different aspects of the same problem. Successful resolution of the problem in one area requires (and contributes to) successfully solving the other two. Other Adlerian writers seem to be more flexible recognizing that the variable adjustment to these three problems is likely and that such different levels of fulfillment may not seriously restrict the individual's functioning. For example, we may not be equally prepared to meet all three areas of living and may do better in one but not the other. Success in one area may help compensate the other areas we have yet to train or develop. According to Way, for the ordinary man "the fullest satisfaction is gained by responding to all three demands, although even here a special achievement in one direction may be of use to help compensate failure in another."[4]

In this book, we will call the first three tasks originally postulated by Adler the basic life tasks: work, love (intimacy), and social relations (including friendship, family, and community relationships). They represent three homework areas we are given to fulfill as we meet the demands of life with social interest. In Chapter 2, we presented the "subjective" steps of social interest as innate aptitude, the abilities, and the evaluative attitudes. It is through the training of these three bask life tasks that individuals are connected to the "object" and outer world with their *abilities* to cooperate and contribute.

Being and Belonging: The Existential Tasks

Some Adlerians are also willing to look beyond the three life tasks at other questions regarding the nature of living. Two additional tasks have been offered in an attempt to more adequately describe the demands of human living. Mosak and Dreikurs postulate a fourth life task as the necessity of the individual "to learn how to get along with himself, how to deal with himself.[5] It is important that the individual learns to live with himself, to accept his strengths and weaknesses, and to lose the fear of being wrong. By so doing, he stops fighting with himself and gives his inner resources an opportunity to reach fruition. This task is also called self acceptance or *self care*.[6]

The *fifth life task*, relates to the problem of man establishing himself in relationship to the universe. We are only part of our total environment that was here-to-fore beyond our comprehension. This, then, presents a need for us to adapt in the light of new problems that go beyond the solution of the immediate problems related to our existence on this earth. It requires a form of *cosmic embeddedness* that will allow us to find significance for the existence of mankind of an existential or transcendental nature. The fifth life task has been called several names: the spirituality task or "the spiritual, the existential, the search for meaning, the metaphysical, the metapsychological and the ontological."[7]

The fourth and the fifth life tasks are existential by nature and, in this book, we will call the ability to get alone with self the "being" task (harmony with self) and the ability to get alone with the universe the "belonging" task (harmony with the universe.) The belonging tasks address our psychological need to belong to our community as well as our spiritual well-being. We are endowed with innate *dispositions* or *aptitudes* to be in harmony with ourselves and the universe to which we belong. The tasks of being and belonging are the subjective, evaluative attitudes that transcend the three basic life tasks that require our development of abilities.

The existential tasks operate like a well spring from within and from without enabling us to love; to work; and to related to family, friends, and others. Our endeavor in the basic life tasks are outward expressions of these harmonious tendencies that reside within us. Whereas we learn and train for the basic life tasks, we acquire the existential strengths by genuine respect for what is and affirmation from communal experiences. Together, the three basic tasks and the two existential tasks form the movement that determines our characteristic *attitudes* and approaches toward life.

Contemporary Adlerians such as Sonstegard and Bitter recognized the tasks of kinkeeping (the care of children and the elderly extended across generations), spirituality (connectivity to the largeness of our world) and the task of coping with change. It is only when we successfully meet these life tasks that we may experience and express a sense of belonging.[8]

The Normative Ideal

To illustrate the *normative ideal* that is indicative of an ideal state of mental health represented by the concept of social interest, the life task map is

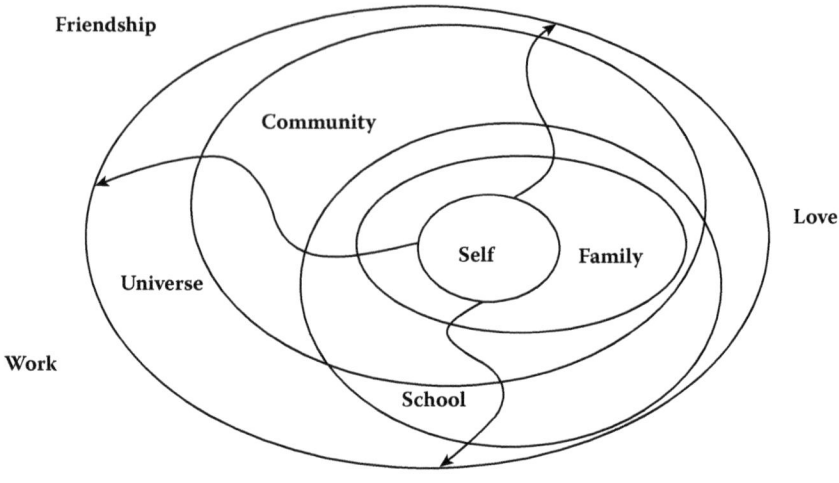

Figure 3.1 Life task map. Copyright 2008 by Julia Yang.

presented in Figure 3.1. By drawing nonconcentric circles around the individual, we can illustrate one's unequal relationship to the chain of organizations of which the person is a link. Moving outward from the individual's self, the larger systems of the community are represented beginning with the smaller units of the family and peers, and continuing until the most extreme ring, the universe. Although it is reasonable to assume that any spacing can be applied to the distance between man and the various circles, the first three from the individual are drawn with shorter distances to emphasize the fact that these levels, for the child and adolescent, tend to be more pronounced and are representative of the groups within which they are primarily concerned. The outside ring may be considered extremely important since it represents the level of *community* into which the child and adolescent are in the process of emerging. In effect, it is possible to view these various circles as developmental steps of increasing importance as the individual grows older. Thus, we are provided with a notion of an ever-widening and ever-expanding grouping of the various systems of which man is a part of and in which social interest can be evidenced.

This total system of circles, beyond oneself, can then be divided into three unequal parts, each representing one of the basic life tasks. This apparent inequality, a reflection of the unique import of each task, is provided, since in most cases, as well as in a hypothetical general instance, balance in fulfillment of these tasks is only proportional to the balance in the character and personality of the individual. Since the individual serves as the basis for the expanding circles, the fourth life task (being) is incorporated as an integral and focal point of the model. The implication is not that the individual is the center of the universe, but that it is only when he learns to live with himself that he is capable of effectively fulfilling the other tasks. The fifth life task (belonging) is also incorporated into the model by the arrows pointing to the outer ring of the cosmos or universe. Although the largest ring is drawn as a solid line, our knowledge of the largeness and finality is incomplete in that we have as of yet to learn what might lie beyond it.

The whole of Figure 3.1 is permeated with the quality of social interest. As a totality, it is representative of the blending of the *gemeinschaft* with the *gefühl*, the complete concept of social interest, and depicts its extent and intensity if it is maximally developed in the individual. When viewed from the vantage point of this model, social interest describes a picture of *what can be* rather than *what is*. It establishes an ideal rather than a norm or median as the direction for the strivings of an individual. It is more than a concept of adjustment since it implies courage, initiative, and creativity, and it places the whole of the person's existence upon a dynamic foundation of movement and improvement, belonging and cooperation. Since this does represent an *ideal norm* it can be used as a standard to which the functioning of the individual can be compared. The differences noted herein could then serve as a type of relative index of the individual's mental health status.

The Evasion of Life Tasks

The curved arrows in Figure 3.1 depict the nonlinear development as the individual reaches out to broader life settings. The life problems pertain to the interactions between our characteristic approaches and the world we live in. In fact, we believe that all human problems stem from our inability to fulfill these life tasks. Wolfe used the analogy of a three-ring circus and sideshows to describe our tendencies to avoid life challenges (i.e., main-tent activities with social interest) although a good life is only attainable when we can face the basic life tasks with wisdom and courage.[9] Our attitudes toward life, if with insufficient social interest, can misguide us and engage us in the sideshows that prevent us from entering the main tent or socially useful activities. Another way of evasion is to focus only on one or two tasks and neglect the rest. This is problematic as the life tasks are inseparable since we deal with the whole person.

> The human being does not necessarily develop himself at all equally, and may find himself much better equipped for the solution of one of these problems than for the others. He may succeed in occupation, but not in love, or love and social contacts may both be easy to him as compared with the difficulty of earning a living. Psychosis

generally involves a breakdown before all three problems at once, whereas neurosis, though general adaptation may be poor, is usually a breakdown in one or two directions only, with social interest preserved in the others.[10]

Individuals who creatively evade life responsibilities in one or more areas show patterns of behaviors and perceptions that are motivated by fears. They fear rejection, failing, not being enough or too much, being trapped, being judged, the unknown or ambiguities, too many or too little choices/responsibilities, being controlled or having no control, and the list goes on. Instead of having the courage to participate in life by cooperation and contribution, these individuals focus their energy on comparison and competition that usually result in either over- or underresponses to life demands. They lean on many habits to avoid dealing with their fears: dominance, conformity, imitation, dependence, arrogance, indecision, procrastination, addictions, and other methods that are seen as commonly useless or bad compensation.[11]

These useless or fear-based life attitudes often perpetuate the individuals to put forth sideshows (as opposed to main-tent activities) that are of false goals, and they impede one's normal functioning and have negative consequences of exclusivity and isolation in social, family, and work relationships. Examples of these sideshows are the problems of excessive family loyalty, remaining idle, inadequacy, laziness, busyness, depression, and neurosis. Those who creatively choose not to face life problems and needs unfortunately escape the initiatives or responsibilities they could take to build a good life, and, ironically, with their fear-based striving, what they fear may just come true.

It has become clear that courage is the only solution to problems caused by evasion of life tasks or bad compensations. Adlerians found that the common denominator of the "sideshow artists" is a very discouraged early life. The best cure for these individuals is to realize that the main-tent arena is actually safer than the sideshows and for them to recharge courage for social interest by taking actions to ride out the difficulties and help fellow men and women with the same obstacles. In general, courage can be seen in the individuals who are optimistic, creative, and prepared to cooperate and contribute for the benefit of other people. Lack of courage and social feeling, on the other hand, accounts for all failures in social life (i.e., work, love, and friendship).

To Adler, courage is a precondition to real cooperation, to move from the useless side to the useful side of adjustment, to face life tasks, to risk mistakes, and to feel the sense of belonging. The courageous individual also has a better developed social interest with a better developed relationship with his/her world. A lack of courage, in contrast, breeds feelings of inferiority, pessimism, avoidance, and misbehaviors. The resolutions to life-task-related problems are to equip the individual with new insight about one's fears and recognition of one's safeguarding tendency or actual evasion with life tasks so that he/she can develop the courage to move away from the fear-based, commonly useless psychological sideshows to participating in main-tent activities with social interest.

> We consider a person who has a love relationship that is an intimate and full co-operation, whose work results in useful achievement, who has lots of friends and whose contacts with people are wide-ranging and fruitful. We may conclude that such a person sees life as a creative task, offering many opportunities and no irreversible setbacks. His courage in confronting all the problems of life is to be construed as saying: "Life means being interested in people, being part of the whole, and contributing my share to the welfare of humankind."[12]

Closing Thoughts

In Part I, we attempted to provide conceptual definitions and understanding of how courage and gemeinschaftsgefühl are reciprocal forces that interact to move each of us toward our life goals. In the present chapter, we focused on the introduction of the life tasks and how they form a normative ideal that defines the fullest or most effective functioning that is indicative of an ideal state of mental health. Insofar, we have presented the conceptual foundations of courage, community feeling, and life tasks in the Individual Psychology framework.

We are now ready to proceed to the specific life tasks where we will further our understanding of the individual characteristic approaches to the problems and the ideal of our social living. In Part II, we will illustrate how the feeling of community can inspire and prepare us to face life problems with courage and to take responsibility for ourselves and others. Specifically we address each life task with the attitudes of the individual and the extent to which an individual has the courage to cooperate with and contribute to the solution of the whole of life's problems.

PART II
The Courage of Social Living

CHAPTER **4**

The Courage to Work

To laugh often and much; to win the respect of intelligent people and the affection of children; to earn the appreciation of honest critics and endure the betrayal of false friends; to appreciate beauty; to find the best in others; to leave the world a bit better whether by a healthy child, a garden patch, or a redeemed social condition; to know even one life has breathed easier because you have lived. This is to have succeeded.

—**Ralph Waldo Emerson**

Emerson's quote was read at Burt's funeral. Burt died of multiple heart attacks after a typical workday when he normally sent his staff home first and stayed afterward to care for unfinished business himself. Burt had been around for a long time. He loved his work. His students and colleagues often sought him for advice. You would hear his laughter well before you saw him. He always responded to others' curiosity about his unusual work spirit with a statement: "Life is a good place to be." To Burt, work meant self-worth, other directedness, helpfulness, and joy. To others, as we will see in this chapter, work means many different things.

What Is Work?

Work is the most important life task for an individual's survival, family provision, and social living. In addition to providing the financial means for survival, work has many layers of psychological and social meanings. When we work, we work with love not only in the interest of ourselves but also in care of others. Occupation in the Adlerian framework is defined as "any kind of work which is useful to the community." Work includes the activities of play, house chores, schoolwork for the children, and the paid or unpaid jobs we do in fulfillment of our life roles throughout our life span. Spiritually, work is a journey through which we express our self-concept and achieve our life goals and belonging via mutual dependence.

When we work, we seldom work alone. The courage to work requires our cooperation with others and our contribution in fulfillment of the needs of a better world. Work, when viewed in the context of social interest, can chart our goals and actions that shape our feelings of uselessness or usefulness. Courage helps us determine whether feelings of self and community could either hinder or promote our participation in work.

To work or not to work is *not* a question. The only question is whether we overwork or underwork. We must work or we starve. "Life without work is a living death."[1] For those who do not work, they rely on others' work to support them. They are low with social interest but high with self-interest. In Individual Psychology, work is one of the three basic tasks to attain a good life. As we require societal protection, we work by cooperation and contribution within the social system. Work is not done in isolation. Although our use of work as compensation for inferior feelings is justified, our work must also bring contribution to our fellow human beings.

SOCRATIC DIALOGUE 4.1

Following are some of the common assumptions people have about work.[2] Ask your family members, friends, or colleagues their thoughts about these assumptions and compare these thoughts with your own. In what way are you surprised by the differences or similarities?

- There is one occupation for which each individual is best fit.
- Once a field is chosen, the choice is irreversible.
- One can succeed at whatever interests one.
- Effort and motivation can overcome all obstacles.
- Intrinsic job satisfaction is better than extrinsic job satisfaction.
- Most people dislike their work.
- Most people would not work if they did not have to.
- Educational choice and vocational choice are nearly the same.
- In the future, people will work less and less.
- The younger a person is when the choice of career is made the better.

Individual Inferiority

In today's society, work is the most acceptable way for individuals to attain recognition, wealth, power, status, and prestige. To most people, work is the road to success or a sense of superiority. The individualistic and capitalistic values of our society demands workers to produce, perform, and compete. In our fear of not keeping up with an expected living standard, we work for a conformist style of living and the accumulation for security. As a consequence, many are simply working to retire. Another contribution to individual inferiority in our work life is that we are bound to experience fears from within and from without. This fear is exasperated by cooperate decisions that are autocratic and punitive. As we meet external job demands and seek advancement, we work harder or manipulate to overcome our fear of mistakes, disapproval, and failure.

On the individual level, our work problems mostly stem from the need to safeguard against failures by total or partial evasion of home, school, and work responsibilities by overworking or underworking. Upon completion of our required education, many enter the workforce ill prepared for the challenges of work. Young adults, who grew up pampered and protected, return home to their parents after college with or without employment. The fluctuation of economy and unemployment, while bringing devastation to many, seems to give excuses to some who cannot find a job that suit them, who do not have the motivation to work, and those who cannot hold a job due to various interpersonal reasons.

> I just wanna make sure I do something with my life. When I am ready to have a family, I can make sure if I wanna go to church on Sundays I can have Sundays off. Make a lot of money so that my family is well off. Make sure they are all taken care of, no matter what happens. But if I do get a lot of money I'd want my kids to earn it for allowance and stuff because that's where I think a lot of things happened. In my high school and in our district, it's like basically a richer school which is really not that rich, where the rich kids go and basically it's predominantly white in my town. A lot of the kids who go there are like snooty, are like jerks; they get whatever they want. I don't want my kids to be like that. I want them to work.
>
> —Jose

Al asked Jose, 18, where he was headed. Jose stated that he was fed up with what he saw in his school: unequal treatment and disparities between the poor and the rich. Jose has chosen to drop out of the community college to join the Navy. Classes in high school or college were either too difficult or too easy. Being fair and just is important to this young man who has experienced injustices in school and at home where he and his stepfather had several physical confrontations. He planned to pursue a career in criminal justice at a later date.

Jose's ideal of a good life where one's hard work will lead to wealth unfortunately will be confronted with a very different reality. Our belief that a good education will lead to a good career is an unfounded assumption that does not apply to all. Many adolescent and adults share with Jose the irony of underpreparedness and the dream of accumulation, possession, social hierarchy, and stability.

SOCRATIC DIALOGUE 4.2

Is Jose's career goal realistic or fictive? What strengths do you see in Jose who dropped out of college so he could drop in the Navy?[3] What is Jose's view of himself, others, and the world? What are some of Jose's general attitudes toward life? Are they more fear based or courage based? How could Jose be more prepared and adaptable in his thoughts and decisions about his career?

We develop negative work attitudes when we attempt to avoid dealing with fears of work. Instead of meeting work challenges with courage, the discouraged worker is drawn to the side shows of timidity, procrastination, laziness, indecisiveness, entitlement, victimization, and a lack of motivation. Basically what these behaviors manifest are inadequacies in the individuals who underwork to avoid the perceived threat of failures.

Such inadequacies are compounded by our own ambition, perfectionism, the perception of insufficient time/resources, and other conflicting responsibilities. We never quite attain our goals, as perfection is subjective and does not really exist. Perfection is only part of our fictional beliefs. Other fictional beliefs such as *I must rule, I must control,* or *I must get* cultivate discouragement within us and with problems in our work life.[4]

For those who work for recognition and extrinsic rewards, work becomes meaningless when the recognition and rewards are absent. When we overwork to compensate for our inadequacies, we knowingly or unknowingly compromise or loose sight of our intimacy, social relations, self-care, and a deeper sense of the meaning of work or of life in general. The discouraged worker expresses such familiar complaints as fatigue, stress, lack of vitality, self-doubt, role overload and role conflict (at home and work), and lack of personal control.

Collective Inferiority

Individual and institutional inferior feelings characterize a discouraged workplace where perceptions and actions are based on fears. When individuals feel insecure about their own identities, they create settings that deprive other people of their identities as well. When workers believe that work is a battleground, the perception of we must do or die becomes a self-fulfilling prophecy for many.[5] It is not uncommon that leaders encourage foreclosure of the potentials out of fear of negative consequences. Fears in the workplace are best expressed in rigidity of rules and procedures by which blame could be easily placed on certain individuals when there are failures or losses.

Often these seemingly personal fears surface in the workplace as collective "better than" or "less than" attitudes that breed a climate of competition and rationalize the practice of inequality and discrimination. A typical example is the controversial concerns of affirmative action for equal education and occupational opportunities (i.e., quality vs. quota.)

A White person doesn't have a chance.

Mixed feelings ... When things have been unfair and distinctly so, then there is some deliberate effort to correct it. Then I think what we end up with is those that have been in the down end, as they gain a foothold, to push for all those things they haven't had.

I realize Whites have given Blacks trouble in history, but there must be a limit to concessions given.

Black students may not be academically prepared. I try to form the attitude I have toward all the students based on what I consider the merits of their performance rather than anything else.

It's baloney. White Americans have had their way all the time ... Blacks have always been segregated, and nowadays they are involved in what Whites always had.[6]

The above statements were made by college staff, students, and professor in a small predominantly white university who participated in a campus wide study on racial climate. A Hispanic graduate student offered her comment in a very different voice, however.

What is it that Caucasians don't get it –they have had a lifetime of the benefits of affirmative action?

Work problems, already challenging with the constant change of economy, are intensified with human rights issues in the institutional, social, and cultural levels. Throughout human history, laws and policies have been made and implemented for the exclusion of what is perceived as the "out-group." The out-group is held in a less than status to maintain the status quo.

> I've always been a performer and excelled in whatever I do and part of it is to overcome the negative stereotypes, to show that I am capable.
>
> —A gay man[7]

This gay man's narrative is also shared by women and workers of color. Power differential based on gender, ethnicity, and sexual orientation underscores inequalities in work attainment, retention, compensation, and advancement. Individuals with the assigned less than or minority status often experience many barriers of becoming successful in their careers. They cope with perseverance and their coping strategies often include working harder. They may also internalize the external values that are oppressive in nature; they feel "not good enough" and will not ultimately see themselves as worthy of their work.

SOCRATIC DIALOGUE 4.3

Recall a particular event when you first realized things are not equal at work. How has that experience influenced the way you think, feel about work? Do you work differently because of the awareness?

New Fear: Protean Career

The time of institutional career and linear career development that promised success has come to pass. The 20th-century dream of career for middle-class workers was never realized for many and is dead for a person like Jose in the new millennium. The best choice for Jose is to become adaptable taking advantage of the first job opportunities, building social networks through present job offers, and continuing the development of new skills and employability.

The career of the 21st century will be protean, driven by the person and reinvented by the person from time to time responding to the changes within and outside the person. Whereas the traditional career concept focused on the institution, advancement, low mobility, salary progression as success criteria, and organizational commitment, now the courage to work for the worker who has a protean orientation is to succeed with a focus on his or her autonomy, a core value of freedom and growth, high mobility, psychological success, satisfaction, and professional commitment.

The protean career is a process which the person, not the organization, is managing. It consists of all of the person's varied experiences in education, training, work in several organizations, changes in occupational field, etc. The protean person's own personal career choices and search for self-fulfillment are the unifying or integrative elements in his or her life. The criterion of success is internal (psychological success), not external.[8]

We are faced with new worries and fears when we shift the transition from the traditional concept of work to a protean career. Proteus, the god of sea in Greek mythology, was known to be changeable, but could not commit to a form unless he was seized and chained. The dilemma of the "Protean Man"[9] is best described with the ambivalence of the incessant change to reflect the continuously changing world and the need for identity and belonging.

Many factors come into play to influence a worker's job attainment, satisfaction, and retention. Most workers do not have an alternative plan in case they lose their job. Men and women are experiencing issues of work and family interface that require them to reexamine their gender and life roles. The barriers of our development are often contextual that require the system's intervention. That "little engine that could" is not only confronted with the uphill test but the many sideway distractions and impediments imposed by a vast, changing society that no longer provides a clear path for our journey.

SOCRATIC DIALOGUE 4.4

How do you go about solving problems at work? Do you and people at work welcome or resist change? What fears do you have for your career and work life? How do we better prepare ourselves for a protean career? How may we use these fears constructively to move toward our life goals?

The protean concept encompasses any kind of flexible, idiosyncratic career course, with peaks and valleys, left and right turns, moves from one line of work to another, and so forth. Rather that focusing outward on some ideal generalized career "path," the protean career is unique to each person—a sort of career fingerprint.[10]

The intriguing concept of the protean career liberates us from the external control of our work life with a sense of vitality and freedom at the price of more fears of the unknown future. In Individual Psychology, we do not believe in the demise of fear but recognize the purpose and the use of fear. As we have discussed in Chapter 1, when the fear is larger than our problems, fear becomes worry and anxiety. It can be used as a way to express our discouragement and defying attitudes, to avoid change, or to safeguard the imagined failure. The answer to the new challenges the protean career presents requires us to counter our fears with creative power and courage as we train ourselves to be adaptable and to imagine possible resolutions. Our fear is a gift when we can listen to it, not exaggerate it, and use it to facilitate change.

Career Construction in Style

Individual psychology coincides with the new mind-set of the protean career in viewing work as a task of life that requires a holistic understanding of the individual's characteristic attitudes toward life. The meaning of work is in the making of the individual based on the perceptions of self, others, and the world. To understand work and work choices, the traditional "test 'em and tell 'em," best fit (trait and factor), and linear developmental approaches are now less useful.

> Congruence may not be based solely on the objective work environment criteria used in Holland's job classification. Rather, it may be how the individual perceives the work environment which determines its fit with the worker's lifestyle.[11]

Understanding of an individual's life style (i.e., unity of action, emotion, and thinking) helps to explain how an individual will function, adjust, and thrive in the new protean career environment. We contribute and construct our own career stories. Our traits, as described by many typology approaches (e.g., Holland type or Myers–Briggs Type Indicator) are actually our coping strategies or a "success formula" we naturally use to respond to our work environment. Likewise, the character traits we associate with our birth order may be related to our career choices and achievement patterns. Children learn about work attitudes and values from their early play and work at home and in school. Family constellation and atmosphere influence one's life style that will later find its expression in one's work task. Both chronological and psychological birth-order positions are aligned with specific characteristics or personality traits (see Chapter 6) that actually function as career strategies.

The Individual Psychology framework is obvious in the career construction theory that stresses individual life themes, personality traits as attitudes toward life, as well as career adaptability. We can have access to the individual's guiding beliefs that invite opportunities or constraints to an individual's career stories, strengths, or weaknesses as well as needs/problems and resolutions.

SOCRATIC DIALOGUE 4.5

- What are your earliest recollections (stories) about things you recall happening to you when you were 3–6 years old?
- How would the headline read for each story?
- Who was your hero when you were growing up?
- What is your favorite saying?
- What is your favorite magazine and TV show?[12]

The way we remember (choose) our early memories indicate our preoccupation (needs, goals, and what should have been), and the qualities of our hero(s) or role model(s) as we remember them represent the strengths we identify with or possess to resolve the problems and meet the needs. In career construction theory, creative methods are utilized to facilitate understanding of an individual's thinking, feeling, and acting.

We can find useful information embedded in a person's preferences of activities. For example, in the individual's favorite saying we can see self-advice, in the person's favorite magazine we learn about the person's concerns for the environment, and in the person's favorite TV shows and characters we can guess the person's approaches to people and struggles. What we are looking for is not really the individual's preferences but the unique style or unity of the person's attitude toward work or life.

Calvin, a White male in his early 40s, has been a hard worker since his school years. He holds a very interesting work history that includes roofing technician, architectural drafting, and installation technician and troubleshooter (where he was promoted to sales engineer and regional technical manager). He indicated that he went through a career crisis as he reached a career ceiling. After some meditation on life satisfaction and meaning, Calvin decided to return to school. He is now a college professor. His Holland type is Social, Artistic, and Enterprising. His favorite quote is by Michelangelo: "I saw the angel in the marble and I carved until I set him free." The following is one of Calvin's early recollections:

Our home was older and in need of repair. One summer day while my parents were at work I decided to repair a rock retaining wall supporting our back porch. I mixed the concrete and repaired the wall. I remember my mother and father being impressed because I could do this repair at 12 years of age. I felt proud to be able to fix the wall and make the house look better.

SOCRATIC DIALOGUE 4.6

How would you describe some of the traits (including strengths) Calvin has as a worker? What are Calvin's lifestyle themes? How does Calvin use his Holland type in his career transitioning? What other variables would help you understand his career development? How does Calvin's early recollection reflect his adult career transitions? How would you describe his attitudes toward life? Fears? Courage?

The Encouraged Worker

I love my job. It is like throwing a party; you get ready before people come and you clean up afterward with the hope that every one had a good time. I did not know my job would put me into touch with the world so much. There was a family who knew that the person they were going to visit had just passed way in the hospital shortly before they boarded. We were part of the journey with the Katrina evacuees. Not knowing where they would end up going, all we could do was just to give our best providing a little comfort in the midst of these individuals' pain and loss. There was this 9-year-old unaccompanied minor, who had to sit in his seat to keep his flight phobia under control. He needed to go to the toilet. With some help, he made it to the door of the toilet but had so much fear of going inside by himself. I told the boy, you have made it this far and now you can stand here being afraid or just get in there and pee! And he did!

—**Christina, a flight attendant**

Christina's work attitude is an exemplary illustration that our career satisfaction is positively related to social interest. To have the courage to work is to contribute to the community feeling what we do. That is, through our work, we make the world a better place not only for us but for others as well. This courage to work in the interest of others is demonstrated in an everyday worker like Christina as well as in the well-known figures like Dr. Schweitzer and Florence Nightingale who made contributions to humankind with their selfless acts.

According to Losoncy, the encouraging workplace uninvites the private goals of recognition, power, revenge, and withdrawal but focuses on "creating a positive, productive work climate by building people's skills to bring out the best in each other." Encouragement in the workplace translates into actions that foster the worker's feeling of choice, respect, and meaning as well as a sense of community.

> Encouragement is an uplifting process to build totally committed, inner driven, goal directed people by centering on their strengths, talents, interest, possibilities and contributions to their team, the company's vision and the world.[13]

Many techniques and strategies based on Individual Psychology are readily available to help build an encouraging workplace where workers and leadership experience mutual respect and positive attitudes. The emphasis is on intrinsic rather than extrinsic motives, natural and logical consequences rather than punishment, encouragement rather than praise or rewards, and contribution and cooperation rather than accomplishments by competition and comparison. Encouraged workers respond with a yes attitude when their work fulfills their needs, they are earning a living, they feel useful, and they are making a difference in the world. In the presence of difficulties, they act as if they were unafraid and competent.

Vocational barriers and chance events (happenstances), paradoxically, are a part of our vocational identity. *Happenstances* are no longer viewed as random events, but as growth opportunities.[14] This process can only occur if we are willing to be positive, encouraging, and trusting of ourselves as we make choices, and view these circumstances as opportunities rather than negative events. The process that promotes the use of happenstances often follows a particular path and can be integrated into the process of becoming our vocational self, especially if we believe that it is influenced by our spiritual self. As a result, our life work becomes our vocation as we trust and accept our self and the happenstance events that come into our lives.

Encouraged workers are, therefore, capable of self-encouragement and build self-encouraging people. Whereas discouraged workers complain that they are overworked and that they do not have a life, encouraged workers celebrate that what they are doing is a life work.

> **SOCRATIC DIALOGUE 4.7**
>
> Find out from the following whether you are an encouraged worker. Give yourself and others courage by helping them become self-encouragers. If there are areas you are not as encouraged in your work life, how could you go about getting charged with more intrinsic motivation?
>
> - Recognizing personal growth through your work
> - Appreciating your technical skills and task mastery
> - Reflecting on your career advancement and potential
> - Sensing the social meaning in your work
> - Sharing your team's challenges and accomplishments
> - Respecting your contribution to your company
> - Finding customer fulfillment in your work
> - Experiencing inspirational meaning in your life work

Work Is Sacred

Work, like other tasks of life, is the expression of our longing and laboring to be connected with ourselves, others, and the universe. It is interesting that we often allow the workplace to be dominated by function and efficiency. The emotional complaints of our work life such as emptiness, meaninglessness, vague depression, loss of values, yearning for personal fulfillment, and a hunger for spirituality are, for the most part, ignored. Work, often seen as a secular space, is in fact a spiritual pathway through life, a gift, and a life calling. In work, we "find communion with that which is deepest within oneself and that which is greatest outside oneself."[15]

> Finding one's true career or calling, an enlightening and fulfilling path mocking and haughty to the laboring j-o-b, often means embarking on a journey that is markedly spiritual, introspective, and highly personal. It goes beyond survival, a new consciousness where you are the choreographer of life rather than a dancer in someone else's dream. Instead of placing value on external, quantifiable rewards, intrinsic motivation creates meaning in what is immeasurable. When I look externally at what I have to gain specifically through employment, I lose sight of the spiritual reckoning of career whereby, rather than profiting from what society owes me, I stand to the universe, and to a higher power. It's taking the outward lens that we have of ourselves in relation to the world and turning it inward toward the expansiveness of the soul and heart where rational, sensible things like money, prestige,

power, cost of living, upward mobility, perks, location, amount of flexibility, benefit package, and other tangibles seem more like limits in a vast and invisible stream of endless, divine opportunity.

As creatures of habit, limited by fear, doubt, responsibility, and the need for security, we often make the costly error that sees life and purpose only in the realm of the physical; time, effort, and insight are needed when moving to the next level where experience is sifted through a spiritual funnel as well. It seems time consuming and the noise outside can be so utterly deafening; why bother? Because a higher calling is our purpose and I would argue without it, what are we?[16]

The undercurrent of work problems often signals the individual's quest for meaning and spiritual direction. Where in my work am I moving toward becoming the person I am capable of becoming? What would a more spiritual workplace mean for me? What can I do at work that will give me purpose? Where did I come from, where am I going to, and why am I here? How I have touched others' lives? How does my work make the world a better place? Our vocational journey is *not* about spirituality as the answer but about spirituality as the question. And in this questioning, we notice the deepening of our own spiritual experience at work.

Clint, 44, entered career counseling with the stated concerns: "Travel too much, don't want to be on the front line anymore, and want to do something fun that can make a difference in other's lives." He had been in healthcare information systems sales for 8 years. He was having trouble enjoying it. He felt as though he was "hunting for new prospects." It was "eating at his soul." Looking back at the process during a recent interview he remembers wondering if he could ever achieve enough and that the answer to that question was no. He now sees that time as a struggle with the question: What was he after, success or significance?

Clint's struggle was a tension between his rational goal and spiritual fulfillment at his workplace. Instead of finding the meaning of work, for Clint, work was a frenetic place filled with fear and greed. Clint's counselor was able to work with him on finding a space, away from his routine of course, where he could get hold of his resource of energy. Clint discovered that he felt plugged in and the lamp that he had was lit up when he was in relationship with others. His gift was one of being a facilitator or liaison between people (e.g., between his company and his clients). As a result, he only found it necessary to change companies and not careers. His new work environment afforded him the opportunities to establish rapport and cultivate customer relationships rather than "hunting them down." He felt he was more in a position of giving than taking, which ironically resulted in him ultimately making more money than in his previous position.

Lucy thought she was a square peg in a round hole. Lucy was quite unsettled as to whether she was in the right career direction. She was judging herself by a financial measure: the six-figure income she'd earned as an account executive of a large group insurance company versus the profit she was yet to make in her 2-year-old business. And yet, somewhere inside there was a disconnection with the financial success. For nearly 6 years prior to her leaving her corporate position she'd "prayed for some change." For Lucy, the workaholic, who'd labored 60–80 hours a week for 9 years, her prayers were answered. She was diagnosed with colon cancer. To her credit she did a lot of work healing physically, grew stronger in her spiritual beliefs, and also did a lot of work on her own to develop a more fulfilling life style including the training necessary to build a new career.[17]

What we have learned from Clint's and Lucy's stories is that work-life problems are profound opportunities for life-work development. Work helps us to mediate our subjective aspiration and its objective usefulness. The challenges of external demands and our inner striving for significance suggest a profound life work of developing our identity and universal connectedness. Our responses to these challenges and changes require courage by which we may gain insight of the happenstances that actually lead to positive and transformative changes. These life events enabled Clint and Lucy to bring together their vocational and spiritual selves to experience the wholeness of life.

SOCRATIC DIALOGUE 4.8

Answer any questions that call to you … or make up your own![18]

- Have you ever felt called to something? How did this call *feel*?
- What led you into your present career?
- What questions did you hope your work would answer?
- As a child, what did you hope to give to the world?
- Deathbed questions: What would you regret *not* doing? What would you feel proudest of accomplishing?
- What problems in the world call out to you to address?
- In what type of activities do you lose track of time?
- When are you at your best?
- What human problems or groups emotionally touch you the most?

Closing Thoughts

Work deepens our understanding of self, others, and the world. Our assumptions about work and its contexts help us appreciate the complexity of career, especially in a time that is characterized by fast and vast changes. In the wake of a protean career, we now have to have the courage to show concern and develop adaptability.

In our work task, we have many fears as we cope with our personal and collective inferiorities. We fear failures with our work task as it is directly linked to the provision of our physical and social existence. We respond to fears by either overworking or underworking. Work can be problematic when people's self-interests outweigh social interests.

Work means more than making a living for our survival and overcoming of our inferiority, however. We cooperate as we work within the social structure and we contribute to make the world a better place for all.

The courage to work means to give courage to self and others at the workplace and to see career barriers as happenstances that propel us to grow and change. Life is larger than work. Work is what we use to construct our meaning of life, and seek social and spiritual belongingness.

> But I say to you that when you work
> you fulfill a part of earth's furthest dream,
> assigned to you when that dream was born,
> And to love life through labour
> is to be intimate with life's inmost secret …
> And when you work with love you bind yourself to yourself,
> and to one another and to God.[19]

CHAPTER 5

The Courage to Love

> Being deeply loved by someone gives you strength, while loving someone deeply gives you courage.
>
> —Lao Tzu

We are created to love and to be creative for our loves. *Relationship* is a word used most often in American culture to describe the intimacy between two adults. In this chapter, we prefer to use the word *love*. Love in different relationships in non-English languages is expressed with additional distinctive prefixes such as familial love, friendship love, intimate love, parental love, spousal love, and so forth. In this chapter, we will discuss love in the contexts of our intimate, sexual, and marital relationships.

What Is Love?

Love has many layers as we come into touch with ourselves and others. Four Greek words are most frequently used about our love experiences. They are *storge* for affection, *philia* for friendship, *eros* for intimacy, and *agape* for God's love. Affection is fondness through familiarity and is embedded in all types of love. Love in the parent–child relationship is the best example for affection. Friendship love is a bond between people who share common interests or values. Whereas eros is a sense of "being in love" with or without physical attraction, agape is an unconditional love toward one's neighbor that makes experiences such as tolerance, forgiveness, and reconciliation possible.

The first three (storge, philia, and eros) are natural loves, whereas agape is love from God. In all of these loves, one finds the three intertwined

53

elements of love: need love, gift love, and appreciative love. We have affection for nature and the living things in nature. We also have affection for others in family, work, and communities. Some of these natural loves are based on needs and some are unconditional gifts we give, receive, and appreciate. Although need love is both necessary and prevalent in our popular culture, gift love is the answer to our heart's longing. All loves are insufficient and vulnerable without the ultimate agape love. The agape enables us to love both what is lovable and what is, by nature, not lovable (e.g., individuals who have made serious mistakes and caused unbearable consequences).[1]

Agape love, expressed in Individual Psychology, is the community feeling to which we strive with our love for ourselves and our fellow humankind. In our discussions of intimacy/marriage, friendship/family/community (Chapters 6 and 7), and the spiritual sense of belonging (Chapter 9), we will use the eros love (motivated by fear) and agape love (motivated by courage) as conceptual opposites to illustrate relationships that differ on the basis of self-interest and social interest.

The Use and Misuses of Sex

Love is not confined to sexuality. Adler originally used *sex* when referring to the task of love or problems of intimacy, which is reflective of our attitude toward one's sexual urges and sexual role in life. Starting from a physical sensation, the function of sex develops slowly over the life span, always in the company of other impulses and stimulations. It eventually evolves from one's relationship with oneself to his/her relationship with a partner, which requires not only wishful thinking but also cooperation. To Adler, even masturbation has a hidden component of imagining the latter development, because sexual function is a task for two people.

> Sex is not a field of causes: sex is the field of results! It is a mirror in which we reflect our own character accurately and fully. It is—what we are![2]

Sex is an expression of the individual character. The sexual sideshows (i.e., perversion, diversion, and conversion)[3] of intimate relationships can be examined by the magnifier of one's use or misuse of sex. Sex used in pervasive ways is for those who evade the problems of love and marriage. Sex used in context other than love and marriage is for those who divert their sexual life to some false social or other ends. Sexual activity substituted for activity in other life tasks areas is called the conversion of sex. These sexual practices are expressions of the life style of isolation and timidity, and, therefore, are choices made away from social participation. This reveals the individual's fear for a superior or authoritarian power, and actions of defiance toward that power.

Marriage should be a partnership of two people for the world and not a sideshow of two people against the world.[4]

With the concerns of social interest, Adler warned his readers of the danger of the early completion of the sexual function. To Adlerians, the problems of love, sexuality, and marriage are viewed as social problems of true cooperation. Intimacy is the strongest and closest emotional relationship that can exist between two human beings.

SOCRATIC DIALOGUE 5.1

What would Adler say about sex before or outside of marriage? What would Adler say about falling in and out of love? Love at first sight and being in love?

The Myth of Romance

> My father died of cancer when I was in high school. I believe I chose to marry my husband mainly because he is capable of offering me the kind of love my father used to provide for me with which I would feel protected and secure. Our children have grown and left home. We are going through what they say a midlife crisis. The other day it occurred to me that this father–daughter ordeal is gone. What he needs is a lover.
>
> —Cathy

Cathy, during a group session on early recollections, shared her insight about her marriage; she started out seeking marriage with a man she saw as an opportunity to quickly fill the gaps in her life, which she had been too cowardly to develop for herself. For Cathy (and many others like her), love and marriage is equated to a fictive romance or a shortcut that they wish to use as a personal solution for escape, as a cure, or as goals that are perceived to be unattainable.

Individuals develop mistaken expectations of what love and marriage can accomplish for them based on their private and unfulfilled desires guided by eros love. Some common examples are when love/marriage is built on external factors such as economic security; perceived prestige; one's pity for another person; unplanned pregnancy; remedy for personal problems; and pressures related to age, gender, and cultural values.

There are other problematic loves that appear in real life and the drama of love stories we see in literature and popular media. As each topic in the following dialogue box deserves debate and discussion, the Adlerian principles suggest that discouraged love relationships and problems of love originate from fear that limits the individual's ability to be real and respectful to oneself and the other. All these problems will become manageable when, in a relationship, one cares for the other more than himself or herself.

SOCRATIC DIALOGUE 5.2

What do love and marriage mean to you? Can someone fall in love with more than one partner at a time? Is unattainable love still love? How do lovers know when to end a relationship? How do they depart? Why do people get married when there seems to be other alternatives? Living together without marriage? Trial marriage? Are people happy in their marriages? What problems have we seen in marriages? Are there right and wrong reasons for how people come to the decision of marriage? What contributes to the high divorce rate?

Men and women would be far happier if they planned their marital relationships according to the deep compatibilities of social, intellectual, and occupational interests, responsibilities toward children and their community, mutual helpfulness, and acted "as if" love might be the reward of five or ten years of successful cooperation.[5]

Dependent individuals who come into a relationship not ready to cooperate or contribute will only look for the private satisfaction of romance, personal recognition, and the desire to be pampered. Individuals who long for eros love hold infantile attitudes, beg for recognition, make decisions out of fear, and sense no freedom. In isolation and loneliness, these individuals take no initiative to change and in the long run, they become the emotionally unemployed. Most likely, these individuals are eros lovers who will experience fears that result in problems of self-serving interest, self-guards, exploitation, and superiority. When one partner dominates and possesses another, the other will be subject to submission, conformity, mutual blame, or hostility.

It is surely easier for a camel to pass through a needle's eye than for a spoiled child to be happy in the cooperative venture of marriage.[6]

On the contrary, intimate love that is inspired by agape is naturally content with mutual respect. With unconditional acceptance and respect, each partner regards the other's interest as more important than his/her own. The

Table 5.1 Effects of Eros versus Agape on Love

Eros Love (Self-Interest)	Agape Love (Social Interest)
Sex	Love
Leaning (dependent)	Self-sufficient
Personal recognition	Inner potential
Begging attitude	Content
Emotional poverty	Fullness
Infantile possessiveness	Freedom
Partiality	Nonpartisan
Attraction and aversion	Acceptance
Critical, evaluative	Capacity
Judgmental, hidden	Nonjudgmental
Fault finding	Encouraging
Seeker, taker	Giver, doer
Hypersensitive	Okayness regardless
Wishful thinking	Hopeful
Willpower	Creative, playfulness
Defective love	Fulfillment
Double mind	Free mind

agape lovers are independent individuals who are giving and free minded. They are both compatible and interdependent. Table 5.1 presents descriptions that characterize the difference between eros love and agape love.[7]

Problems of Love and Marriage

The intimacy task can be totally avoided if one chooses the compensations of work and friendships. To live the love task, however, is to have the courage to meet the challenges of mistaken expectations, cooperation, and gender equality. True intimacy demands companionship, commitment, and mutual respect. Sexuality, love, and marriage are tasks of two equal persons. The tasks of forming a unit can only rightly be solved if persons are trained for sufficient social interest. Love means so much more than the romantic feeling and it is very different from a marriage of which the marital functions are mainly geared toward functioning for the family and society.

Individuals who experience marital happiness express equality, self-worth, and cooperation with their spouse. They also feel needed and well in their marriage where they know they are irreplaceable in their life journey and they simply feel like a friend to each other. Such intimate feeling is attainable to men and women who are secure about themselves, certain of their occupations, and capable of social relationships.

Contrary to these positive marital qualities, the picture Tim and Christina painted for 32 years for their marital relationship appears rather different:

> Tim, 63, and Christina, 57, have been married for 32 years. They are a much-respected couple in their extended family and community. Tim retired from the Navy at the age of 45 and took on a second career as a government employee. He enjoys the social aspects of his job and has been very successful at it. Christina recently retired from her schoolteacher's career after 30 years of service. They raised two girls. The husband admitted to the lack of sexual intimacy in the marriage, which has been as long as two decades mainly due to his wife's frigidity and his impotence. The wife felt that the husband had been too critical about keeping their home spotless. She suspected that the husband had had affairs over time. They came to counseling first to talk about their concerns of their daughters who both started their rebellious behaviors during their college years.

Couples like Tim and Christina often put forth a nice front, concealing troubles and challenges they have in their relationship. Instead of facing their marital challenges, they externalize their concerns to their children's behavior problems. Many couples stay in the marriage for the sake of their children thinking the children need both parents for normal development. Infidelity in the Adlerian perspective is a form of sexual competition for one spouse to use as punishment for his/her mate and simultaneously express sexual superiority (male) or rebellion (female) against the imposition of false masculine authority.

> Denying ourselves the pursuit of our interests does not make us cooperative, but merely submissive. One cannot establish a good relationship on the basis of submission and appeasement. One does not gain respect in this way, and without mutual respect no harmonious and lasting equilibrium is possible.[8]

Tim and Christina operate from fear and the need to be right and good in the eyes of others. As individuals and as a couple, they need to examine (with or without professional help) their own life attitudes expressed in Table 5.1. They then can decide if they wish to develop new skills that allow them to move from the eros marriage to the agape marriage (Table 5.2) via personal growth and retraining for the mature love that is reflective of courage and social interest. According to Adler, "It is also a great mistake if a marriage is contracted out of fear and not out of courage. We can understand that courage is one side of cooperation, and if men and women choose their partners out of fear it is a sign that they do not want real cooperation."[9]

Table 5.2 Effects of Eros and Agape on Marriage

Eros Marriage (Self Interest)	Agape Marriage (Social Interest)
Enslaving	Liberating
Envy	Appreciation
Dominion or submission	Egalitarian
Obedience	Respect
Romantic myth	Gifts of give and take
Fear and distrust	Faith
Power	Productivity
Mutual blame	Mutual respect
Demanding expectations	Companionship
Against the world	For the world
Pampering	Affirmation
Infantile attitude	Independence
Resentment	Disagreeability
Happy ending of fairy tale	A working relationship
Growing apart	Growing apace
Coercion	Commitment
One-upmanship	Partnership

Same-Gender and Transgender Love

Reflective of his time and culture, Adler regarded the social function of sexual intimacy to be for procreation and his biased views of homosexuality were that it was a deviation from the normal development and that gay men lacked courage (to be heterosexual) and social interest (inability to cooperate) that originated from inadequate childhood preparation. He suggested "curing" the individuals with same-gender orientation as an alternative to the then-prevalent jail treatment.

Efforts to depathologize same-gender orientation in Individual Psychology have been built based on our confidence in Adler's beliefs in equality, respect, and acceptance (as he had endeavored to advocate for women and the children), and his proactive view of collaboration for the ideal of community feeling. We are confident that Individual Psychology, as a psychology of courage, has the capability to "critique, correct and expand"[10] for it to be more inclusive and sustainable in the tests of time and diversity.

> Maria, a mother of a 2-year-old boy and a 4-year-old girl, decided to disclose to the family counselor what transitions she had been going through. Maria's husband, Joe, was transsexual and had decided

to undergo the medical procedure that would help him become a female. He had asked her to call him by the new name Joyce. Maria knew about Joe's gender identity issue when they first met and fell in love. The couple had worked together on this decision for more than a year and had just recently begun to tell their family, friends, and coworkers about the upcoming change. They decided to get a divorce soon so the children could still go under Maria's medical insurance plan. Maria felt that they could deal with others' reaction but feared that her children were already confused about what their daddy was doing wearing female clothing when they woke up in the middle of the night. In addition, Maria said, "I love Joe and what I love is the person, not his gender. I am not sure what his new gender would make me to be. I never thought that I would become a lesbian."

SOCRATIC DIALOGUE 5.3

What are the fears individuals with same-gender attractions, bisexual orientation, and transgender concerns would say they have about intimacy or relationships? What are the compensating/coping strategies that the individuals with same-gender orientation have identified as encouraging and effective as they respond to these fears? What are the compensating strategies that might not help?

The inferior feelings of gay men, lesbians, and bisexual and transgendered men and women in regard to the love task need to be understood as their response to the prejudiced and oppressive heterosexual norm. For these individuals, challenges and preparation of the love task need to be addressed as part of a whole life style by which these individuals address other life tasks of work, friendship, self-acceptance, and spirituality.

To develop a deeper understanding of the issues of love task that confront individuals with alternative sexual orientation, we asked a colleague, who specializes in the area of marriage and family counseling, to contribute with her response to the questions in Socratic Dialogue 5.3:

> Some of the issues that GLBT and transgendered people have are similar and some are very different. There is a difference between gender orientation and sexual (affectional) orientation. People who are gay, lesbian, or bisexual often feel comfortable within their bodies, but they are attracted to same-sex people and that attraction tends to be marginalized by larger society. Transgendered people feel like they are born in the wrong body. That their internal sense of gender does

not match their biological sex. Transgendered people carry the stigmatization and marginalization attached to being transgendered, but also may have to deal with physiological/medical issues.

Any group with a minority (a group with less power than the majority and are often stigmatized by their group identity) has different relational and life coping strategies to deal with oppression, marginalization, and internalized oppression. Sexual minorities often internalize many of the negative messages that they hear about themselves. Some may fear that their relationships with romantic partners are "unnatural" or internalize the stereotypes that somehow their relationships are not worth as much as opposite-sex relationships or that same-sex relationships cannot be healthy or last. Relationships in general are difficult enough, but when one adds societal oppression to the mix and perhaps a lack of family support it can add extra stress to a relationship. In addition, having very few social sanctions (like marriage) for one's relationship can also add to the feeling that somehow one's relationship is not worth as much as opposite-sex relationships.

Because same-sex relationships have been marginalized there have not been as many public examples of healthy relationships as there have been for opposite-sex relationships. Some may fear that they do not know how same-sex relationships are supposed to work because there are few role models and there aren't gendered roles to emulate. Also, there is very little open discussion about how to be a caring, loving, sexual partner for opposite-sex couples, and there are fewer opportunities for these types of discussions for GLBT people as they are growing up until they, perhaps, connect with the GLBT community.

As in many oppressed groups, there are healthy and unhealthy coping mechanisms for dealing with a stigmatized identity. Some of the healthy coping mechanisms are creating families-of-choice. For other types of minorities (e.g., ethnic, racial, religious), they have the comfort of knowing most, if not all, of their family members share that identity. There is solace in numbers and shared experience. Because most GLBT people do not share the same sexual (affectional) or gender identity with their family, they often become involved in a community of similar people and make them their family. Those who are "out" and connected to a social network of accepting people tend to be healthier than those who do not have a social context in which they can own their identity. As with other oppressed groups, one also tends to see some unhealthy coping styles that sometimes culminate in alcohol abuse, drug abuse, depression, and higher rates of suicide.

It takes courage to accept, love, and be proud of oneself. It takes even more courage to accept, love, and be proud of oneself when surrounded by messages that one is different, unacceptable, or unnatural. It is not because a person has an identity of GLBT that sometimes makes it more difficult for sexual minorities to have the courage to embrace their identities—it's because society lacks the courage to love, accept, and encourage those who are different from the majority.[11]

SOCRATIC DIALOGUE 5.4

In what way can concepts about intimacy in Individual Psychology be useful for individuals with same-gender or transgender orientations? Are our discussions about sex and marriage, training for the love task, and agape love applicable for gay men and lesbians?

Although sharing the same ideal love relationship as their counterparts, same-gender relationships meet unique challenges that produce more social discouragement and variable compensating strategies. It is harder for gay and lesbian individuals to find relationships, acceptance by others and support from families, and legal equality of marriage and parenting. Compensating strategies for discouraged gay men and lesbians are variable and often include escapes (e.g., overuse of alcohol), denial (e.g., married to a spouse of opposite gender), avoidance (e.g., being with a married partner), and promiscuity (e.g., the ambivalence of looking and avoiding love).[12]

The hurdles gay men, lesbians, and individuals with transgender orientation encounter in a heterosexual social system are overwhelming. The time has come that we as a community act on our true beliefs of social interest and further educate ourselves so that we can be prepared to facilitate gay men and lesbians to recognize their fears of social rejection; improve self-acceptance; reject social discouragement; and develop integrated, healthy relationships with oneself, others, and a higher power.

Training for the Love Task

Like happiness, love may be achieved only where each partner is not only confident of his value to his mate but also to humanity at large, and is willing to assume that his mate, likewise, is well adjusted and useful not only to him but to humanity.[13]

To prepare for love and marriage, training is necessary. Intimacy is a task that can be developed. Such training is missing in many cultures that discourage early interests of youth intimacy and expect individuals to know how to be a mature intimate partner once they become adults. Instead, the courage to love starts with the belief that we can prepare to recognize the suitable qualities of our future partner by learning from our parents' marriage (e.g., the presence or absence of harmony) and making adjustment in our original family life. We will learn, sometimes in hard ways, which self-centered and pampered adult children make the worst possible candidates for intimacy.

> Infantile love follows the principle: "I love because I am loved."
> Mature love follows the principle: "I am loved because I love."[14]

We should avoid these individuals who do not know the arts of mutual respect and equality. Examples of behaviors of these individuals that discourage and frustrate a relationship are lateness, blaming, need to lecture, indifference, dominance, insensitivity, intolerance, and intimidation. Individuals with too much feeling of inferiority also show signs of weakness early in the courtship; they are under-prepared for a long-term and committed relationship. Behaviors characteristic of these individuals are indecisiveness, pessimism, overly sensitive due to feelings of inferiority, and a delay in choosing an occupation.

SOCRATIC DIALOGUE 5.5

What is the importance of friendship and work in preparing us for the task of intimate love? How does the family atmosphere in which the individual was brought up help us see his or her fitness for marriage? What can we learn from the not-so-successful marriages about early identification of problems and know the best course of action before marriage? How should partners be prepared for marriage? What should we know about courtship? What are the criteria of choice? What do you think of the reasoning of the Adlerian advice to avoid choosing a mate who is a pampered child, has more self-interest than social interest, and is a neglected child?

Once we can let go of the romance myth about love and marriage and appreciate the benefits of the social usefulness of an individual and a relationship, we can also prepare ourselves to choose our future life partner by developing the capacity to retain their friendship, the ability to be interested in his/her work, and, ultimately, to become interested in the ones we care for more than ourselves.

The Perfect Love: *Agape*

> But perfect love drives out fear, because fear has to do with punishment. The one who fears is not made perfect in love.
>
> —1 John 4:18 (New International Version)[15]

For many cultures, marriage represents spiritual unions and the bonding of two families and the communities they represent. Intimacy is therefore not only an individual choice but also a spiritual gift.[16] This gift is a reflection of agape. Agape is the divine, selfless, and egalitarian gift love that is for the well-being of the other. Agape makes possible the love in spiritual teachings such as "love thy neighbor" or "love others as you would love yourself." Agape love appears in our everyday lives. We not only receive agape love from our lover, friends, or relatives, we also benefit from the agape love of strangers and unsung heroes who do not seek reward or recognition from us.

Aversion will not be seen in the independent person who is capable of agape love. The agape lover will not choose to fall back on control. He or she is self-sufficient and will offer choices, respect, and freedom to his/her partner. The individual with agape love chooses the useful approaches toward resolving life problems of work, love, and friendship. He or she shows characteristics of altruism, courage, hope, and empathy. He or she has the courage to seek meaning and endure the ambivalence life often presented to us. Agape love is a gift love that does not ask for anything in return. The gift love in agape not only fulfills the need loves we naturally have but also enables us to love those who are not naturally lovable. Social interest or community feeling, from the Adlerian psychology vantage point, is a love that is closest to agape love.

Love can be experienced by individuals in or out of a relationship. There is equal importance in being loved, loving, and lovable. There are differences in how eros and agape loves affect our sexual behaviors, friendships, family ties, and work relationships.[17] If we only focus on eros love, our desire will bring us pain, attachment, greed, emotional poverty, dependence, and disappointment. The dependent person seeks close attachments with mutual use and controls. Eros love will eventually result in hurt feelings, misunderstandings, boredom, dullness, tensions, anxieties, hostilities, and struggles to possess, dominate, and use the partner. On the contrary, agape love empowers us to develop the qualities of self-sufficiency, fullness, capacity, confidence, and strength.

> Love and hate are but two different ways of depending on someone else. Love (eros) is gratified dependency. Hate is our resentment at being frustrated at being dependent. There is a love (agape) which has no opposite and seeks no favors or return. It exists when we are wholly

impartial in our interest and are willing to live-and-let-live in coexistence. Such love makes no demands and seeks no benefits, since it arises from our acceptance of the situation or person without any desire to change it in any way. We are in a state of affirmation or acceptance of reality, and living, at least for that moment, in the here-and-now.[18]

Closing Thoughts

The goal of love and marriage goes beyond the relationship of two individuals and their immediate family and community. Problems of intimate love and marriage stem from a lack of preparedness and cooperation. As we strive toward our perceived perfection, we recognize that the supply and the going of our love are not only from/to the natural loves of affection, friendship and eros love but also from/to agape love.

Social interest is the psychological expression of the spiritual implications of agape. Our striving toward a fulfilling love and marriage, community feeling, and spiritual belonging is accomplished by our human contribution and cooperation. Just as social interest is the ultimate measure of an individual's mental health, agape love is the best indicator of the strength of love and marriage. The agape that holds the world together is the agape that brings intimate relationships to life.

CHAPTER **6**
The Courage for Friendship and Family

> If he makes friends he is already making his family a part of the wider society around him.
>
> —**Alfred Adler**[1]

We put the topics of friendship and family together in the present chapter, as they are inseparable and often grouped together as the social relationship task in Individual Psychology. When the family prepares the child for friendship, friendship prepares the same individual for all other social relationships. These relationships require the attitudes and skills of cooperation and contribution. To have the courage for friendship and family is to acquire the necessary training for the social attitudes characterized by social interest, equality, and democracy.

Understanding Friendship

The meaning of friendship is rooted in the Greek word *philia*. The subject of friendship is sparsely covered in psychology. Friendship is often neglected because it is the least required concern for our biological survival. Friendship loses its primacy when we acquire intimate relationships and later assume child-rearing roles. Friendships developed in the workplace have to sustain the scrutiny in others' eyes where there is evaluation of performance. Unfortunately, popular culture holds much bias about friendship and often colors it with homophobic views for same-gender friendships and sexual connotations for opposite-gender friendships.

Friendship is least required for one's survival adjustment when compared to work, love, or family relationships. Nevertheless, friendship assumes a rather important role as we meet the demands of living because we are social beings. Friendship means more than an acquaintance, as it is a natural love given to the individuals who not only share common interests or values but also a sense of life direction. Adler and his followers equate the friendship task to terms such as fellowship, interpersonal relationships, social relations, and social contacts.

> Our real friends are those for whom we have a warm willingness to participate on a live-and-let-live basis. The number of our friendships is limited only by our ability to be a friend.[2]

There is a downside to the friendship task if it is not handled with discernment. All real friends share the danger of following each other into a bad course of choices, and close friends (just like close family ties) can function to exclude others in our group or community and thus hinder our social/cultural inclusiveness.[3] Having true friendship is often deemed impossible by many in a society where competition is valued and mistrust is the adopted way of dealing with the fear of failure. Evasion of the friendship task is either seen in the judgmental attitudes one holds about others or in relationships meant only for mutual use.

Successful friendships are established by individuals with constructive attitudes that form the basis for cooperation: social interest, confidence, equality, and courage. On the other hand, the absence of cooperation will result in encountering attitudes such as hostility, distrust and suspicion, feeling of inferiority, and fear, respectively. As Dreikurs describes,

> Another characteristic of the good comrade is his readiness to demand less than he offers. Nowadays most people brought up in large towns are spoiled children, who measure their happiness and satisfaction only by what they get. This is a grave error, for which thousands pay in unhappiness and suffering. ... None but those who can seek their happiness as a part of the whole, that is to say, in the contribution they themselves can make to the commonweal, can feel satisfied with themselves and their lives. The social interest, therefore, is expressed by willingness to contribute without thought of reward.[4]

The constructive attitudes facilitate the equal relationship in social interactions characterized by mutual respect, shared decision making, mutual influence, invitation, and freedom. On the other hand, individuals with the oppositional negative attitudes (hostility, distrust and suspicion, feeling of inferiority and fear) cater friendships that focus on external standards, competition, apathy, control, chaos, punishment, intimidation, or seduction.

Making Friends

Al: When you were growing up, who were your friends?
Rachel: I didn't have many friends growing up ... up to about when I was 15.
Al: As you think about that now, what was that like for you?
Rachel: Alone, feeling alone. Wishing I could be like the other kids.
Al: How would that be for you? Being like the other kids.
Rachel: I watched the kids going to swim with their families. I watched them play. But I only watched them. I wished I could be part of the activities but I never participated much.
Al: How is that for you now?
Rachel: I think my life has a different story now. I still don't have a lot of friends but my friends are lifelong friends.
Al: How does that affect you in your career, or family, or relationships?
Rachel: I have enough social network to sustain me in tough times like divorce or work challenges or single motherhood. I seem to be able to establish new friendships easier now than when I was young.
Al: How did that change for you?
Rachel: Somehow I woke up to the reality that I had to take care of my own future, as my family was not capable of giving me the support I needed. Then I realized likeminded friends could connect me to a world very different from my family. I recall making a conscientious choice to join and accept others for some school-related activities.
Al: So you went from being a watcher to more of a doer?

Making friends by participation did not come naturally for Rachel. It was a choice. Rachel was the middle child who grew up in a poor family where her parents were too preoccupied with family provision to be psychologically present for her and her siblings. She was always quiet and cooperative, secretly wishing her parents would pay more attention to her as her schoolmates' parents did. Her attitude changed from that of leaning on her parents' recognition to appreciating her new friendships as her life circle expanded. In fact, friendships later greatly contributed to Rachel's adjustment after her divorce.

Friendship begins with curiosity, nonjudgmental listening, encouragement, and mutual admiration. The foundation of good friendships is rooted in the healthy attitudes of the individuals toward themselves and others. Friendship is a descriptive measure of our distance to the world front and is directly related to the Adlerian concept of cooperation and is ultimately the best measure of social interest.

Table 6.1 Effects of Eros Love and Agape Love on Friendship

Eros Friendship (Self Interest)	Agape Friendship (Social Interest)
Mutual conformity	Lifeblood of community
Fear	Security, risk taking
Competition	Cooperation
Greed	Needs
Exploitation	Equality
Mutual babysitting	Unconditional
Invented busyness	Free-flowing
Pretense goodwill	Authenticity
Irresponsibility	Willingness to participate
Mutual advantage	Mutual enrichment

> **SOCRATIC DIALOGUE 6.1**
>
> Growing up, what were your friendships with others like? Who was your best friends? Whom did you get along with best in your family? Were you close to either or both of your parents? Who was your best teacher? Describe these relationships using the descriptions in Table 6.1.

In general, the way we make friends reveals our attitudes toward society. In fact, the natural affection, appreciation, and gift love we have allow for friendships to be found in relationships at home, school, and work. Friendship between two individuals could also convert to intimate (eros) love. In addition, our interest in others beyond our family prepares us to become community minded, ready to participate in life with a higher level worldview. Like an intimate relationship, the ideal friendship is inspired by agape love. The ultimate agape love may not be attainable as we always have flaws as humans in our social relationships.

Birth Order and Family Constellation

The Greek word used for love in the family is *storge* and it means "natural." Family is a place where this natural affection is expressed among family members but it often faces obstructions. If looked at as a system, the family dynamic is expressed by the individual members' interacting behaviors, their characteristic goals, and life styles.

> In the life pattern of every child there is the imprint of the child's position in the family and that much of the child's attitude towards

life depends on this factor ... It is from the family constellation that the child first draws conclusions about life, about his/her own worth as compared to others, and interpretation of his/her position, he/she develops a unique attitude and behavior pattern which serves as a way to find a place in the group.[5]

Adler was among the first to discuss the individual's character traits according to one's natural and psychological birth position in the family. Development of these characteristics is, in general, based on the child's creative endeavor to overcome inferior feelings and responses from parents and siblings as well as others significant to the child's early life decisions and behaviors. For example, a new sibling often brings to an only child or the youngest child a feeling of being "dethroned" and the child may decide to regain the perceived "superior" position by being a good child or give up and become "the best of the worst."

Firstborn children are regarded as overly responsible, internalizing parental values and expectations, perfectionist, less oriented to friendships during school years, academically excellent, directive, and dominant. Middle children tend to be the opposite of the firstborn in school, housework, or friendship. They feel that they need to work harder to gain recognition. They are uncertain about their own abilities, rebellious, good at social networking, and they are empathic. Last-born children are typically pampered, spoiled, sweet, and easily discouraged. There are limited expectations of success for the last-born children but they often become the most successful in the family. Only-children are unique, self-centered, lonely, and are used to being the center of attention and comfortable in the presence of adults. They work harder to achieve an adult level of competence and they may be good at misbehaving while feeling they are not good enough.

Variations to these typical traits of differing birth positions should be considered when we take into account the factors such as family size, individual and cultural differences that are expressed through the child's abilities/disabilities, health problems, age gap between siblings, tragedies/illness/miscarriages in the family, sibling competition/rivalry, parental attitudes (e.g., favoritism or neglect) and responses to the children, and so forth. Psychological birth order is often found to be more descriptive of the individual's self-concept and patterns of his/her thoughts and feelings than physical birth order.

> Dave, 27, is the last of four kids. He has two brothers and one sister. There are 7 years between him and the firstborn. He is the first one in his family to receive a master's degree. Dave initially expressed that he was "picky" about choosing a girlfriend for a long-term relationship. There is a problem in that none of his brothers have sons; they all have daughters. Dave was certain he wants children, especially at

least one boy to carry on the family name. He would not continue to date a girl if he discovered that she did not want kids, as having kids will be a condition for marriage.

Dave has many fears when it comes to having a long-term relationship. Biologically, he is the youngest son, but psychologically he assumes the position of the only child. He has the social responsibility of the firstborn now that he is the only one who can carry the family name. He feared failure of marriage and the inability to have a male child. These fears contributed to his indecisive and evasive attitudes toward having a long-term committed relationship. Whereas no one definitely knows whether a marital choice is going to be a "right" one, Dave needs courage and confidence to move onward in the face of this social pressure.

> The family constellation is a socio-gram of the group at home during the person's formative years. This investigation reveals the individual field of early experience, the circumstances under which he developed the personal perspectives and biases, the person's concepts and convictions about one's self and others, one's fundamental attitudes, and one's own approaches to life, which are the basis for the person's character and personality.[6]

The best way to understand the dynamic makeup of a family constellation is for us to gather insight about how sibling competition, parent reactions/favoritism, and critical family transitions all contribute to the family atmosphere, which is the phenomena of how each member strives, in his/her own way, to belong and feel significant. A visual drawing of family birth positions chart like Figure 6.1 provides a beginning point when an individual's biological birth order is first made clear, and more information about the individual's possible psychological position and family constellation can be obtained via Socratic questions (see Chapter 10, Tool #3).

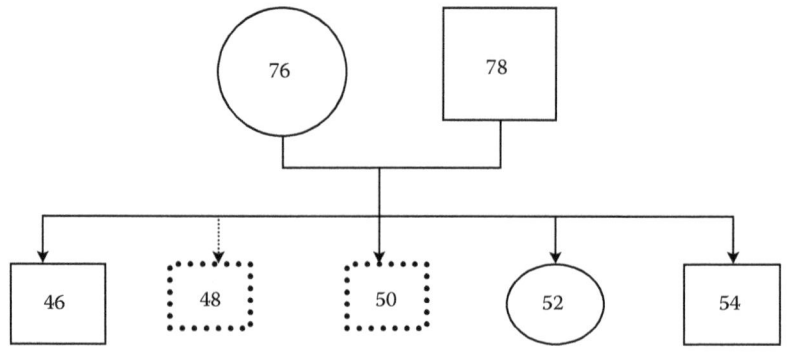

Figure 6.1 Rachel's family constellation.

SOCRATIC DIALOGUE 6.2

As shown in Figure 6.1, Rachel is the only female child of a family of three. Rachel's mother had two miscarriages (male fetuses) before she gave birth to Rachel's younger brother 6 years later. Rachel was the youngest child before the baby brother came along. What adjustment did Rachel have to make? What did the miscarriages and the gender of the fetus mean to the family and Rachel?

Birth order and family constellation provide us viable information about how people view themselves in relation to their view of life. Every child copes with inferior feelings in their creative and unique style; some gain social approval, whereas others receive a reprimand. The characteristic strategies children use to meet early life demands can be best observed in play, school experience, home chores, and relationships with siblings and parents and friends.

The Use of Children's Goal-Seeking Behaviors

Timmy's parents came to the United States from China a year before Timmy was born. He has a sister 5 years older than him. Timmy was 2 when he began to have separation anxiety toward his mother leaving for work every morning. One day, I offered to babysit for Timmy. This is what I observed. Timmy began to whine and cry when his mother picked up her purse and walked toward the door after she said goodbye. His mother left his sight without turning around to comfort him like she normally did. Timmy cried louder and choked on his mucus and began to cough. His mother came back to check on him and then left again. Just as the mother disappeared, Timmy stood up and walked to the sofa where he stumbled and screamed as if he was injured. I walked to signal the mother not to return. After two minutes of crying, Timmy began to play with his toy as if nothing had ever happened.

SOCRATIC DIALOGUE 6.3

What made Timmy the way he is? Consider how these factors came into play for him in his family: birth order, gender, age difference between Timmy and his sister, parental responses, and social/cultural background. In addition to being the youngest of the family, what would you guess is Timmy's psychological birth order? (Consider the fact that his parents come from a culture that favors male children.) What are the goals of his behaviors?

Individual Psychology believes that all human behavior is goal oriented and manifests the life attitudes children acquire in their early years. A child's inferior feeling is typically propelled by fear of disapproval, defeat, and not having a place to belong in the family. This fear is intensified in those children who have physical disadvantages and those who grow up in any of the three following home situations will have difficulties meeting life demands: *pampering, hostility,* or *absence of love and warmth*.[7] Although the ultimate goal for these children is to achieve belonging and significance, they often creatively use uncooperative behaviors to engage their caretakers to fulfill their immediate needs.

For discouraged children who are under the age of 10, their misbehaviors are directed toward the four goals postulated by Dreikurs: attention getting, power struggle, revenge, and display of inadequacy (Table 6.2).[8] The attention getting goal is only revealed when the misbehaviors continue after the child is reprimanded. In the power struggle goal, the child will use all interrelationships as an opportunity for challenging the perceived superiority. The child with the revenge or getting even goal may have been hurt and adopted the distorted belief that hurting back serves to attain some power. For those who choose to withdraw from participating in the outside world, they are using a real or imagined deficiency as a means to safeguard their inferiority.

Table 6.2 Children's Goals and Misbehaviors

Goal	Behaviors
Attention getting	(*I belong only when I am being noticed or served.*)
	Active–constructive (the model child, exaggerated conscientiousness, bright sayings)
	Active–destructive (showing off, obtrusiveness, instability)
	Passive–constructive (the clinging vine, vanity)
	Passive–destructive (bashfulness, dependence and untidiness, lack of concentration and stamina, self-indulgence and frivolity, anxiety and fear, eating difficulties, speech impediments)
Power struggle	(*I belong only when I am in control or am boss, or when I am proving no one can boss me.*)
	Disobedience, stubbornness, temper tantrums, bad habits, masturbation, untruthfulness, dawdling
Revenge	(*I belong only by hurting others as I feel hurt. I cannot be loved.*)
	Stealing, violence and brutality, bed-wetting
Displayed inadequacy	(*I belong only by convincing others not to expect anything from me; I am helpless.*)
	Laziness, stupidity, violent, passivity

To Adler, a child purposefully selects his/her own symptoms according to his/her own private logic and life goal. Symptoms and problems are to be looked at as "creations, as work of art."[9] The child's goal-seeking behaviors are examples of how one's inferiority evokes one's creative power as a response to the environment as the child sees it. The creative power enables the child to adopt behavioral strategies as he/she moves toward goals of self-preservation. In this movement, our emotions, thoughts, and behaviors are consistent with the child's private logic as well as his/her life plan.

To decide which mistaken goal the child is using, we have to first observe how the child responds to our correction when they misbehave (Table 6.2). Our awareness of how we feel in response to the child's response to our reprimand/correction also helps us to recognize the child's goals. For attention-seeking behavior, the goal of the child is to keep us busy and our reaction is one of *annoyance*; when the child's goal is to show he or she is the boss, our reaction most likely will be *anger*; when the child's goal is to get even by hurting other's feeling or actually physically hurting others, our reaction is *hurt*; and last, when the child's goal is to be left alone, our reaction is to give up with *hopelessness*.

There is an interesting parallel emotional and behavioral reaction between the misbehaving child and the adult that makes the relationship both challenging and promising. Typically when the child demands undue attention, the adult may give in by giving what the child wants to avoid a worse reaction from the child. When the child wants power, the adult would show power over the child. When the child hurts the feelings of the adult, it is easy for the adult to hurt back by punishment, and when the child displays inadequacy, the adult either takes over the child's responsibility or lowers his or her expectations of the child.

Individual Psychology suggests that if the adult communicates an accurate observation of the child's misbehaving goal, the child would respond with a recognition reflex that "usually expresses itself though a smile, a grin, an embarrassed laughter or a twinkle in the eye."[10] Given that the child's misbehaving goals are rooted in his/her creative power, the adult can creatively engage the child in goal disclosure and acquisition of insight. We should be mindful, however, of not labeling the child's goal and losing insight to the totality of the child's life movement. We must be able to observe the child's reactions to our reprimands and our own related feelings before we are able to identify the child's chosen path to achieve his or her goal (see Part III, tools #8, 9, and 12 for activities that facilitate goal closure.)

Parents and teachers can take corrective measures after they successfully identify and communicate the goals of the child's misbehaviors. Overall, parents can learn to use the techniques of encouragement (instead of praise or rewards) to cultivate a democratic family atmosphere. Parents

Table 6.3 Parents' Efficient and Mistaken Methods of Training

Efficient Methods

Maintaining order	Family atmosphere, domestic rights and obligations, consistency, decisiveness, natural consequences
Avoiding conflict	Restraint, flexibility, arousing interest, winning the child's confidence, relieving the situation, withdrawing
Encouraging	Commendation, guidance and instruction, mutual confidence, "may" instead of "must," endeavor, disclosures, the family council

Common Mistakes

Spoiling the child	Lovelessness
Excessive affection	Withdrawal of affection
Anxiety	Frightening the child
Excessive Draconic severity	Mortification
Physical punishment	Rigid supervision
Excessive talking	Neglect
Urging	Extracting promises
Retaliation	Insistence on blind obedience
Nagging	Faultfinding
Belittling	Ridicule

Source: Based on Dreikurs and Soltz (1964).

give attention to their children when the children are not demanding attention with inappropriate behavior. They do not give in when their children are involved in a power struggle. They do so by giving choices with clearly stated natural or logical consequences. They do not hurt back when the children hurt their feelings. They are keen to know how their children might be discouraged by themselves or others. They recognize that there is a relationship problem behind their children's misbehaviors. Finally, the parents never give up on a child even when the child may decide to give up on him- or herself. They exercise unconditional positive regard and find opportunities for the child to experience small successes (see Table 6.3).

Victoria was in third grade when she began to come into her parents' bedroom and climb into their bed every morning around 2 a.m., indicating that she had had a nightmare and was too afraid to stay alone in her room. For a couple of weeks her parents tried coaxing her back to her room. This did not work and they began to allow her to continue to sleep with them so they could get some sleep. Victoria began to keep her parents awake after she came to bed. The father became frustrated and would spank Victoria. She was strong willed and was eventually allowed to stay in the room per her mother's plea to the father. The couple later sought professional consultation when Victoria's grades dropped and the teacher complained to them on several occasions about her lack of compliance with classroom rules.

SOCRATIC DIALOGUE 6.4

For what purpose can children use fear? Is fear real? If children experience constant fear, what is the parental responsibility? What is the difference between punishment and discipline? In what ways was the parents' care for Victoria both harsh and pampering?

Lifestyle Goal Seeking for Teens and Adults

Our views and responses to difficult youth are often limited to our own professional training. Most approaches focus on deviance of the youth: deviant, demonic, diseased, disturbed, disordered, delinquent, deprived, dysfunctional, disobedient, and disabled; each points to a very different set of intervention strategies. In Individual Psychology, we look at difficult youth in the context of inadequate childhood experience at home, school, and community as well as the forming of their lifestyle goal-seeking behaviors.

If children's mistaken goals are not corrected in the home and school, the children's private logic (private sense) of what they must do to overcome problems of inferior feeling or belonging will develop further away from what is commonly acceptable (the common sense). Their self-interest increases as their approach toward others becomes indifferent or hostile. Children and teens who perceive themselves to be inferior to others can seek alternative resolutions that put them at risk of alienation, early exposure/experience with at-risk behaviors, academic failure, early pregnancy/parenthood, and early substance abuse. Children and teens who seek belongingness with an improper reference group may become antisocial or oppositional defiant against rules and laws. These children and teens carry with them the false beliefs into their adulthood with persistent self-defeating or antisocial behaviors.

In addition to the four goals for children under age 10 (attention getting, power struggle, revenge, and display of inadequacy), Dinkmeyer and Carlson indicated that teens may seek the goals of excitement, peer acceptance, and superiority that give the adult feeling of nervousness, worry, and

78 • The Psychology of Courage

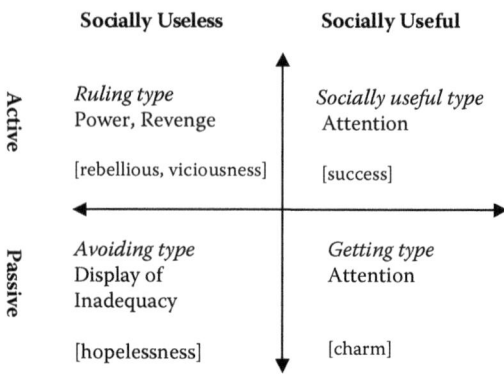

Figure 6.2 Active, passive, socially useless, and socially useful goals and behaviors.

inadequacy. What is in the goal-seeking behaviors for the child could be in the lifestyle goal-seeking patterns for teens and adults. Figure 6.2 highlights the two dimensions of the Dreikurs–Adler synthesis connecting the four goals and the four types of social-interest activities or temperaments: *socially useful type, the ruling type, the getting type,* and the *avoiding type*.[11] The active–passive and the socially useful–socially useless dimensions intersect to create four quadrants by which we could geographically locate and recognize a child's goals and behaviors.[12] If the child continues to rely on these four misbehaving goals, we may speculate that they later adopt the adult style of behaviors as expressed by the four types of temperaments (in italics).

SOCRATIC DIALOGUE 6.5

Rosie's teacher complains to Rosie's mother that Rosie, 15, is argumentative and contradictive. Rosie continues forbidden acts, temper tantrums, and many other bad habits. How would you help the mother conceptualize Rosie's mistaken goal(s) using Table 6.2 and Figure 6.2? How could you help parents or teachers who work with a teenager who has problems of untruthfulness, dawdling, laziness, disobedience, stubbornness, and/or forgetting?

Thoughts on Parenting

There were conflicting views about the use of punishment and whether the Bible advocates physical punishment of children. There was the idea that "sparing the rod" would result in "spoiling the child." In Biblical times, the rod was used to guide sheep and to keep them together for their protection from predators. It was not used to physically strike or hurt the sheep. In the Bible, the rod is used as a metaphor for guiding and disciplining. Punishment inspires fear in children. Parents want to inspire love in children. Punishment is inconsistent with inspiring love. The New Jerusalem Bible renders 1 John 4:18 this way: "In love there is no room for fear, but perfect love drives out fear, because fear implies punishment and no one who is afraid has come to perfection in love." That scripture speaks for itself. Punishment and fear do not inspire cooperation; knowledge, especially that which is derived from natural and logical consequences, is what inspires cooperation with the family's goals. Mistakes are golden opportunities to teach children and impart knowledge to them. Knowledge empowers children. Parents need to empower children so that they can make wise choices. Punishment discourages children and robs them of their confidence. Punishment lowers children's self-esteem. Punishment is counterproductive. No humans are perfect. Parents make mistakes, too. They have to deal with the consequences of their mistakes and that is usually enough for them to learn from and prevent a repeat of those mistakes. In the spirit of the "golden rule" should children not be afforded the same opportunity?

—Georgia[13]

This is a parent educator's self-reflection on the controversial use of physical punishment in Christian homes after running a parent education group with parents from her church.[14] Parenting is closely linked with our personal social upbringing as well as our cultural and religious beliefs. In patriarchal societies and some religious communities, the absolute authority is given to the father to discipline the children. This often involves physical punishment. The courage to be a parent is to be aware of his/her own cultural practice in child rearing and to discern the timeliness of methods by which one uses. It is imperative that parents and teachers do not confuse discipline with punishment.

Parents (and teachers) are people makers who, if untrained, replicate the values and attitudes of what their parents and teachers imparted to them. This replication, though unintentional, may negatively impact parents' present relationships with children. The dilemma of parenting is tied to the best intention most parents have about preparing their children to go into a world where there is danger and competition. Our own sense of inadequacy often is expressed in the forms of our high expectations or our fears that our children will suffer if we fail to prepare them to be "better than" others. We overprotect our children either by being too demanding or too permissive, or worse, by doing both. Knowingly or unknowingly, we lean on autocratic methods in response to a child's misbehavior at home and school under the influences of the social/cultural pressure that is often driven by fear.

Most parents either follow the way they were parented or take an oppositional approach compensating for their childhood regrets when they provide care and discipline for their children. Very few parents seek or receive training about being a parent. Even though we now live in a social climate that allows more democratic thinking and relationships at home, we still live under the shadow of autocracy from the past that influences us in our thoughts and actions about using our power as we rationalize how we parent our children.

> The cult of personal greatness, the elevation of "uniqueness" and "being different" arises out of the sense of inferiority born of family competition.[15]

The family is the first training ground where children learn to see the world and develop their life strategies. Parents, untrained themselves, make mistakes of overprotecting, pampering, spoiling, or being overdemanding of their children. The motivating factor for this parental behavior is a fear of their children not making it. Parents end up underpreparing children for the courage of discovering the world firsthand and a willingness to compete openly. These children cannot face the world without parent intervention (or interference).

Many individuals fail to meet the challenges of living because of a lack of understanding and training in socially useful devices and, instead, have ineffective attitudes that seem to make their lives more complicated. The many social sideshows we see adults play as they respond to their life tasks are directly derived from the influence of family life. Many adults either enter marriage and family without reeducation, or they fear marring or having children mainly because of their family difficulties as they grew up.

The primary purpose of the family is to prepare the young for vocational, social, and love relationships. The family is the testing ground of the social feeling, providing children opportunities for social cooperation. The courage for family love is embedded in the family members' attitudes toward social interest that resemble the characteristics of agape friendship and family (Table 6.4).

In Individual Psychology, the family atmosphere is mainly determined by the parents' marital relationship and the parental relationships with the children. We can guess whether one's family atmosphere is democratic or autocratic by the children's characteristic thoughts, feelings, and behaviors toward themselves, others, and life in general. These characteristics are summarized in Table 6.5. A good example is that in an autocratic family or education system, physical punishment is used as discipline to elicit fear.

Table 6.4 Effects of Eros and Agape on Family

Eros Family (Self Interest)	Agape Family (Social Interest)
Staying together forever	Standing-alone individuals
Autocratic	Democratic
Control	Confidence
Manipulation	Let go and let live
Secret	Openness
Praise	Encouragement
Punishment	Choice and consequences

In a democratic family, consequence is used instead of fear to encourage choice and learning.

Closing Thoughts

We gain our basic training for social relationships via friendships and family during our formative years. Our abilities to make friends prepare us to choose a mate and have a family. Birth order and family constellation provide dynamic information for understanding the individual. Understanding that behavior is goal oriented, and that children, teens, and adults behave according to their perceptions and attitudes allow us to recognize and create new approaches to understanding and working with children. We approach the task of friendship/family with attitudes that are not unrelated to our cultural and religious practice. Individual Psychology believes the use of encouragement and consequences as discipline instead of praise and punishment. The best practice of parenting is accomplished in a democratic family atmosphere where democratic methods of parenting are utilized.

Table 6.5 Autocratic and Democratic Methods of Parenting

Characteristics of the Child	Autocratic Parenting Methods
Submissive	Being arbitrary
Dependent	Give few choices
Obedient	Punishment
Fearful	Make threats
Follower	Intimidate
Passive	Give rewards
Domineering to those under him	Dictate
Obedient to those over him	Do things for them even though they are capable
Lack of self-respect	
Not original or creative	Talk about their mistakes
Indecisive	Make decisions for them
Not responsible	Criticize in others' presence
Not motivated to value what they want	Tell them what they need
Knows what is right and wrong according to the dictator	Break up their fights so they are not hurt
Feeling guilty	Blame and compare them to others
Characteristics of the Child	**Democratic Parenting Methods**
Creative	Let them make decisions
Sense of equality	Hold them responsible for what they decide
Responsible to the demands of the situation	Don't do things for them that they can do themselves
Flexible	Encourage
Asks why	Let them know they are accepted
Takes time to understand the mistakes they made	Help them repair mistakes
Respects self and others	Respect them
Encouraged	Let them know they are accepted
Self-disciplined	Be kind and firm at the same time
High self-esteem	Help them learn how much they can do
Has the ability to influence others	Let them help you
Is not afraid to make mistakes	Use consequences
Ability to promote agreement	Be understanding
Can be either leader or follower	Do not blame or compare
Honest	Do not use double standards

CHAPTER 7

The Courage to Belong

> When we successfully meet these life tasks, we express an essential feeling of belonging. This feeling of belonging, of having a place with our fellow humans, mitigates the experience of fear, loneliness, and desperation. Our sense of belonging gives us—courage-and in many cases, confidence—as we move toward our personal and collective goals in life.
>
> **—Manford A. Sonstegard and James Robert Bitter**[1]

The feeling of belongingness is only attainable when we are able to manage the basic life tasks of work, love, friendship and family with courage and confidence. Specifically, it is through our relationships with self, others, and the world that we acquire a place to belong. The feeling of belongingness is both psychological and spiritual. There are the contextual and cultural factors in our community living that either facilitate or hinder our psychological sense of belonging. Social equality is the resolution to the problems of belonging. Social interest, as a timeless and transcultural concept, helps us strive toward the ideal state of belonging and harmony. Community feeling works best where there is kinship in suffering that inspires the courage for acceptance and mutual help.

Problems of Belonging

We are a part of the whole and our desire to belong is a natural goal of our striving. Nevertheless, the sense of belonging does not come easy for many. Zeig, a Brazilian, reflected on her cross-cultural marriage to an American psychologist. Although language was not a problem, she encountered the challenges of the bureaucratic irony and social/political barriers in her immigration process. She also felt deprived of her family and social network. Zeig experienced psychosomatic symptoms caused by the conflict inside her and this conflict also caused problems in her marriage.

> The most difficulty I think was the fact that my husband did not understand what I was going through; it is very hard to explain water to fish. Culture is something in which we are all immersed, the "silent language" the anthropologist Edward Hall describes so well in his work. Only when a fish is outside of water does it misses it. My husband was not outside of water, I was.[2]

Rachel, a Chinese American who has been in the country for a quarter century, was very tired of being asked where are you from or when will you go home at social or professional occasions. Iris Chang's voice for Chinese Americans represents the voices of the many generations of immigrant workers from all over the world. She asked: How many hoops do we have to jump through to be considered "real" Americans?[3]

Rodney, an African American father, taught his three boys how to drive safely. The first instruction was "Leave your hands on the steering wheel when you are pulled over by a cop" to avoid the deadly mistake of being shot, a tragedy that occurs too frequently among black males. A White faculty commented on racial conflicts on college campuses with the ambivalence that racial violence is a result of the ills of the past of which he was not a part.

> I think there is a growing sensitivity, particularly in young people who are in that competitive game, who will lash out. I think a lot has to do with the economy. There is no doubt in my mind that these people [the Blacks] have been downtrodden. We can't kid ourselves, but the ills of 20–100 years ago I'm not sure should be put on people … I didn't have anything to do with that …

The road to belongingness is full of predicaments for many. Five participants out of ten individuals with same-gender sexual orientation in a study on social discouragement admitted attempts at suicide. Harry was one of them.[4] "I, actually that year, attempted suicide as a result of having to deal with all of the issues, my sexuality and my addiction."

> It is not funny but we laughed anyway. Roger, an African American man in his late 60s, and I, 30, a first-generation immigrant from China, found a common use of coffee and soy sauce. Our family and friends discouraged us from drinking coffee and dipping too much

soy sauce when we were young. The fear was that they would make us look darker!

—Claudia

The collective attitudes of "better than" or "less than" are a root cause to the problems of prejudice, discrimination, and oppression. Racism, sexism, and other prejudices as individual beliefs, although not necessarily oppressive in themselves, can lead to oppression if they are acted on and institutionalized via unjust exercise of authority or power. Our approaches to coping with discrimination and oppression range from confrontation, self-control, and self-defense to self-denying and resignation. The most negative outcome of the collective inferiority is the internalized oppression when the marginalized group uses the methods of the oppressor against itself.

The problems of belonging we have described become overwhelming when we examine the results of colonization, genocide, and cultural/spiritual deprivation that have happened to the native people throughout the world. To Jack Lawson, the results of racism are the loss of tradition, community, and a sense of identity for the native people. Simply put, they become the stereotypes.

> One hundred percent of Native people are affected either directly or indirectly by alcoholism. Underlying this are a host of complex problems related to the loss of culture, identity, and disruption of the family unit, all symptomatic of a long history of genocide and oppression. There are also a lot of anger and anger-related issues, depression and hopelessness, health problems, and unusually high rates of suicide and homicide, especially among the young. There has also been a serious increase in the diagnosis of HIV in our community, mostly related to IV drug use. Among Native people who are incarcerated, alcohol and drugs is a major contributor to their incarceration.[5]

SOCRATIC DIALOGUE 7.1

Are we born equal? What are your thoughts on equal opportunity?

Our problematic individual attitudes underscore the problematic social dynamics and therefore contribute to our problems of belonging. These attitudes stem from our fear of being inferior to others. It is this fear that triggers war within oneself, between sexes, in the family, and at work as well as within and between countries. We are conditioned to be afraid either via autocratic training at home, school, and community, or the overconcern of political correctness. We fear punishment, failure, and rejection.

The obstacles to social equality are our fear and inferiority that things are not equal and the consequent apathy and the loss of our confidence. Instead of confronting inequality, we become the conformists playing games where we compete against ourselves and others to achieve and succeed.

- We fail to see others as equals.
- Our needs for respect and inner freedom are conflicted with the hierarchical system that gives superior position to males, parents, and authority figures.
- We are deeply but differently influenced by the social demands of class, prestige, and power.
- We are mistaken with the need to be good or right according to these cultural norms.
- We often fail to recognize that behavioral problems are not the cause but the result of relationship conflicts.[6]

The Courage of Social Equality

Society is not imposed upon individuals; it is composed of them. We tend to forget this because we underestimate our own social significance. We have the same mistaken attitude toward society as we have toward life: we consider both as if they were outside us, whereas actually both life and society are embodied in us. We are life and society.[7]

The answer to the problems of belonging is our courage of community where there is mutual understanding and cooperation on the basis of social equality. The courage for social equality starts with the courage for self-affirmation in the face of a hostile environment where there are superior others that attempt to deny us equal status.

We must first have confidence in ourselves and others before we can have the feeling of belongingness. To have confidence is to have courage to believe in our ability, responsibility, and belonging.

We cannot fully participate in our relationships or society when there is no common ground or when the unchallenged goal of striving is to protect the status quo. We cannot, however, expect the society to function for us when we are not in it ourselves. The same problems we encounter in our work, love, and social relationships surface in our problems with the society and the universe. To free ourselves from assumptions of social or collective inferiority, we must have the courage for knowing our strengths and limits, letting go of our habitual prejudice, believing in ourselves and others that we are good enough and equal, discarding the obsession with success and failure, and avoiding the urge to compare and compete.[8]

Most of the conflicts in our relationships can be attributed to the absence of equality that leads to the dangers of competition and comparison, dominance and control, and superiority and discrimination. Instead of trying hard to overcome deficiencies and to strive for perfection, we can develop *the courage for imperfection*[9] and risk doing what we know would be best for ourselves and others. The courage of social equality therefore is the courage to see ourselves and others as equals, not to be consumed by the fictional belief of superiority, and to participate and collaborate. Once we are able to modify our social attitudes, then we can bring the concepts of equal opportunity for access to life with a focus on the common good.

> Man can function in a democratic era only as an equal among equals; he can do so only if he can extricate himself from the assumption of individual inferiority that hold him enslaved, blind him to the realization of his strength, deprive him of his inner freedom, and of his peace and serenity.[10]

Equality is both the basis and the goal of democracy where our rights are respected and our identity is developed. We recognize the need for early training and education. Our family, friends, and school/work relationships are good training grounds for mutual respect, trust, and cooperation (see Figure 7.1).

We can learn to listen and become sensitive to others' private logic, fears, and insecurities, and, consequently, their misbehaviors. We use natural and logical consequences with choices instead of replicating our last generations' use of punishment that is fueled by hostile emotions. Even in so-called dysfunctional relationships, we can find opportunities to learn. As an example, we can refrain from what we should not do and practice self-encouragement.

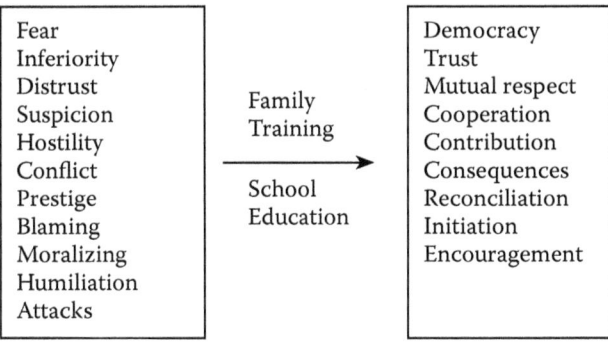

Figure 7.1 Training for social equality.

SOCRATIC DIALOGUE 7.2

What role does our society and culture play as we make decisions about ourselves, others, and the world? How do factors of race, gender, ability/disability, age, sexual orientation, and class interact to cultivate feelings of inequality?

Cindy reflected on her Native American experiences. She realized that things are not equal. Cindy's cultural and spiritual heritage, however, guide her to draw from strengths of the community feeling that helped her to help others to unlearn the negative effects of oppression.

As a young person (around 14) I began learning about Native American culture/history. I also learned about oppression and how Native people were put on reservations, forced to go to White schools, and saw firsthand how they lived in poverty. I also learned that Native Americans had suffered a lot of hardships and for those reasons had a lot of prejudice against White people. So, if you were White and Indian, nobody really wanted you. However, I also grew up without a lot of money and I understand the culture of poverty.

I have a vested interest in righting the wrongs as I can through empowering people and helping them understand that they are worth much more than they probably give themselves credit for. I realize that we may all do this, but especially among any people of color, I see that this has been a great tragedy in having people sell themselves short. This in itself is a result of oppression. I see oppression as those who take away validation in any way from others as human beings. For the workplace, not only can a worker of color (red or black or yellow) feel "not good enough," but employers treat people of color as not good enough. Not only will they be the ones to do the work, but they will not ultimately see themselves as worthy of their work without coaxing.

In my cultural tradition, all living things are seen as coming from one source and that all people are one. I use this idea in my life to not raise anyone above me nor put them below me. I understand oppression to be fear that has been created because the person has been blocked off from the group or others in society, and in losing that connection to what we call "great mystery," they are left with a hollow space that is filled with all other things like fear, anger, doubt, and oppression.

To unlearn about oppression, people need to understand where they come from, that they are all from the same life force and that to strive to understand those they really fear will help to ease their own hearts. Since we are all one, those that are oppressing are really also oppressing themselves emotionally and spiritually.

SOCRATIC DIALOGUE 7.3

> Our longing for democracy is not without ambivalence as we have yet to counter the fears we acquired in our home, school, and work where autocratic beliefs and practices are still present. As we strive for the ideal democracy and equality, how do we overcome inequalities and the problems of belonging?

Harmony: The Human Best and the Ideal Society

> There can be no harmony and stability in the community unless each member of it has his safe place as an equal to all others.[11]

What is the philosophy behind equality and democracy, and how may we be at our best facing the problems of belonging? Cindy's narrative teaches us the value of being in harmony with the whole of life, the cosmic community feeling that goes beyond oneself and others to include the universe. The courage of such wholeness is only attainable when each individual, as its own element, functions not only for him- or herself but for the health of the whole. Our strengths are only useful when they are useful for others. To Adler, individuals who become unreasonable, being motivated by the goal of superiority and with disproportional private intelligence, transgress the limits of common sense. The loss of common sense to an overdeveloped private sense is the ultimate root of our problems of social living.

The courage for community feeling and harmony is Individual Psychology's response to social inequalities, differing from the contemporary social justice approach that appears to be based on materialistic, individualistic, and political aspects of human rights.[12] Social harmony as an ideal state, focusing on global human rights, interconnectedness, partnership, and compassion is a social ideal commonly shared by world cultures and spiritual traditions. The value of global humanity is best expressed in Individual Psychology that coincides with the world philosophies that have survived the passage of time.

As we have pointed out in Chapter 1, Adler and his thoughts have been compared to Confucius in the East and Socrates in the West.[13] Their similarities are striking in the concepts of social interest and *ren* (仁, "two persons"). Social interest and ren are both the innate character trait in the individual as well as the virtue that guides one's behaviors. They share the same interest in self-cultivation, family value, and early education. Most important, they both despise self-interest and embrace the love for all, *agape*. Concerned with the problems of men and of society, Adler shared with Confucius the same wisdom of proper social relationships that are first embedded in one's ability to abide in the highest of good, to love the masses, to harmonize one's family, and to ultimately cultivate one's character. One seeks a coherence that reconciles the self to the other.

To Adler, happiness or meaning of life is when the individual can meet the five life tasks (work, love, friendship/family/community, self, and universe) with courage and social interest. To Confucius, *ren* is the "human best," the true self actualized in the five principle relationships the individual has with his/her society (e.g., ruler to the ruled, father to son, elder brother to younger brother, husband to wife, friend to friend). Embedded in social interest and ren are many other directed character traits, the paths by which we can strive toward the ideal state of community. Ren represents the human best with the multifaceted qualities of love, wisdom, discernment, righteousness, justice, empathy, filial piety, and courage.

To achieve harmony, according to Confucius, is to follow and allow the centrality and constancy (the golden mean) of our experiences. Courage, in the ideal society with reasonableness and perfect balance, is the common sense of the common people who believe in the ideal of social harmony and in the movement against the competitive beliefs of wealth, fame, power, and success.

> When the perfect order prevails, the world is like a home shared by all. Virtuous and worthy men are elected to public office, and capable men hold posts of gainful employment in society; peace and trust among all men are the maxims of living. All men love and respect their own parents and children, as well as the parents and children of others. There is caring for the old; there are jobs for the adults; there are nourishment and education for the children. There is a means of support for the widows, and the widowers; for all who find themselves alone in the world; and for the disabled. Every man and woman has an appropriate role to play in the family and society. A sense of sharing displaces the effects of selfishness and materialism. A devotion to public duty leaves no room for idleness. Intrigues and runners do not exist. The door to every home need never be locked and bolted by day or night. These are the characteristics of ideal world, the common wealth state.[14]

As Taoism is deeply embedded in Confucianism, Individual Psychology has a counterpart expression in the Taoist thoughts of equality and harmony. Equality in Taoist tradition is existential and naturalistic, strongly linked to the concept of acceptance, allowing, and following. One of the

Taoist principles is the notion of complementary opposites (the yin and the yang). To achieve harmony is to have the courage of complete obedience/harmony with the natural law that guides the individual in the direction of life's fulfillment. The individual is a reconciler of the opposites. The ideal of social living is to live in harmony with the opposites via inaction and thereby avoid falling into one extreme or the other.[15]

> Mankind has lost its paradise, if it ever had one. Life is always full of conflict, hardships, and predicaments. But a courageous person feels that he belongs to this life, is sure of his place in it, can look at it as a medium in which he lives, acts, produces, participates, and creates. ... This world belongs to the one who accepts himself as an integral part of it. In living, we are life.[16]

To Adler, the balance and harmony of our social living is inherent in our balanced give and take, contribution, and cooperation. To be in harmony, the community/group functions as a perfect whole in which each individual functions not for oneself but for the common welfare. Doing one's work within the bounds necessary for social harmony, however, is also conducive to individual happiness.

Our desire of belongingness and significance springs from the awareness that we cannot survive in isolation. We function as parts of the whole, and the ultimate protection and provision for our survival is not by competition or comparison but by cooperation and contribution even in the face of inequalities. In Individual Psychology, we are to act as if we are the equal of the equals when we interrelate with others, society, nature, and the universe. Our problems of belonging are our attitudes manifested in how we approach life in general. The courage to belong is to strive toward the ultimate social equality and social harmony in the face of collective inferiority and social inequalities.

We are endowed with a natural desire for overcoming barriers to belonging. Adler wrote: "Social interest ... means feeling with the whole, *sub speice aeternitatis*, under aspect of eternity. It means a striving for a form of community ... as it could be thought of if mankind had reached the goal of perfection."[17] The concepts of social interest and its related character traits have spiritual values similar to agape, a life force that allows our creative power to move us forward in times of difficulties (see our discussions on creative power in Chapters 1, 5, and 9).

> On one side, prayer is our capacity to enter into that vast community of life in which self and other, human and nonhuman, visible and invisible, are intricately intertwined. While my senses discriminate and my mind dissects, my prayer acknowledges and recreates [sic] the unity of life. In prayer, I no longer set myself apart from others and the world,

manipulating them to suit my needs. Instead, I reach for relationship, allow myself to feel the tugging of mutuality and accountability, take my place in community by knowing the transcendent center that connects it all. On the other side prayer means opening myself to the fact that as I reach that connecting center, the center is reaching for me.[18]

Observing how spiritual needs fostered human equality from earlier Christian and Buddhist faiths, Dreikurs called for a *religion for democracy* in which courage was one of the most essential requirements. To have freedom is to have the courage to face uncertainties and to recognize creativeness. It was his belief that the interdependence required in this new religion will "stimulate devotion to the common good, to stir up our willingness to feel with each other, to live with each other, to belong to each other in a long-delayed fulfillment of humanity's most cherished and ancient dream: the brotherhood."[19]

In the following, we present an actual account of how this dream of brotherhood has been realized via a worldwide community initiative for individuals in need.[20]

Community Feeling at Work: The Courage of Recovery

We are people who normally would not mix. But there exists among us a fellowship, a friendliness, and an understanding which is indescribably wonderful. We are like the passengers of a great liner the moment after rescue from shipwreck when camaraderie, joyousness and democracy pervade the vessel from steerage to Captain's table. Unlike the feelings of the ship's passengers, however, our joy in escape from disaster does not subside as we go our individual ways. The feeling of having shared in a common peril is one element in the powerful cement which binds us. But that in itself would never have held us together as we are now joined. ... The first requirement is that we be convinced that any life run on self-will can hardly be a success.

—Alcoholics Anonymous[21]

The causes of addiction are complex and beyond the scope of this book, but we have discussed from the Individual Psychology point of view that addiction is an effective way of evading life tasks for individuals who lack courage to participate in their social relationships. In the process of this evasion, the addicted person becomes extraordinarily self-centered and uses his or her addiction to deal with all aspects of life. This maladaptive approach significantly slows or delays normal development and alienates the individual from self (from their core values) and society. The addicted person is simply surviving with no sense of belonging or significance.

One alcoholic with 6 months of successful recovery found himself making a decision that would dramatically improve the prognosis for a countless number of alcoholics. The genesis of this decision was a spiritual awakening when he became convinced that by helping another alcoholic, he could save himself. Devastated by life circumstances yet once again, in a strange city, he knew that the comfort of alcohol was only a half dozen drinks away along with the downward spiral of his alcoholism. But this time he knew he also had another choice and that choice was to "fellowship" with a yet sober, hopeless alcoholic like his former self.

This man, William R. Wilson (known as Bill W.) from New York City made a decision that would change history. Instead of reaching for the false seduction of alcohol, which he knew so well, he located his hopeless alcoholic comrade, Dr. Robert Holbrook (known as Dr. Bob), a local MD. In this meeting Bill W. and Dr. Bob merged into animation and action. Bill W. introduced his concept (experiment) of recovery to Dr. Bob. In summer 1935, Bill W. and Dr. Bob began to sketch the framework of what in 4 short years would become known as Alcoholics Anonymous. The 12-step program Bill W. created has also generated successful programs for other addictions and people affected by others' addictions around the world. Aldous Huxley called him "the greatest social architect of our century." Bill W. was named by *Time* magazine in 2000 as among the 20 heroes who exemplified courage, selfishness, exuberance, super human ability, and amazing grace in the last century.

Why does Alcoholics Anonymous work? Although there are many factors that contribute to the answer to this question, in a sentence, it is because A.A. gives hope to the hopeless by providing for them, among other things, fellowship and a community of others who understand, can provide support, and who will not judge. Once they are introduced to the fellowship of A.A., the kinship in suffering allows alcoholics a daily reprieve from certain self-destruction (one day at a time). Although confined and constricted in their own addiction, the community support and the call to help others connects them with others. The courage of recovery begins.

The A.A. community approach in the 12 steps and 12 traditions strikingly resembles the tenet of Adler's social interest.[22] The impression is reinforced by many A.A. expressions such as "Fake it till you make it" (a paraphrase of "live life as is" or "act as if"), "progress not perfection," "do the next right thing," and "it works if you work it." There are many other such examples throughout the Alcoholics Anonymous text and the rich correspondence of Bill W. Much of the transformative power of A.A. seems to be directly traced to key elements of Individual Psychology.

Is there any clear evidence that Bill W. had knowledge of Adlerian thoughts? There is.[23] Throughout Bill W.'s life, he had an unusually close but odd relationship with his mother. It is very possible that it was his mother from whom he learned the major concepts of Adlerian theory. Emily Griffith Wilson (his mother) "had studied in Vienna with Freud's sometime colleague, Alfred Adler, and … was a practicing Adlerian analyst in San Diego."[24]

Closing Thoughts

All problems of living are individual problems and social problems. Adler's resolution to the problems of belonging is straightforward with his concept of our striving for the community feeling via our work, love, and social relationships. The dimension of the communal feeling can be expanded to be of cosmic social interest that goes beyond oneself and others to include the universe, or "to the whole of life."

The pathway to the sense of belonging is both psychological and spiritual. Our self-confidence and acceptance, the recognition of our fear of the others, and the ability to treat self and others as equals are our psychological resolutions to the problems of belonging. Social harmony, according to the philosophical teachings of the East and the West, is attainable when each individual works for the common welfare as he/she overcomes individual inferior feelings. Social interest, as a universal law of social living, guides us with a goal of commonweal for all. The return of community is the answer to the problems of belonging. Specifically, to many individuals and cultural groups who are oppressed by the social illness of collective superiority, community feeling mediates and reconciles the lost self to a feeling of at home.

Alcoholics Anonymous is a successful example of a community effort that gives courage for recovery. If the history and development of A.A. is studied in depth, the influence of Individual Psychology is clear. The core beliefs of belonging seem to have informed the conception and development of A.A. The courage to belong, then, is our action to form a community where our value and labor for one another can be learned, and the transformation of personal and social inadequacies experienced.

CHAPTER 8

The Courage to Be

Once upon a time, I, Chuang-tzu, dreamed I was a butterfly, fluttering hither and thither, to all intents and purposes a butterfly. I was conscious only of following my fancies as a butterfly, and was unconscious of my individuality as a man. Suddenly, I awoke, and there I lay, myself again. Now I do not know whether I was then a man dreaming I was a butterfly, or whether I am now a butterfly dreaming I am a man.

—Chuang-tzu[1]

The existential task of *being* (getting along with oneself) and the task of *belonging* (getting along with the universe) are two inseparable transcendental forces that affect the resolution of work, love, and our participation in social relationships. As mentioned in Chapter 7, to have the courage to belong is to first become aware our fears, our internal and external goals of striving, and to grow our self-acceptance. The task of being in harmony with self or self-acceptance is not easy, however, as we experience the ambivalence of our desire to being ourselves and the desire of being part of our society.

The "No" Attitudes

In response to the individual inferior feeling and/or collective inferiority we face, many individuals join the social norm of self-elevation. When we are not "better than," then we are failures. In our longing to belong, even with the best intentions, we adopt more "no" attitudes toward life in fear of loss and failure of our place in any group to which we wish to belong. In our choice to conform, however, we live with the consequences of indecision, lacking self-knowledge, overconcern, and many preoccupations that deprive us from authenticity. Knowingly or unknowingly, we partake in the familial and social pressure for success in school and career only to feel fatigue or inner emptiness and meaninglessness at the end. Our inferiority actually increases when we work harder to attain our goal of perfection.

It is a universal phenomenon that our inferiority feelings are constant and they prevail in all aspects of living. We compare ourselves with others to ensure that we do not fall behind and we compete to get ahead. We vary, however, in how we perceive the obstacles we encounter; how we take in the influences our family, school, and community have on us; and how we respond to life challenges with our feelings, attitudes, and actions. It is through our striving in response to the life challenges of work, friendship, and love that we express our characteristic traits.

> The tendency to compare oneself with others is a natural human process. It is the interpretations that we give to these reflective comparisons that determine whether we are able to get along with ourselves well. People who are self-critical, pessimistic, anxious, perfectionistic, guilt-ridden, or overly impressed with their imperfections and weaknesses tend to retreat from the task of getting along with oneself.[2]

Our characteristic movements toward our life goals say a lot about what we are and who we will become. In general, we can observe individuals' differences by their oppositional attitudes or how they approach difficulties. For example, there are those who are optimists and some pessimists; some going straightforward and some taking detours; some aggressive and some defensive. Referring back to Figure 2.1 of Chapter 2, judging by the individual's capacity to cooperate and contribute, we can estimate the direction the individual is moving toward or away from social interest, and, thus, we can also estimate the distance and balance between one's subjective power and social responsibility.

The consequence of evading our life tasks is discouragement. Adler reminded us that we have to see these characteristic traits in light of social life (not moral judgment). He called social life the evaluation of the quality of our relationship to the society in which we live.[3] It is in our relationship to our society that we establish our sense of self-worth and belonging.

> Martha, 80 years old, lived alone and had rejected the ideas of any other living arrangement, indicating that she could not really get along with anyone else, including her children. Martha stayed in her very unhappy marriage for 20 years mostly for the sake of her children and sought divorce in her early 40s. Although she was in many relationships she would not consider marriage again. Keeping good

health, looking beautiful, and being independent are most important to Martha. No one could tell that she was illiterate from how she dressed and conducted herself. She had showed some interest in learning to read but did not follow through. Martha worked in some blue-collar jobs she was not proud of. She stopped working as soon as her children were old enough to support her. She took her volunteer role in a local church very seriously where she also received much respect as being warm and helpful. Martha recently began to feel that church had become too political for her.

In many ways, Martha's life as she narrated it was rather ambivalent. She seemed to value love but her doubt of men's intent seemed to keep her from having a long-term relationship. She was capable in her volunteer activities and yet she seemed to have evaded her work task with the excuse that she did not really fit a lower class occupation. She worked very hard to keep her beauty and put forth a social front so others would not learn of her illiteracy and her financial inadequacy. In her old age, she seemed to have an active social life where she received much affirmation although she doubted the trustworthiness of the people she worked with.

All nervous manifestations of this sort originate at the point where the nervous individual becomes frightened of the problems she must solve, problems which are really no more than the necessary duties and obligations of everyday life.[4]

Martha's problem was the problem of distance, the disparity between her self-interest and a genuine social feeling. Our responses of yes; yes, but; and no are indicators of our feelings of courage or inadequacies, and our social interest or our retreat to self-interest as we meet the demands of life.[5] Overall, Martha seemed to have said no to most of the tasks of living because of her fears and discouragement. Martha's life outlook gave an impression of the "plus gestures." The more we feel inferior, the more gestures we use to appear bigger, richer, and better. Normally, in isolation, these individuals make an effort to maintain these make-beliefs, as the fiction of power is much more easily attained than real power and satisfaction. Martha's self-perception of not getting along with others is actually rooted in the problem that she did not get along with herself and, therefore, the inability to cooperate is permeated in her approaches to all three basic life tasks.

According to Adler, this "no" life attitude actually underscores the aggressive and nonaggressive character traits.[6] The aggressive character traits are vanity, ambition, playing God, jealousy, envy, and greed—all are connected in hostility, negligence, and the need to dominate and to be right or better than. Among the nonaggressive traits are withdrawal, anxiety, timidity, absence of social grace, and the detour syndromes (such as laziness, frequent change of occupations, petty crimes, and so forth). These are all diversions for these individuals who say no to life.

The issues of self-acceptance do not only concern individuals with the inferior status but also those with superior status in our society. The yes attitude for some individuals of minority status often means rejecting the social rejection and increasing the social acceptance first by developing self-acceptance.[7] As a result, these individuals may develop a better sense of self than those from the majority status who were not afforded a need for such self-exploration and definition. For example, when asked the question "What does it mean to be White?" White individuals often respond with surprise, accompanied by a perplexed and cautious searching for expression: "Good grief!" "Never thought about this." Or, "Maybe it means more advantages and hassle-free life." For Whites, White is neither a race nor a color and something they do not think about. A color-blind perspective is prevalent suggesting the lack of insight of one's own racial/cultural identity and underpreparedness to respond to diversity.[8]

CHARACTERistics with the "Yes" Attitude

> We have tremendous inner resources if we would only believe in them and thereby believe in ourselves as we are. When we stop trying to "control ourselves," we will soon discover that our actions will in no way be different, for we always do what we decide to do anyhow. After this discovery, we shall be ready for the next step: to change our decisions. Then we will be more likely and able to decide what is good for both ourselves and others, and be less afraid of the wrong things we may do.[9]

None of us can be totally perfect. Nevertheless, it lies within the power of us to adjust our striving away from our personal mistaken goals and lifestyles that are not effective. The conflict or doubt we often experience is an expression of our striving for overcoming/compensation, superiority, security, or power. Conflict is deeply connected to our style of life. The following dialogue illustrates Eva's yes attitude as she worked toward the changes in the home and community environment that imposed much fear on her. She always had the desire to work toward becoming what she was intended to become. Eva was an African American in her mid-40s who came back to school as her daughters entered college.

Al: How would you describe the neighborhoods?
Eva: The neighborhoods where I lived were Black, totally Black where it was not unusual. It was unusual to have friends that had fathers at home. My mom was a single parent. We went to school, I didn't know I was poor, I had no idea. I knew that there were differences, I knew

about racism, didn't know what it was called, just believed it was the way of the world. That's the way things were, that's all I could see except for what was on TV, and TV was understood to not be real, so in our neighborhood we just went to school. I was the oldest of three so I have a sister who is almost 2 years younger than me, and a brother who is 6 years younger. I didn't notice also those differences, speaking from the female perspective, how my brother was revered over the two older girls. I remember thinking that that was unfair. My mom as a single mom was very powerful, a very strong woman which she had to be very afraid but I can't even imagine today her admitting being afraid.

Al: Do you recall what that fear was about?

Eva: I think there was just a basic fear of life and existence and those things that she grew up with. She grew up in the south. And she was dark skinned, my family is dark, dark skinned. I am the lighter one. I have a different father from my brother and sister, so it was really rough for her … so much lack of understanding, well we've come so far of course.

Al: [Changes] have been very rapid when you look at the time so that the shift from her experience growing up to yours it's probably been real dramatic.

Eva: Even those changes that she made so that things would be better for her children.

Al: Are you aware of growing up with a sense that this is not a safe world, so that survival was really important?

Eva: Survival, yes, definitely. That reminds me of the saying about the crabs or the lobsters in the crate and how they are trying to climb to the top and then they get pulled back by each other. I thought about that saying and how it wasn't necessarily that way. It would seem that way from outside and it kinda had that feel but after a while in looking back, I can see that it wasn't fear, it was a protection mechanism actually, because if you don't aspire to get ahead or to be somebody then you don't get hurt as much as if you do.

Al: How did that influence you, do you know? 'Cause here you are working on a master's degree. You've stepped out of the box, the cage. You're somewhere else.

Eva: Thank God. I think that, too, that it helped. There were other things that I think helped. I don't know why I believe in purpose. I believe that this all had a purpose.

Eva and Martha are individuals of the "less than" status: race, gender, divorce as well as their financial struggles. We clearly see that Martha's

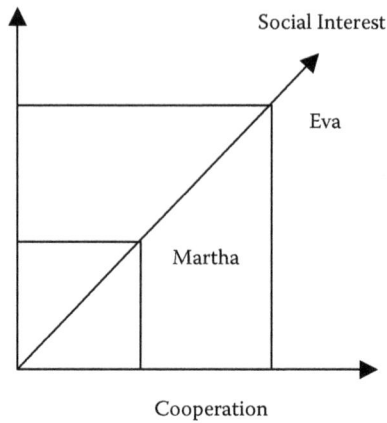

Figure 8.1 Measuring social interest by cooperation and contribution.

approach leans on *blaming*, whereas Eva adopted the *building* attitude of her efforts. Unlike Martha, Eva had the yes attitude to move on and did not allow the lobster to fall back into the crate. Eva had to make a choice when she had to negotiate between conforming to the cultural expectation (of lack of expectation) with fear or proceed to pursuing her ideal. Eva's striving was with self-respect and a sense of purpose as well as cooperation.

SOCRATIC DIALOGUE 8.1

Considering the yes; no; or yes, but attitudes and the abilities to cooperate and contribute, where would you position Martha and Eva on the diagonal model of social interest–mental health as illustrated in Figure 8.1 (also see discussions about Figure 2.1 in Chapter 2).

For Adler, the single criterion for success in life was embodied in the extent to which the individual possesses social interest, the ideal state of the individual's mental health or what we might term today as *character*. Social interest or character has to be consciously developed. With the development of one's social interest comes the development of the capacities for cooperation and contribution, which are primary components of character. Furthermore, character is related to the Adlerian concept of self-respect, "the feeling that one is a worthwhile human being in spite of one's faults and imperfections."[10] The courage to be oneself, therefore, is the courage to be imperfect, the key to the development of character. Our self-respect (or character) is subjective and does not depend on external evaluations. Table 8.1 lists 36 "character"istics or components that help

Table 8.1 CHARACTERistics: The "Yes" Attitudes

Components of Character	
Acceptance of unpleasant reality	Lovability
Accomplishment	Maturity
Approachability	Positive regard
Appropriate anger	Power and control
Appropriate responsibility	Power of choice
Belonging	Relief
Confidence	Relief from guilt
Counting one's blessings	Relief from fear and anxiety
Courage	Security
Courage to succeed	Securing cooperation
Equality	Self-acceptance
Identity	Self-respect
In touch with reality	Serenity
Independence	Success
Intellectual self-respect	Tolerance of pain or disappointment
Less vulnerable to temptation	Trust
Liberation	Trust in one's judgment
Living in the present	Unselfish

to define one's yes attitudes. These serve as the traits or qualities that give us everyday opportunity to draw out and help develop social interest and character in others (see Chapter 10, Tool #4).

The Use of Emotions

According to Adler, our characteristic approach to life tasks not only finds expressions in our behaviors and thoughts (e.g., bad luck or fate for Martha) but also in our mood and temperament. "Emotions comes from two Latin words, *ex* or *e* which means 'out of,' and *movere*, which means to 'move.' Hence emotion helps one 'move out' of a situation in a way that is consistent with the lifestyle and one's immediate goals."[11]

> Emotions provide the power, the steam, so to speak, for our actions, the driving force without which we would be impotent. They come into play whenever we decide to do something forcefully. They make it possible for use to carry out our decisions. They permit us to take a stand, to develop definite attitudes, to form convictions. They are the only basis for strong personal relationships to others, for developing interests and for building alliances of interests with others. They make us appreciate and devaluate, accept and reject. They

make it possible for use to enjoy and dislike. In short, they make us human beings instead of machines.[12]

For example, the feelings of being neglected and being discriminated against, if not appropriately acknowledged, can perpetuate the destructive character of jealousy, whereas the feelings of hopelessness can be related to envy. Anger, grief, disgust, and fear are regarded as *disjunctive* or disruptive feelings turning people away from social feeling. Disjunctive emotions are the feelings that set us against others and are disrespectful of ourselves. For the *conjunctive* feelings, there are joy, sympathy, and humility, which are the expressions of social feeling instrumental for facilitating overcoming of difficulties.

Comparison and competition are motivated by fear. Those who are competitive generally can be understood in that they desire praise for what they do. They strive for recognition and rewards. Their response to failure or the less-than-perfect outcome is punishment for themselves or others. Competition leads one to become dominant with begging or infantile attitudes. Conformity to the external standards of success or failure or one's own fictive perfection allows no risk taking but conceals resentment and hostility. Individuals who are being dominated appear dull and dependent, and are soon trained to only perform the sideshows of leaning/blaming, manipulation/control, enslavement, arrogant demands, wishful thinking, double bind, passivity, idolatry, inadequacies, and exclusiveness. Those who compare themselves to others lose their originality and either compensate by imitation or not taking initiatives. They approach life tasks without creativity and risk taking. There is no playfulness and joy in what they do as they are captives of their fears. In their isolation and loneliness, they are blind to their birthright of freedom. These individuals are preoccupied by disjunctive emotions best described by the "move away" words (as in Figure 8.2) and rejection movements that are characterized by the no attitudes.

On the contrary, a very different picture can be painted if we are in cooperation with ourselves and one another. When we have the courage to create and re-create, we become self-reliant. With a sense of autonomy, we venture to connect as we realize our ideals. The individuals with self-reliance are free to be explorative, independent, flexible, thoughtful, unique, energetic, liberal, and spirited in all their relationships. Those who experience self-realization and fulfillment become confident, contributing to the world outside of them. They possess a high level of social interest. Those who have the courage to cooperate are those who know when to wait for their chance and live in the present. They have quiet persistence and exercise mutual respect in their social interactions. They experience/express conjunctive feelings described in the "move forward" words (i.e., Figure 8.3) and the forward

The Courage to Be • 103

Figure 8.2 Disjunctive emotions, rejection movement.

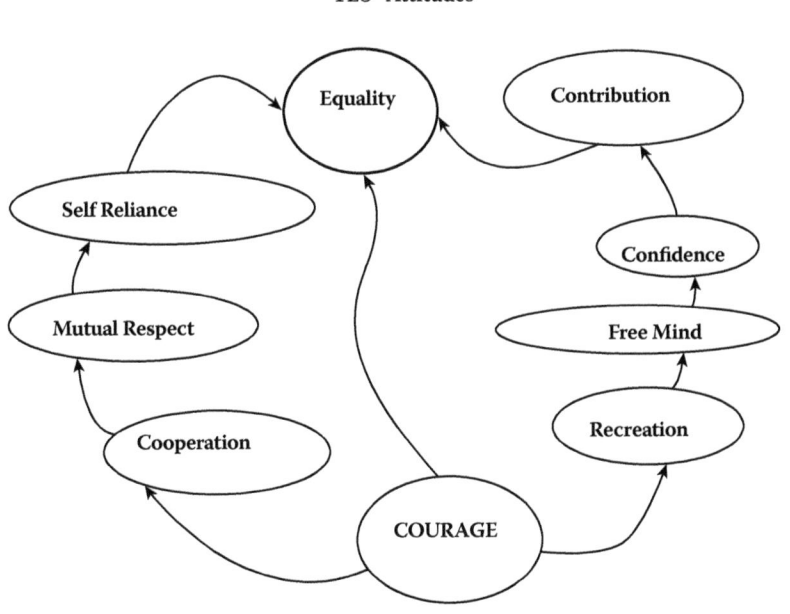

Figure 8.3 Conjunctive emotions, "move forward" words, encouraging movement.

movement that enables them to treat themselves and others as equals. They live to greet their life challenges with yes attitudes even in the face of fears.

As feelings are purposeful, we can identify them when we investigate individuals' goals or behaviors. Depending on our feelings of annoyance, anger, hurt, or hopelessness, we can guess the misbehaving goals of children: attention getting, power struggle, getting even, or withdrawal, respectively (see Chapter 6, Table 6.2). In Individual Psychology, there is a purpose in every emotion and depression is not an exception. Depression is the socially acceptable front of anger and may represent "frustration, disappointment, denial, a feeling of unfairness, loss of control, or any combination of these attitudes."[13]

To Adler, *anger* is the feeling that most typifies the striving for power and domination, whereas the original feeling of frustration could have been easily addressed through the mutual respect of two equal individuals. *Grief* occurs when someone cannot console him- or herself for a loss or deprivation. Mentally, *disgust* is the feeling that consists of tendencies and attempts to "vomit" matter out of the psyche. *Fear* arises when we anticipate defeat and experience a thirst for superiority, and demand for protection or exceptional privilege. Fear can help us evade the demands of living and it can also be an instrument to enslave others. *Hostility* is a strong inferior or superior feeling toward others that finds disguise in forgetfulness, sleeplessness, worries, and clumsiness.[14]

SOCRATIC DIALOGUE 8.2

Do you worry? How does worry help you? Is the cost of worrying greater than the cost of changing? What is the purpose of your worrying? What stops you from changing? What are some of your yes; yes, but; and no attitudes toward solving the problem you are worried about?

The Use of the Neurotic Symptoms

In the previous chapters we have discussed in several ways about the approach toward life in general and toward each of the basic life tasks using opposite pairs of attitudes (i.e., fear-based vs. courage-based attitudes; the contrasting effects of eros and agape loves on intimacy, friendship, and family) to illustrate the differing directions of movement toward or away from social usefulness. In this chapter, we have attempted to illustrate whether individuals get along with themselves by using the yes and no attitudes and emotions. These are examples of how our characteristic style depicts our life movement and finds its expressions in our thinking, feeling, and actions.

> Originally it was fear of "sin" that kept man from being "bad." Today is becoming increasingly obvious that the "sin" of modern man is fear itself.[15]

The same movement (i.e., of overcoming the "felt minus" and striving toward the "perceived plus") navigates our relationship with ourselves, which often is the problem that obstructs the fulfillment of other tasks. Consequences of evading the task of getting along with oneself or avoiding can be costly. There are many devices used to evade the issues of social participation and emotional being. They are characteristically based on faulty make-beliefs, exaggerated worries, jealousy, and possessiveness that establish neurotic problems or symptoms that are prevalent in normal people who first adapt these behaviors when confronted with a crisis.

Tracy had a tough life: car accident, foreclosure on her house, divorce after her husband's many suicide attempts, family death, and her autoimmune disorder. She recently attended a few Alcoholics Anonymous meetings as a spouse of an alcoholic. She admitted that she got out of the "sober social" more about herself than about the addicted person. She quickly came to terms with her making judgment about something she knew nothing about. She attributed this blaming attitude to be about her and her fear. She also realized that her overeating behavior has something to do how she had used her illness.

> The thing about the soft addictions as well as the hard addictions is that you can't escape yourself; wherever you go, there you are ... and sooner or later you have to face it head on. ... I can honestly say that food is my friend ... and I like it that way; it doesn't talk back, disappoint, drink or hog the covers, make me sick or take time out of my day. I know that I sometimes use food to ease loneliness and boredom, to insulate my feelings, and to forget the difficulties or sadness in my life. I just don't know how to do the work in the middle to become healthy. Perhaps this "safe" place is my chance to start facing my issues and begin that road to recovery and wellness.
>
> —**Tracy**

We believe that fear is the root to all neuroses as it works to assist the individual escape from the difficult tasks when feelings of inferiority are present. In fear of exposing our weaknesses to others, we actively and creatively participate in our neurosis. To Adlerians, neurosis, regardless of the type, is concealed hostility with a clever design. Neuroses are low in social interest.

Instead of facing and resolving the problems, we resort to fighting ourselves using the functions of our mind and body, feelings, and thoughts.

> In our fight with ourselves, we choose symptoms according to our style of life. Certain syndromes are linked with types of personality. A rigid person with high conscience and inability to admit his rebellion and defiance to himself may tend to develop compulsive symptoms. Timid and dependent persons may find fears and anxieties more suitable. Persons who believe in their own strength and ability may prefer an organ symptom which seems to be out of their control.[16]

Neurotic individuals are those who have lost their courage as they journey through life challenges. Discouragement and isolation are the common denominators to problems such as neurosis, depression, crime, suicide, perversion, addictions, and other forms of insanity.[17] The more discouraged an individual becomes, the less fitted he/she feels to fulfill the requirements of life, and the more determined and more likely he will evade the life tasks. If taken from the psychological factors (versus hereditary or physical causes), neurosis is merely a pretense of sickness, a subjective escape from social demands as a response to conflicts. According to Wolfe,[18] the characteristics of neurosis are

- Ignorance of the meaning of life and the value of social cooperation
- Primacy of the individual ego and the cult of individual uniqueness
- An emotional undercurrent of fear
- Establishment of a subjective sense of power and security
- Purposiveness in the attainment of the neurotic goal
- Substitution of "I cannot" for "I will not"
- Creation of a scapegoat
- Cult of personal irresponsibility for failure
- Futility
- Isolation and the constriction of the sphere of activity to the bare minimum consonance with life

Using the analogy of a battlefront to represent the demands of life tasks, Wolfe conceptualized and discussed the five neurotic patterns of escape and the neurotic traits of the individuals (Table 8.2).[19] To Adlerians, neurosis is what one uses to announce one's helplessness and serves as an excuse for not participating in the common tasks of life. It is a creative strategy of the evasion of life problems. Schizophrenia (excluding organic inferiority factors) is a neurotic fiction in which the neurotic acts as if he were ill in order to escape the responsibility demanded of an integrated personality. The nature of the response to conflicts distinguishes the types of psychiatric disorders.

Table 8.2 Patterns of Neurotic Traits

Evasion of Reality By	Neurotic Traits
Superiority complex	Aggressive, intense, ambitious, paranoia, fear, trail of unhappiness
Hesitation at distance	Indecision, procrastination, hesitation, doubt, time-killing, perfection in details, conflict between good and bad, in need of safety, resistance to risk, unprepared for life demands, melancholia, depression
A detour from the arenas of human endeavor	Clever, confused by one's own strategy, chief work for praise, physical symptoms with a social value, high blood pressure, stomach ache, sleeplessness, a vague pain, nervousness, fatigue, sinusitis
Frank retreat	Open retreat admitting inferiority, reproduction of childhood conditions of dependence and security, refusal to grow up, helplessness, adult infants, schizophrenia, organ inferiority
Destruction of the self	Suicide or self-sabotage that resemble suicide in its psychological value: self-mutilation, paralyses of hysteria, etc.

Living in Harmony with Oneself

Six weeks before her death, Marina commented to me that our oncologist seemed so serious lately. I stated that it had been a long time since he had any good news to give us, and unlike the previous 7 months when all was going well, he probably felt it inappropriate to appear light and humorous. I mentioned to her that if she initiated humor, the doctor would probably appreciate it. So one day, even though she was in a great deal of discomfort due to her poorly functioning liver (as she said, she looked to be 10 months pregnant). As he came into the examining room she put her hands on her distended stomach and announced, "This is yours." The doctor almost collapsed with laughter, but she was not through. As he denied any involvement, Marina said, "No, I'm pretty sure it is yours."

Mark told this story as part of the eulogy at his wife's funeral. The couple was married for 33 years. The courage and humor of Mark and Marina in the face of death were both beautiful and real, communicating their cooperation with life (i.e., acceptance of death) and their care for others. The same courage and love Marina expressed throughout her dying process became the courage and love that later supported her husband and children to move on after her death.

At the age of 12, David was diagnosed with muscular dystrophy, which would gradually weaken all of his muscular functions. Some doctors predicted that he had 10 years left to live. Right before graduating from senior high school, David was seriously injured in a traffic accident. After the hospitalization, he could no longer stand on his feet. He was forced to leave school. He stayed at home for 8 years feeling very frustrated and sorry for himself. During that time, David's parents spent all of their money on his treatments. Sometimes they had to pawn some valuables to pay the medical expenses. His doctor encouraged him to take part in social life by taking David out to concerts and other activities. At one point, David took a watch repairing class hoping that he at the least could earn a living as a watch repairer. The classroom was on the second floor without any lift. He had to sit on the stairs and move upward step by step. After the training, David thought to himself, "If I can overcome the stairs, why can't I overcome the challenges of moving around on a college campus?" David entered a college majoring in English and he studied very hard and won scholarships every year. As of now, with the help of technology, David has worked as an English tutor in his home for 24 years. David even ventured to travel overseas a few times. He deeply believes in the saying that God helps those who help themselves.

Like Marina and Mark, David possessed many of the tools (i.e., the yes character traits) that helped him to live out his life to the fullest extent. He values education and he enjoys work. He is tolerant of the physical limitation. In fact, his coping with the disease brings about his courage and social usefulness. He takes a deep interest in life.

Tracy embraced the same "yes" attitude of Marina, Mark, and David toward life challenges. To Tracy, the courage to be is expressed in a feeling of at ease with her new awareness of her soft addictions and is achieved as she practices and reflects on her new sense of serenity.[20]

> Serenity ... what is that? For me, the true test of serenity was about being okay when I was by myself. Being okay or serene is being calm in mind, body, and spirit, not obsessing about things or persons I have no control over, or situations or circumstances that I do not own. So much painful growing is encompassed but what remains for me are clarity, purpose, and direction. Serenity for me is that centered, grounded, tranquil quality that allows me to just be where I am and in the moment. I draw on my serenity in the midst of the chaos and complexity of daily living and I use the reinforcing and empowering feelings that serenity generates to push ahead even in the darkness. Darkness is personal.
>
> —**Tracy**

SOCRATIC DIALOGUE 8.3

Beethoven had to transition from keyboard to composition when he began to develop deafness. It was in this transformational process that he moved from contemplating suicide to finishing the masterpiece of Piano Concerto No. 3, which was considered his first "new self." In the face of adversities and obstacles, how do some individuals retreat to the neurotic style of behaviors, whereas others seem to retain their strengths and continue living? Is neurosis curable? Is it possible for one to be in harmony with oneself when life seems to be full of contradictions and when problems of living appear so demanding?

Affirmation and Ambivalence

We are at odds with ourselves mainly because we have doubts about ourselves, fear of failure, and inadequacy feelings when we are confronted with the contradictory duality in human nature. We fight against ourselves, and yet we live with the ambivalence knowing that we will never be good enough as perfection does not really exist. In fact, the purpose of ambivalence may well be avoidance, as we cannot move in two directions at the same time.

Mark had recently lost his wife of 33 years to cancer and he described the ambivalence he was experiencing. After the despair had lifted, he experienced great growth, excitement, and energy, but he was also beginning to experience a normalcy or comfort pervading his reality and he saw this in a negative way:

> That participation (in life and her death) was very important and I think it gave me, if I can continue it (the energy) gives me a sense of life that I couldn't experience any other way. But I think that excitement is beginning to ebb a little bit; it is beginning to have a ... there's a tendency with me I've noticed to kind of fall back into comfort and it's almost as though I need to continue moving (growing and experiencing), otherwise I get too comfortable. It's about authenticity—it is living in a spiritual world and living in the nonspiritual world. The nonspiritual world doesn't require very much, we know the rules. We work hard, we put money away, we live in a nice house, we drive a nice car, we talk foolishness with each other, and we know those rules. It's solid and yet it has no meaning, no real meaning. And I

know the difference; the depth in comfort is nothing. But, it takes work but it's honest, it's hard, it's meaningful, but it's also very easy to kind of plateau. I must keep asking what it means to live a life that matters and how is that. That it is fluid and how is that changing and if I can give myself a baseline of what that means now, and then I can revisit that and say okay yes I am coasting, yes I am taking a breather (seeking comfort). But, also not being seduced by the comfort, or in I guess another way, seduced by the adventure, the excitement ... and then as I mentioned the journey, it's the route, it's the progression and movement. It's the space, it's the peace, it's the spiritual nature of it and I had a chance to experience that.

Last week when I was learning, actually relearning to snowboard, and how you really have to let go in order to really experience it as opposed to trying to control ... controlling becomes fairly meaningless. In snowboarding it's a confluence of the mountain, the snow, the board the balance and then the head, all kinds of movement but there has to be a letting go; there can't be that need to control. With snowboarding, you're moving from edge to edge and there is a constant interaction of the balance and everything else. When I started snow boarding, my tendency was to lean back—leaning back is very intuitive—it is being very secure, very simple. You'll never take a hard fall but if you get too far forward or catch an edge, the tumbles are great, they're great, they teach you so much, but there is that potential that you may not get up right away—they can really hurt. The beauty of it is finding that line.

As mentioned in Chapter 1, people existentially have the desire to avoid death and to procreate. Our courage to be is intimately related to the idea of will to power in which *will* is a given feature we have at birth and we have the *power* to affirm our living with strengths and commitment and the ability to overcome life hurdles. The psychological force Mark experienced after the despair of loosing his wife is part of the creative energy that we call courage that allows him to overcome the incompleteness and strive for completion in the same time.

May, in his book *The Discovering of Being*, stated that "every existing person has the character of self-affirmation and the name given to this self-affirmation is *courage*."[21] Our self-affirmation has two distinguishable but not separable sides: the courage to be as oneself and the courage to participate in the world. Mark's experience of ambivalence, although potentially generating anxiety, is the path that eventually leads to freedom and healing.

"To venture causes anxiety, but not venture is to lose oneself"...
Availing oneself of possibilities, confronting the anxiety, and accepting

the responsibility and guilt feeling involved result in increased self-awareness, freedom, and enlarged spheres of creativity.[22]

Mark's courage to move on is revealed in his insight about the confluence of many factors that come into play as he learned to be in harmony with his snowboard. He has the courage of self-affirmation in spite of how the ambivalence between his stepping into the open space of life after his wife's death and seeking comfort, which tend to bring him doubt. Mark has the courage to be himself and to self-realization when he accepts the ambivalence and finds the balance between availing himself of new possibilities and meeting the life demands.

The courage to be is the courage to accept oneself as accepted in spite of being unacceptable.[23]

Closing Thoughts

So many people live within unhappy circumstances and yet will not take the initiative to change their situation because they are conditioned to a life of security, conformity, and conservatism, all of which may appear to give one peace of mind, but in reality nothing is more demanding to the adventurous spirit within a man than a secure future. ... You are wrong if you think joy emanates only or principally from human relationships. God has placed it all around us. It is in everything and anything we might experience. We just have to have the courage to turn against our habitual life style and engage in unconventional living. It [the light] is simply waiting out there for you to grasp it, and all you have to do is reach for it. The only person you are fighting is yourself and your stubbornness to engage in new circumstances.[24]

This quote was written by Chris McCandless, a 22-year-old who possessed many preoccupations that deprived him from authenticity. The quote came from a letter he wrote to Ron Franz, an older gentleman he met and befriended. After McCandless graduated from college he sought solace, comfort, and himself by forsaking materialism and existing to a great extent on his own ability to survive. His odyssey took him into the wilderness and his death posed many controversies and challenges for us to ponder. What made his encounters with others on his journey life changing? A message of his last words he left behind was "HAPPINESS REAL ONLY WHEN SHARED."[25] What do we learn from his pursue of authenticity in his courage to be and eventually to belong?

Existentially, *being* is a verb. The courage to be is the courage to live. In our being, we strive toward what we are intended to become. Being is a generalization of the concept of life, of willing, acting, and becoming. According to nature, we want to live and to live is to achieve the tasks set for us. Our courage to be is the natural life force that affirms us even if conditions of living are ambivalent and challenging.

In Individual Psychology, the courage to be is a life task in which we gain self-acceptance and confidence while we recognize our life plan and the ineffective detours or sideshows that prevent us from taking responsibilities in love, work, and society. We do so by measuring the distance we have away or toward community feeling or by listening to our yes or no attitudes and their undercurrent emotions toward solving problems. To not be constricted in our private sense or fear of failure, we need to adopt the yes attitudes and decision-making capabilities to be part of the whole.

We shall conclude this chapter with thoughts of a contemporary Adlerian who believes we should:

> Live life "as if" we are with one human being ... questioning what we are up to, spot disjunctive emotions and thoughts, replace them with conjunctive emotions and thoughts, recognize the courage and love of self and others you are manifesting at that moment, encourage yourself at these moments ... Just be it.[26]

Risk It

To laugh is to risk being a fool.
To weep is to risk appearing sentimental.
To reach out to another is to risk involvement.
To express feelings is to risk exposing your true self.
To place your ideas, your dreams, before the crowd
is to risk their loss.
To love is to risk not being loved in return.
To live is to risk dying.
To hope is to risk despair.
To try is to risk failure.
The person who risks nothing,
Does nothing,
Has nothing and is nothing.
They may avoid suffering and sorrow,
But they simply cannot learn,
Feel, change, grow, love or live.
Risks must be taken because,
The greatest hazard in life is to risk nothing.
Only a person who risks is free.

—**Author unknown**

CHAPTER **9**

The Courage to Spiritual Well-Being

I thought that my voyage had come to its end
At the last limit of my power,
that the path before me was closed,
that provisions were exhausted
And the time comes to take shelter in a silent obscurity.
But I find that thy will knows no end in me,
And when old words die out on the tongue,
And where the old tracks are lost,
new country is revealed with its wonders.

—RABINERANATH TAGORE, SONGS OF KABIR

Spirituality as a Life Task

Our discussions on the tasks of being and belonging are incomplete unless we look at the spiritual context of which we experience the deeper problems and resolutions of the individual and the society. This chapter addresses the existential task of being in harmony with the universe, or the spiritual task. In Individual Psychology it is proposed that there are five subtasks we fulfill to meet the demands of the spiritual task. These tasks about our relationship to the universe are (1) our individual decision to believe in God or not, (2) our attitude toward religion, (3) our conception of the place of man in the universe and the psychological movement to which this conception leads, (4) the way we address ourselves regarding the issue of immortality, and (5) our answer to the meaning of life.[1]

The most obvious aspect of my life would be my disability known as cerebral palsy. Because I've been assigned this body, my perspective could easily have been "who should I blame for my circumstances?" But, on the contrary, I have acquired an appreciation for how my life story is unfolding. This is because I realize that having a mind, spirit, and soul that is housed in a body that is uniquely woven together, has taught me and is still teaching that my presence on Earth has to go beyond what most people consider to be the American dream. I have to accept that my creator has plans for my life, which only I can fulfill. Because I have come to understand and accept this honor I have made a conscious effort to appreciate everyday for the gift it brings.

—Tonya

Tonya was an African American female in her mid 30s. In response to her questions of why me, is my illness part of a larger design, and what is the purpose of my living, Tonya found the ultimate insight of her disability, unemployment, and challenges in her development, marriage, and single parenthood. Her courage to persist and excel despite the adversity life presents to her is amazing. Tonya not only had an optimistic vision of what she could become, she also had the psychological strength to help her reach her life goals.

I believe in karma. I accept all that have happened to me as parts of my fate. I cannot change my fate on this earth but I know that my next life and my children will benefit from my good deeds.

—Lily

Lily, 77, lived by herself with very limited financial resources. She attributed much of her pain or dissatisfaction about living to the lack of virtuous acts of her previous life. She loyally volunteered in a Buddhist temple where she assisted the believers in worship and asked for God's advice to resolve their financial and relationship difficulties. To Lily, the temple felt like a home where she found herself useful.

SOCRATIC DIALOGUE 9.1

Tonya and Lily share the similar courage to accept life as it is. Although in very different belief systems, their faith finds expressions in their sense of social usefulness. They both hold a set of values or a roadmap that point in the direction of a spiritual life beyond the physical life. How would the five subtasks listed in the beginning of this chapter further help us learn more about Tonya and Lily's worldviews?

Striving: The Courage to Overcome

Mary was a White female who returned to school as her children entered preschool. After 7 years of being overwhelmed with all that she needed to do to complete her degree and her family needs, she reflected on the inner force that had carried her to where she needed to be.

> Sometimes it's a little scary ... and I ask myself ... "Do I know what I'm doing?" and I find I have not only found my way ... but I have found this force inside myself, this driving force, that gives me hope and a sense of purpose and such complete fulfillment. Wow! I'm sitting here with tears falling down my face and realizing this is where I needed to be ... I feel as a part of me that was small and withered has been infused with lifesaving water and is becoming full and smooth and is beginning to grow and flourish ... I'm paying attention and being mindful of the thoughts and feelings inside myself ... reflecting on them ... giving them space ... letting them surface and giving them life. And I am so thankful that I am here right now.
>
> **—Mary**

What Mary experienced was a force brought to life by what Adler called *the creative power*.[2] The creative power creates an urge for us "as if"[3] we were to overcome imperfections in all things. The creative power moves us toward the goal of perfection as a compensatory response to our environment. The striving to overcome (or striving for power) is also called the goal of striving, which we are born with.

> Striving is the very activity of life. Life is movement towards an end state—not only that which we know, but also that towards which we can only hope and see "as if" it exists. Not only the minus of desire and the plus of satisfaction and completion; but also that striving towards which a given individual lives as his or her ultimate concern, final goal, "eternal destiny."[4]

Inferiority is the cause of striving for superiority. Psychologically, striving for superiority and perfection is the governing dynamic force that is the most important factor to understanding Adler's view of one's unified personality (see Figure 1.2). The goal of striving is also for power, security, completion, overcoming, ultimate adaptation, and self-enhancement when Adler spoke of the normal individuals. Ultimately, striving is a matter of spiritual overcoming or actualization.

"This coercion to carry out a better adaptation can never end."[5] Our striving does not stop at what is deemed as social adjustment. Better put, social adjustment is only a part of the result of our ultimate striving toward meaning of life or spiritual belonging. Individual Psychology recognizes the creative power as a striving life force that moves the individual from the inferior feeling to the goal of overcoming.

In Individual Psychology, spirituality is therefore defined as "the experience of consciously *striving* to integrate one's life in terms not of isolation and self-absorption, but of self-transcendence toward the ultimate value one perceives."[6] Our courage is enacted by the mystic creative power that moves us away from the inferior feeling and toward the goal of social usefulness spiritually motivated by an innate life force. Guided by the cosmic social feeling, the courage to belong is to allow the creative power to do its work as we develop and practice our spiritual attitudes toward life. We are part of the whole and our striving for adaptation to the external world is a precondition to the cosmic relation.[7] The wrong paths of life mean that an individual moves toward the direction opposite of the goal of perfection and evades the tasks of life in order to not suffer certain defeats.

Pain and Suffering

> At the end of the A.A. meeting, one of the women asked me, "What do you think of us?" and when I didn't respond immediately, she said, "What do you think keeps us together and keeps us coming back?" Before I could answer, she said, "It's our pain, our struggle to stay sober, and the fact that we understand this in each other." I thought to myself, can I, the beginning counselor, recognize the struggle and the pain, and allow clients a safe and serene place for recovery? It can happen. I am drawn to these meetings in a "spiritual" way.
>
> —Elizabeth

The inferiority feeling exists not only in our relationships with our self, family, and community. It also exists in our relationships with nature, society, and the universe. It is the *cosmic inferiority* with which we are reminded of our very own smallness and helplessness. Things sometimes happen without making sense. We live in a problematic and hostile world where tragic events may threaten our wholeness, alienating us from ourselves and the society. Death and disease are two sources of the inferiority feeling from which very few of us escape. Pain and suffering are results of losses due to death and dying, conflicts, insanity, abuses, ignorance, corruption, and oppression.

Furthermore, friendships, family ties, communities, countries, or any grouping can work for self-preservation and mutual exclusivity as they compete for scarce resources, power, and prestige. The unfounded collective superior attitudes are the basis of discrimination and oppression that bring segregation or confrontation. Suffering has many definitions that share a common connotation of the bearing or undergoing of pain, anguish, or trouble, implying the sense of pain from physical and emotional injuries. Inherent in our suffering are a deep feeling of physical, social, and moral isolation and a crisis of meaning.

> On the day the second of my two mentally handicapped children was born, I experienced a fathomless despair. I felt that I was drowning and did not even know how to struggle. Yet there was something in me that wanted to grow through this horror, to use it for good in some way. When I reached what seemed to me the darkest depths, I was suddenly aware of being upheld, aware of a promise of strength, if I would only seek it. I know that this was a direct experience of God.
>
> —**Anonymous**

Suffering is inevitable and is a universal aspect of our living. The understanding and relief of our pain and suffering call for the spiritual values that are traditionally not addressed in psychology. Generation after generation, the spiritual and cultural value systems in the world have attempted to find the purpose and cure of suffering (Table 9.1).

> Suffering is God's megaphone to rouse a deaf world where the individuals are not in harmony with the universe and the Creator.[9]

In psychology, we must ask such questions concerning the causes of suffering. How could these conditions be eliminated? How do we differ in our responses to suffering? What are the therapeutic values of suffering? How does courage deliver us from vulnerability? What is the meaning of suffering and under what conditions can it make us more human?

From the Individual Psychology perspective, suffering is an unconscious decision of not appearing defeated. Pain and suffering are the deeper problems of belonging. Suffering serves a purpose. It is a guilt feeling used to stifle recovery, a partial expression with the whole style of life. Prolonged suffering is psychological arrangement for the individuals who have mistaken beliefs such as it's not fair, take care of me, see I am noble, and you can't kick a man when he is down.[10] As a result,

Table 9.1 Causes and Elimination of Suffering[8]

Belief System	Cause	Elimination
Confucian	Injustice	Ethical behavior directed toward all
Taoist	Failure to cherish all things	To cherish all things
Buddhist	Craving/attachment	Elimination of craving or detachment
Christian	Bearing Jesus' cross	Salvation (love for God and man)
Existentialist	Existential anxiety	Meaning
Humanist	Low self-esteem	Self-actualization

instead of taking the task-oriented stance, these individuals suffer more consequences of the self-oriented stance toward all life tasks by running away from the painful situation, taking a detour from direct confrontation, or taking the hesitant approach pretending that the problem does not exist.

> No experience is a cause of success or failure. We do not suffer from the shock of our experiences, so-called trauma—but we make out of them just what suits our purposes.[11]

In our private logic, we only see ourselves as the center of "our" universe and sometimes we cannot comprehend when things happen the way they do. We are our own barriers that prevent us from seeing our connection to the wholeness of life. The feeling that we are deprived from what *it should be* is rooted in our very limited self-knowledge and our fear of the feelings of insignificance and, mostly, the unknown. Unfounded fear and the resulting alienation from oneself, others, and society are indications of the possibility of one's avoidance of social responsibilities, participation, and contribution. The individual's characteristic approach to life and one's life goal of perfection have a defining effect on the courage it takes for the person to see the cause and use of his/her suffering.

The Courage to Heal

> The 33 years we were married we taught each other a great deal about life and about both good and bad, and the last 6 or 7 years particularly were mostly good and even the last 18 months, as negative as that all may sound, there were very few negative moments, even the passing, even the actual process of death, it was sad, it was intense, but it was just part of the continuing process … The 3 weeks after the funeral there was just pure anguish to loss and then to [feeling] lost, but [it] was about 3 months after the funeral, the possibilities seemed infinite, there was a vista. I was lost and now I was found, but that's what the death created. In that short period of time there was an understanding. It was very similar to, I felt so similar [in that third week or second week after the funeral] to that period of time when I was 17. There was fear in the beginning, other fear of losing, of death … I think for me in the sense of being lost. I saw a great opportunity to find and I knew that it was a choice … I knew I was on a path.
>
> —Mark

Mark, 53, paralleled the tragic loss of his wife to the experience of being lost in the mountains for a day and a night when he was 17. He moved from the feeling of loss to the feeling of being lost, and then to seeing the space for opportunity. There was a psychological force (or process) that allowed Mark to see life through his wife's dying and moved him from the deep despair to the wider space where he began to see freedom and choice again. In the face of death, Mark chose life.

Mark had the courage of despair. Twice in his life, he did not see an exit to his immediate crisis. Yet, the affirmation he felt in the midst of despair was mystic. Mark's experience illustrates for us the existential concept of the will to power, upon which Adler conceived his notion of striving for power.

> The striving will continue in any case; but in case of the cooperative individual it will be hopeful, useful striving, directed towards a real improvement in our common situation ... Human striving is never ending and we can always find or invent new problems, and create new opportunities for cooperation and contribution.[12]

Nietzsche's thoughts of the *will to power* and *eternal recurrence,* if considered together, contrasts Schopenhauer's the "will to live" but parallels with the Eastern spiritual thoughts on self-renewal, "generation and regeneration without ceasing." The will to live is secondary to the will to power to Nietzsche. The will to power is more than an innate desire we have to procreate and avoid death as Schopenhauer suggested. There is a greater need to use the power "to grow, to expand and possibly to subsume other 'wills' in the process."[13] The will to power, therefore, is not the will to mere existence, but to the power of being—life. The will to power is the will to more life. The will to power is partially the basis on which Tillich defined courage.

> Courage is self-affirmation "in-spite-of" that is in spite of that which tends to prevent the self from affirming itself.[14]

According to Tillich, our self-affirmation works to affirm the self as a self (individuation) and the self as a part (participation in the world). The courage must be rooted in a power of being that is greater than the power of oneself and the power of one's world. Courage is the two sides of self-affirmation that work interdependently following the harmony principle. Life is the process in which the power of being actualizes itself. The power of being is the source of the courage to be. In other words, courage is the power of life that self-affirms in the face of difficulties.

Existentially, suffering is part of our natural striving toward meaning and toward more life. To heal is to become whole again and to regain a sense of harmonious connection with ourselves, others, and the universe. The value of harmony or becoming whole again indicates an ideal state of being that can be reached by some sort of self-transcendence or transfor-

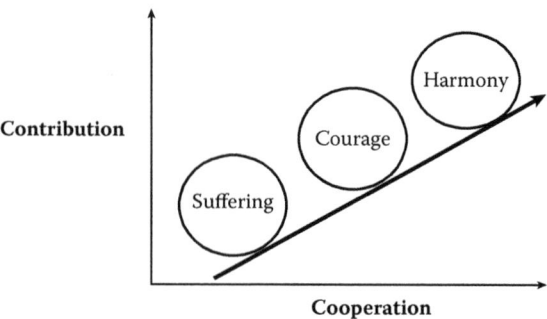

Figure 9.1 The processes of healing.

mation as a result of suffering. In fact, health, from the spiritual wellness aspect, is defined as "the harmonious relationship between every part of the self and the environment."[15]

Figure 9.1 is built upon Figure 2.1 in Chapter 2 where we illustrated a diagonal model of social interest. The movement depicted by the arrow points to social interest is generated by the interaction of the individual's cooperation and contribution. It represents a process of change that moves the individual forward, powered by courage, the self-affirming power of life. We call these processes *healing*.

Adler's stance on healing is based on education for ideal cooperation. Courage is one of the many sides of community for the individual who is capable, through innate creative power, of changing toward socially usefulness. The attainment of healing must start with the individual's courage to cooperate in a positive movement with the yes attitudes toward social interest.[16] The courage to heal, therefore, is the courage to transcend suffering via the process of moving toward one's harmonious relationships with oneself, others, and the universe in spite of the adversities.

This healing experience is best illustrated in *A Grief Observed*, where C. S. Lewis vividly reflected on the loss of his wife. At first, it felt like fear and suspense. He was habitually waiting for his wife to return and learned that his wife would only return to his memory when he was not grieving. After a time of restlessness, there is a sense being quieted. He recognized that his grief was about himself, his wife, and about life (i.e., Where is God?). Suffering only has communal and spiritual value when he was raised above his own pain to recognize others' suffering and his own faith.

> It ends, like all affairs of the heart, with exhaustion. Only so much pain is possible. Then, rest. Of course, it is different when the thing happens to oneself, not to others, and in reality, not in imagination.

Yes; but should it, for a sane man, make quite such a difference as this? No. And it wouldn't for a man whose faith had been real faith and whose concern for other people's sorrows had been real concerns.[17]

SOCRATIC DIALOGUE 9.2

How would the dynamic of movement depicted in Figure 9.1 help us conceptualize our personal insight to such existential questions as: Why me? What is the meaning of all that is happening? Where does the courage I need to meet the challenges come from? Where am I with my love, work, and social life in the face of the obstacles that I have? How, under the same life conditions, would one individual feel the total defeat and withdraw to neurotic responses, while the other is able to transcend the troubles and move on?

Courage and the Allied Spiritual Attitudes

We have mentioned in earlier chapters that ethically courage has to be united with other virtues such as wisdom and passion that help evaluate and decide on goals of actions for the individual and for others. Courage is a matter of heart capable of overcoming fear and negative attitudes. Existentially, courage is the striving power, a universal force of self-affirmation and will for more life in spite of the negating elements of our existence. Courage, which brings all other human characters to life, has to be aligned with other spiritual attitudes for the attainment of the higher good.

Courage is the affirmation of one's being with the forward movement, which has in itself the character of "in spite of." The courage to accept one's uniqueness and the demands of nature in spite of what may be unacceptable can only be justified by *faith*. To have faith is to believe in what has not been accomplished and the courage to accept what is as it is. *Acceptance* is the developed capacity to fully embrace whatever is in the present moment. Tillich termed the courage of faith as the "acceptance of acceptance."

> You are accepted. You are accepted, accepted by that which is greater than you, and the name of which you do not know. Do not ask for the name now; perhaps you will find it later. Do not try to do anything now; perhaps later you will do much. Do not seek for anything; do not perform anything; do not intend anything. Simply accept the fact that you are accepted! If that happens to us, we experience grace.[18]

To accept means to take, seize, or catch.[19] The existential courage of acceptance is best expressed in the Taoist art of action through inaction (*wu-wei*) and its mystic recognition of usefulness of our feeling of smallness and nothingness. Courage in the Taoist thought is to let events take their own course as we comply with the natural life force. Beecher and Beecher (1966) vividly portray this approach of living in the following:

> The fortunate 10 percent who are prepared to meet life on an independent basis show it in everything they do. They seem to pour themselves out on things as if they were pouring out water on parched earth. They seem to have limitless resources and no fear of running dry. They live as if they feel that the world is a good place to be, and they do not feel disturbed if they find things less than perfect. When blocked in one direction, they merely take another and have fun either way.[20]

Existentially, to overcome the inferiority feeling is to have *faith* as we participate in living and become the self we are intended to be. That is to be in harmony with the collective courage and the self-courage.[21] The existential duality to participate and to let it be is deeply embedded in Individual Psychology: The acceptance attitude requires our cooperation on taking what all life has to present to us, and the "yes, in spite of" attitude is our contribution to our fellow humankind. Both of these are guided by social interest.

In Individual Psychology the courage to *hope* is manifested in our striving for a better future that brings not only change of our immediate living but also human progress. To hope is to live the goal of the future as if the future is realized in the present.[22] Hope has the dynamic possibilities of transforming/self-transcendence, as illustrated in Figure 9.1. It is in our hope for the ultimate sense of belongingness that we fulfill our dreams of work, love, and social relationships so that we become connected beyond oneself, away from isolation and self-absorption, and toward the greater community.

> I know quite well that feeling of something strange and wonderful that ought to happen ... and that this hope will someday be fulfilled. ... Perhaps indeed the chance of a change into some world of Terreauty (a word I've coined to mean terror and beauty) is in reality in some allegorical way daily offered to us if we had the courage to take it.[23]

In our hope and faith, courage coincides emotionally with *joy*. Joy is a courageous yes to our spiritual longing: the longing to be acknowledged, to have meaning, to belong, and to transform and become whole.

The Courage to Agape Love

"The beauty of life is while we cannot undo what is done, we can succeed it, understanding it, learn from it and change, so that every new moment is spent not in regret, guilt, fear, anger but in wisdom, understanding, and love. Each action we take can embrace or alienate. Following the great evil is the great good. Courage is always required to accomplish great good." Now it is time for us to demonstrate the courage of nonviolence, the courage to engage in dialogue, the courage to listen to what we do not want to hear, the courage to control our desire to revenge, and follow reason. I am convinced that we are born into the world with inherited good nature and together we must restore our faith and humanity. I believe from this tragedy, courage is the greatest and most endearing honor that we can give in memory of our loved ones.[24]

This quote was part of the message given by a Buddhist community leader in the convocation after the tragic campus shooting at Virginia Tech in 2007. It is only by courage that the adversity could be regarded as the opportunity for the community to unite, to forgive, to reconcile, and to find peace and compassion. The call and attainment of this community feeling can only be achieved by the courage to accept and participate in the agape love that is innate in us.

In Chapter 5, we presented a definition of agape as a love toward one's neighbor that does not depend on any loveable qualities that the object of love possesses. Agape love is a gift love that makes other types of love (intimacy, friendship, family) possible. Agape also enables us to love what is not naturally lovable. Agape love is the perfect love without fear. Agape love is mysterious, mature, and selfless. It is a love that commits itself to the well-being of the other. Agape, the caring for others, has its root in Christian spirituality but has been also regarded as the core value of world religions.[25]

Agape love is the end, and it is the only means. Agape love is the answer to our quest for meaning when we ask such questions as how can we participate in harmony with the life that seems to have endless suffering and short of love. Agape, or unconditional love, is the striving to collective wellness. It is the simple act to love our neighbor because we have been loved. The core concept of innate striving is an expression of our deep longing for this agape love. Using Adlerian terms, agape means the striving to realize the notion of the community feeling.

How do we recognize agape at work around us? Adler called it "social interest."[26]

Table 9.2 Characteristics of Agape Love in Social Relationships

Intimacy	Marriage	Family	Friendship
Love	Liberating	Standing alone	Lifeblood of
Self-sufficient	Egalitarian	Individuals	community
Inner potential	Respect	Democratic	Security
Content	Give and take	Let go and let live	Risk taking
Fullness	Faith	Openness	Cooperation
Freedom	Affirmation	Encouragement	Needs
Nonpartisan	For the world	Choice and	Equality
Acceptance	Productivity	consequences	Unconditional
Capacity	Independence	Collaboration	Authenticity
Nonjudgmental	Disagreeability	Main-tent activities	Participation
Encouraging	Growing apace		
Giver, doer	Participation		
Okayness regardless	A working		
Hopeful	relationship		
Creative, playfulness			
Fulfillment			
Free mind			

Agape is the largest common denominator of Individual Psychology, Confucianism, and humanist psychology, as we have reviewed in the previous chapters. Summarized in Table 9.2 is a snapshot of the characteristics of agape love in intimacy, marriage, and family relationships.

Are characteristics of agape love attainable or, in another word, trainable? Our answer is yes. The Biblical agape has been recognized to be the strategic model of social interest.[27] According to Watts, the attitudinal and behavioral elements of the following verses are indicative of individuals with a high level of social interest and, thus, mental health. These elements are persevering, benevolently useful, trustworthy, humble, altruistic, unselfish, and optimistic. These elements, though originally spiritual qualities, can become operative if regarded as conditions for change that will produce such relational attitudes as those in Table 9.2.

> Love is patient; love is kind. It does not envy, it does not boast, it is not proud. It is not rude, it is not self-seeking, it is not easily angered, it keeps no record of wrongs. Love does not delight in evil but rejoices with the truth. It always protects, always trusts, always hopes, always perseveres. Love never fails.[28]

Agape love and the agape attributes, when regarded as skills and attitudes, can be the facilitative factors of positive change.[29] The courage to agape love is to *act as if* what we do, think, and feel can change in ways that foster growth and healing for self and others.[30] Acting as if is a choice of constructive optimism. Act as if what we fear will not happen. Act as if change is possible, and we grow. Act as if the future is realized in the present, and we have hope. Act as if a good life is attainable, and our striving has meaning. Act as if we are loved, and we then can love.

Closing Thoughts

This chapter concludes Part I and Part II of the book by examining the spiritual life task of Individual Psychology. We first explored the spiritual foundation of striving in the existential contexts of the creative power and the will to more life. The courage to heal is a transformation process with regard to the deeper problems of being and belonging: suffering. To heal is to strive for harmony with oneself, others, and the universe. Courage needs to be united with universal spiritual attitudes such as wisdom, compassion, joy, faith, acceptance, grace, and hope, which are permeated in Individual Psychology. Adler's work of social interest or community feeling has a transcultural spiritual value similar to agape love. We ended the chapter with a discussion of how the spiritual qualities of agape love can be treated as psychological attributes that are useful for facilitating positive change. Finally, we can experience agape love when we have the courage to act as if.

Serenity Prayer

God, grant me the serenity to accept the things I cannot change,
The courage to change the things I can,
And the wisdom to know the difference.
Living one day at a time,
Enjoying one moment at a time,
Accepting hardship as the pathway to peace,
Taking this sinful world as it is,
Not as I would have it.
Trusting that you will make all things right
If I surrender to your will,
So that I may be reasonably happy in this life
And supremely happy with you forever in the next.[31]

PART III
Implications

CHAPTER **10**

The Art of Facilitating Courage

I do believe that life is just a day in school. All our experiences are but lessons in some form or other which condition us for our larger destiny. What matters, and what matters only is what we do with the problems.

—Bill W.[1]

To be mentally healthy, we have to follow the innate social interest that establishes an ideal direction for all of our strivings, both individually and communally. Individual Psychology, with its profound insight about human nature in relation to society, offers a commonsense approach of understanding our experiences, perceptions, and problems as well as how to go about change.

Included in Part III is our attempt to answer the question: How do we obtain and facilitate courage and social interest in ourselves and with others? Or better formulated: How can we creatively facilitate healthy changes that encourage individuals to develop a sense of self-worth and common purpose with a community feeling? The following are several overarching concepts and strategies common to the 22 tools for facilitating courage that are detailed in the last section of the book.

The Courage of the Facilitator

The courage facilitator is someone who gives courage in his/her relationships with self and others.[2] The courage facilitator can be a spouse or partner, a parent or a child, a sibling, a teacher or a student, a friend, a leader or one who is led, or a stranger who possesses social feeling and recognizes the immediacy and value of courage with another fellow human being.

There is no Adlerian way of helping and the courage facilitator is not limited to any one style. There is a link between one's being and one's relationships with others. This implies that the courage facilitator is a warm human who holds more "yes" attitudes than "no" attitudes (see Chapter 6). He or she acts as a whole person, and confidently encourages with feeling, sensitivity, and social purpose. The courage facilitator values quality in a relationship and sees change as a learning process that involves choice and consequences. In a group setting, features of the courage facilitator mirror the descriptors Adlerians use for group counselors: assertiveness and confidence, courage and risk, acceptance, interest and caring, modeling and collaboration, adaptability, and a sense of humor.[3] In addition, the courage facilitator's own attitudes and behaviors reflect some of the agape love qualities in his/her thinking, feeling, and acting (see Chapter 9, Table 9.2). The courage facilitator experiences and believes that social interest and agape is comprehensible and teachable via the development of courage.

Socratic Questioning

To understand individuals' attitudes toward life and how they act upon problems of social living, we must engage in a subjective interview/questioning process. Adler was known to use *The Question*[4] when he asked how life would be different if one was free of the symptoms or concerns. The use of questioning allows us to be active participants in the search for insight or stories of individuals. Socratic questions unravel insight about the internal and external factors that contribute to our life issues. Our response to such questions may reveal our desires, fears, or goals of a deeper level that we would not have reached otherwise.

Socratic-style dialogue serves as the key element of the *Respectful Curious Inquiry (RCI)* process that we will use in many of our tools.[5] The RCI only uses open-ended questions. The dialogue is collaborative; both sides work toward a shared understanding. A Socratic questioner should

- Use the words *who*, *what*, *where*, *when*, and *how*; never *why*.
- Keep the discussion focused
- Keep the discussion therapeutically responsible
- Stimulate the discussion with probing questions
- Periodically summarize what has and what has not been dealt with or resolved

As facilitators listen to the disclosures or responses to Socratic questions, we look for lifestyle themes or patterns in one's thinking, feeling, and acting. Specifically, we facilitate individuals' understanding of their own narratives of their strengths, the what should have beens and as ifs that could be their dreams/needs/goals, problems, and challenges as well as usefulness and uselessness of their problem-resolution endeavors. The FLAVER model in the following enlists six techniques that enhance the level of mutual understanding of Socratic dialogue with others.

> F = Focusing on what the individual wants and arriving at mutually agreed upon goals.
> L = Listening attentively, empathetically, and reflectively.
> A = Assessing the individual's strengths, motivation, resilience, and social interest.
> V = Validating the individual's resources and "character"istics, encouraging the individual's growth.
> E = Enjoying the humor that abounds in the ironies of social living.
> R = Replacing useless information gathering (factophilia) with appropriate clarification, creative intuition, imaginative empathy, and stochastic questions.

Contemporary Adlerians have elaborated on questioning methods that creatively bring out the individual's concerns in a specific life task or one's general life attitudes. For example, the question "What do you want to improve or change in this area of your life?" can be used for each life task area.[6] Presented in Table 10.1 are sample Socratic questions of the life tasks that facilitators can use in either one-on-one or group settings.

The Use of Encouragement

Understanding how individuals adjust and adapt in the face of difficult life tasks, concerning both the welfare of themselves and others, allows us to see sources of discouragement and encouragement. Depending on whether there is an absence or presence of courage, the individual creatively chooses one path or the other (Figure 10.1). One could be mistakenly taking a pathway toward *ichgebundenheit* (self-boundedness or self-interest), or toward contributing and cooperating with oneself and others on the pathway of social interest.[7] Self-bounded individuals are those whose style of social living can be described as pampered or neglected, in another word, discouraged, whereas only the encouraged individuals can display other directedness.

Everyone experiences discouragement from time to time whether in pursuing their self-ideal or chasing after misdirected goals. Discouragement is "an attitude, feeling, or belief that one is unable to succeed in a constructive and cooperative manner, is inadequate, or is a failure in attempts to meet the demands of life."[9] Discouraged adolescents believe that they are unable

Table 10.1 Sample Socratic Questions by Life Tasks[8]

Life Task	Socratic Questions
Work	What constitutes your work and your activities in life? What meaning does it have for you? How do you get along with colleagues, supervisors, and subordinates? Do you feel appreciated for your work?
Love	What are your love relationships like? Do you experience emotional closeness with partners? Do you have any difficulty in expressing or receiving love and affection to and from others? How would you describe men and women? How do you feel about yourself as a man or woman? What do you complain about in your partner? What does your partner complain about in you?
Friendship	Who are your friends and what kind of life do you have in your community? Where do you meet your friends? What activities do you do with them? What is your role with them? How would they describe you? Was making friends easy for you? Who was (were) your best friend(s) growing up?
Harmony with self	Am I moving toward becoming the person I am capable of becoming? How is chaos the precondition to creativity? How is the death of an initiative always a source of new learning?
Harmony with world	Psychological/social belonging: Is there a reality that can be created by another way of doing business: consensual, cooperative, and communal? How is harmony more fundamental than warfare in the nature of reality itself? What gives me the most satisfaction in my work? What brings me to life? How have I touched others' lives? How does my work make the world a better place?
	Spiritual belonging (to believe): Have you ever had transcendent experiences in which you felt connected to something beyond yourself? What was that like for you? What helped you feel connected? When was the last time you felt this connection? What would it be like for you to spend a little time each day relating to God or a higher power?

to cope with life effectively and may attempt to achieve significance and belonging based on faulty goals that produce overt rebellion, disruptiveness, and negative attention-seeking behaviors. The discouraged may have an excessive desire to seek approval and please authority, assuming that they will only be worthwhile when they are better than others. Regardless of what is accomplished or achieved, it is never enough for the approval seekers who are vulnerable to discouragement. Fear and other forms of negative thinking such as "high expectations/unrealistic standards, focusing on mistakes, making comparisons, making pessimistic interpretations, and dominating by being overly responsible" can generate discouragement.[10]

When defined using the root meaning of *courage*, encouragement is the process of facilitating one's courage toward positive life movement.

The Art of Facilitating Courage • 133

Figure 10.1 Life movement and attitudes.

When looked at as a psychological concept, encouragement is the process of giving courage that strengthens the "psychological muscle" of a person. When looked at for its practical use, encouragement is a set of skills, a process, or outcome. When looked at as a spiritual concept, encouragement is a spirit or attitude that can be used to "inspire, foster, stimulate, support, or to instill courage and confidence."[11]

It is through encouragement that the facilitator *gives courage*, empowering the individual to challenge his or her misdirected goals and see a new direction and take action. Through encouragement the facilitator helps the discouraged individual to activate social interest and create meaning and purpose in life. In Adlerian literature, it is often written that human beings need encouragement like plants need water. If social interest can be seen as the backbone of our well-being and courage as the muscle, then encouragement and discouragement can be regarded as the conditions that enable life movement.

When used in helping relationships, encouragement is associated with a wide array of tactics to promote a proper self-evaluation of goals and styles of social living as well as behavioral changes. The Adlerian concepts and strategies of encouragement have been widely applied in educational, familial, therapeutic, and organizational settings. Encouragement thus has become the core of all interventions for those who experience discouragement. Both the professional and the layperson can use encouragement to facilitate courage for change.

How does encouragement work to facilitate change? In Figure 10.1 we present the life attitudes collected from Adlerian literature in pairs of opposites.[12] When we operate from fear we move toward self-interest and we either overcompensate or undercompensate with competition and comparison. These safeguarding devices create for us the perceptions, attitudes, and behaviors of discouragement or the socially useless/no attitudes as displayed in the left word column. On the other hand, we can use good compensation with courage to move toward social interest, that is, develop socially useful/yes attitudes via cooperation and contribution that leads to perceptions, attitudes, and behaviors of encouragement as displayed in the right column.

The attitudes in Figure 10.1 are the expressions of one's life style that were formed by early family training or school experience. Knowledge of these attitudes is accessible using objective interviews with our early memories, information on one's biological/psychological birth position, family constellation, day and night dreams, behavioral goals, and life task assessment.[13]

Our life attitudes characterize the direction of our movement, either toward self-interest with fear or toward social interest with courage. To encourage is to empower (i.e., to give courage) discouraged individuals so that they can redirect their life movement from the left column to the right.

Facilitating Processes

How do we facilitate the courage to change? In Individual Psychology, to change is ultimately to recognize one's mistaken beliefs or life style. The processes of change involve helping the individual to reassess and reorient

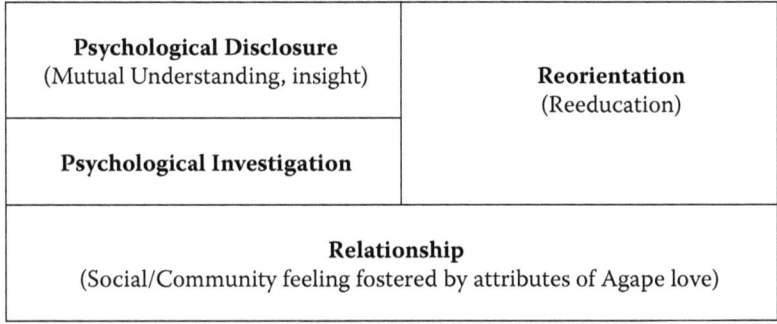

Figure 10.2 Components of facilitating change.

his or her belief system. With the interconnectedness of social interest and the sense of well-being, the Adlerian theory of change is based on the assumption that once one understands one's specific life style and mistaken goals, one can gain courage to reorient oneself toward cultivating the social interest while striving to overcome problems of living in all life tasks.

To facilitate change effectively, the facilitator must be aware of the components of facilitation that sometimes are referred to as change processes or goals in the Individual Psychology literature.[14] As always with encouragement, the facilitator wins over the individual's cooperation and works with him or her to establish and maintain a mutually respectful relationship, to engage in the life style assessment process (psychological investigation), to acquire insight with psychological disclosure, and to redirect and take actions toward new life goals with new strategies (Figure 10.2).

Relationship

Relationship is a component in which the facilitator establishes an effective relationship with the individual seeking change on the basis of mutual respect. The relationship is developed in a democratic atmosphere where there is the presence of mutual respect and equality as well as the attributes of agape love we discussed in Chapter 9 (see Table 9.2). The courage facilitator's being, active listening, and modeling create the conditions of social feeling that communicates patience, selflessness, acceptance, hope, and positive regard.[15] Characterized by active listening and modeling, this relationship conveys the encouragement and support needed for all other components of facilitation.

Psychological Investigation

Psychological investigation is the component of assessment or information gathering for the facilitator to develop a deeper understanding of the individual in relation to the "rules" of social living one had acquired

Table 10.2 Psychological Investigation Tools[17]

Assessment	What to Look For
Life tasks	Coping patterns that individuals use to handle life's problems. Areas of support and dysfunction in daily living (in a group setting, also look for the extent to which group behaviors manifest themselves in other parts of people's lives).
Early recollections	Recollections of danger, punishment, birth of sibling, the first visit to school, sickness or death, a stay away from home, misdeeds, and other interests; one's conviction about the self, others, life, and ethical stances; one's positions in relation to others/community; verification of coping patterns and motivations; identification of strengths, assets, or interfering ideas or mistaken goals.
Family constellation/ birth order	Major influences in the individual's life. Experiences the individual had with parents/caretakers that set a guideline for gender identity. Interpretations of life and society provided by parents/caretakers.
Dream	Expression of style of life, emotions not accessible in waking hours when reason and judgment dominate, warning, getting ready for an anxiety-provoking task, goal attainment, problem solving, forward looking, the fear of loss, overcoming.

in childhood. Techniques for psychological investigation often include investigating the meaning of one's biological and/or psychological birth order, family constellation, early recollection, dream analysis, lifestyle assessment, and personality priority assessment.

While many psychometric instruments are available for mental health professionals, we have included in Part III several subjective and objective interview techniques for the courage facilitator to use or share with others.[16] The purpose is to look for themes or patterns of behaviors/thoughts/feelings that are indicative of individual goals and "private logic." A summary of the Adlerian assessment techniques and the information these techniques generate in helping relationships is presented in Table 10.2.

Psychological Disclosure

The facilitator's task in psychological disclosure is to provide feedback, confrontation, and encouragement with the goal to assist the individual's movement from self-realization to self-actualization. The mutual understanding of the individual's life style can be facilitated by the techniques of goal disclosure and Socratic questioning. The facilitator uses educated guesses to gain useful information and to verify the understanding with the individual (mutual understanding). Guessing is the best facilitators can do as each individual is unique in his or her response to the life demands and movement to his or her private goal of perfection. "Correct guessing is the first step toward the mastery of our problems."[18] This mutual understanding is the goal of the psychological disclosure. It is also regarded as insight that follows the information gathered in the process of psychological investigation and motivates for meaningful actions.

Reorientation

For Adlerians, insight is not sufficient for behavioral change. Insight is only a means to an end. One needs to become aware of personal choice and action. Reorientation and redirection are the most important goals of effective facilitation. The facilitator educates/facilitates the redirection of faulty personal goals, explores alternatives, uses natural and logical consequences, and encourages the implementation of actions. This is a critical process where the individual is facilitated to let go of resistance, take responsibility, develop social interest through cooperation with the facilitator as a fellow human being, and to regain courage for action.

It is in the reorientation process that Individual Psychology, as liaison work, can collaborate with other pragmatic models such as the stages of change (also known as the transtheoretical model of intentional human behavior change) that has been widely used in health fields.[19] This model supposes that change happens incrementally and progressively. The stages of change are

- Precontemplation stage—The individual has no understanding that a problem exists and certainly no desire to change.
- Contemplation stage—The individual knows there is a problem and desires to take action.
- Determination stage (sometimes called the preparation stage)—The individual prepares to take action and may make some tentative movement toward change.
- Action stage—The individual takes action to overcome problems. Action involves the most overt behavioral changes and requires considerable commitment of time and energy.
- Maintenance stage—The individual works to prevent relapse and consolidate the gains attained during the action stage.
- Relapse stage—Relapse to the previous behavior can happen during the action or maintenance stage. When relapse occurs, the individual returns to the precontemplation, contemplation, or determination stage.

The stages of change theory allows both the individual who is attempting change and those who are assisting the individual in the change process to understand how change occurs. An absolute key to this understanding is that change occurs one stage at a time, meaning if a person is in the contemplation stage, she or he can only next move to the determination stage; to attempt to move to the action or maintenance stage will predict relapse. After being in a specific stage, it is then possible to move to the next stage. To facilitate the courage to change in the reorientation process, therefore, means to facilitate patience, persistence, and the courage to use relapse in a constructive manner.

About the Tools for Facilitating Courage

In Part III, we have developed 22 tools based on the theoretical concepts in Part I and Part II. Many fellow Adlerians contributed to these tools with their ideas and experiences of practicing Individual Psychology.[20] Although all tools are useful for strength assessment, users will find that many Adlerian techniques such as Socratic questions, early recollection, family constellation, and lifestyle assessment are embedded in these tools. The tools are as follows:

Tool #1: A Conversation Guide: Socratic Questioning
Tool #2: Attitude Modification
Tool #3: Birth Order
Tool #4: Change in Harmony
Tool #5: CHARACTERistics: Directed Reflection
Tool #6: Constructive Ambivalence
Tool #7: Courage Assessment
Tool #8: Consultation with Parents and Teachers
Tool #9: E-5 Group Session Guide
Tool #10: En-COURAGE-ment
Tool #11: Family Constellation in the Workplace
Tool #12: Goal Disclosure: "The Could It Be's"
Tool #13: Home Page
Tool #14: Hope Is a Choice
Tool #15: In Store: Eleven Seven
Tool #16: Life Style Interview: Variations
Tool #17: Lost or Stuck?
Tool #18: Most Memorable Moment
Tool #19: Recollecting Early Memories
Tool #20: Trust Only the Movement
Tool #21: Ups, Downs, and Sides by Sides: Relationships of Equals
Tool #22: Walk the Line

Each of the tools begins with a brief rationale followed by objectives to connect the activity to the theoretical concepts and the actual implications. Each tool may contain several Adlerian techniques. There are step-by-step instructions for each tool. Some tools come with supplementary worksheets and tables (long tables are located in the Appendix). Those who wish to expand their understanding of concepts or techniques specific to the tool may find the suggested readings or the linkage to the book chapters helpful. At the end of selected tools, a conversational script is provided to illustrate the use of the tool.

As we explained in Part II, all life tasks are inseparable, and our understanding of an individual's psychological pattern has to rely on a multifaceted approach. We would like to assume that these tools can be used in any or all tasks that are of interest to the individual seeking self-understanding or change. Most tools are suitable for both adults and children, but some may be more appropriate for one age group at the user's discretion. We have tested most of these tools in our work in the United States, Europe, and Asia and hope they are cross-culturally applicable not only for individuals but also for families.

The tools can be used in one-on-one interviews/conversations, small groups, and classroom settings. We hope the tools are also supplementary resources for use in training, consultation, and professional presentation purposes. We strongly recommend that users first read the chapters that serve as the conceptual framework for the tool(s). It would be beneficial if the facilitator could practice the tools with him- or herself first before using them with others.

Tool #1

A Conversation Guide: Socratic Questioning

Rationale

Adler has been given the title "the Father of Self Help." He believed that we could gain help without a professional. After all, Individual Psychology is a psychology of common sense. Encouraging and insightful conversations between individuals in various relationships could be therapeutic and facilitative of positive changes. The Socratic questioning technique is widely used in Individual Psychology. The use of questioning allows us to be active participants in the search for insight or stories of the individuals. Socratic questions unravel insight about the internal and external factors that contribute to our life issues. Our response to such questions may reveal our desires, fears, or goals of a deeper level that we would not have reached otherwise.

Objectives
1. To demonstrate Socratic questioning skills that use the words *who*, *what*, *where*, *when*, and *how*, but never *why*.
2. To demonstrate how to use Socratic questioning collaboratively when both sides work toward a shared understanding by keeping the discussion focused, stimulating, and therapeutically responsible.

Suggested Reading
- Chapter 10
- Stein, H. T. (1991). Adler and Socrates: Similarities and differences. *Individual Psychology, 47*(2), 241–246.

Instructions
A. "The Question" in one word
   - How was it for you?
B. Choice
   - What led you to that conclusion?
   - Of all the possibilities, what brought you to _____?
   - What is it about _____ that draws you?
C. Feelings
   - When you consider that situation, are you mad, sad, glad, or scared, etc., or a combination of those?
   - When you are feeling _____, what is that like for you?
   - Where in your body do you experience that?
D. The snapshot
   - Like in a picture or a snapshot, what is it about that moment that stands out for you?
E. The connection
   - How does that connect for you now?
   - How does that play out for you in your life right now?
F. Decision
   - Do you recall the decision you made about that when it was going on?
   - Do you remember what thoughts you had when that was happening?
   - What led you to that conclusion?
G. Ambivalence
   - What would happen if you did that? (What happens when you do that?)
   - What would happen if you didn't do that? (What happens when you don't do that?)
   - What would I see?

- Will you tell me more about it?
- Will you give me an example?
- What would it look like?

H. Goal setting
- How did you hope I might be helpful to you today?
- How do you think I might be able to help you here today?
- How has what we've talked about been helpful to you today?

I. "The Question" of questions
- If I possessed magic power that could make everything change for you to just the way you'd like it, how would things be different for you?

J. Name
- Do you know how you got your name? (If no, ask the person to make something up.)
- Do you know what it means? (If not, have them make something up.)
- What do you like (dislike) about the name you have?
- What would you choose if you were to change it?

K. Career
- What kinds of jobs have you had?
- What was your first regular paying job?
- What kinds of things did you do?
- What did you like (dislike) about it?

L. Personal encourager
- As you were growing up, was there a person who believed in you?
- Who was the person that encouraged you?
- What did they do? How did you know?

M. Of all the …
- Of all the _____ you know, which one do you prefer?
- What is it about _____ that attracts you?

N. As you listen
- As you listen to the stories, always use the client's metaphors as much as you can.
- Identify five or six assets or strengths of your client.
- Record these strengths and assets on a 3 × 5 index card.
- Share the card with your client as he or she leaves.

O. Strengths script
- Here's what I am going to do while we talk. I am going to start to write a list … I am going to listen for your assets and strengths (or, the things you already do well). As I listen, I am going to write a list of things you might be using or able to use in some of the challenges you have. About school, maybe, or

home, or with family or friends ... So, can we just talk for a while? [Allow time for a response.]
- Just before we get done today, I can give you a copy of this list if you want one. Will you help me remember to do that? [Allow time for a response.]

Tool #2
Attitude Modification

Rationale

An attitude is *a predisposition to behave in a certain way.* Positive attitudes are not the problem. Our negative attitudes exist in a context of self-doubt carried over from our childhood. The negative attitude overrides our judgment. Specifically, we hold on to safeguarding strategies or attitudes as we strive for significance or attempt to respond to the perceived threat of failure. We can replace negative attitudes with the positive attitudes with an Adlerian technique called attitude modification.

Objectives

1. To differentiate attitude modification from behavioral modification.
2. To recognize personal negative attitudes or self-guarding strategies.
3. To identity and name areas of personal success and connect them with positive attitudes.
4. To apply positive attitudes to life challenges.

Suggested Reading

Chapter 8

Losoncy, L. E. (2000). *Turning people on: How to be an encouraging person.* Sanford, FL: InSync Communications LLC and InSync Press.

Instructions

A. The old school of psychology believed that our behaviors are learned responses to the stimuli of our outer environment (B = S → R). In Individual Psychology, the person's choice, creative endeavor, direction, and dreams mediate between the environmental input and the final output (B = S → **YOU** → R) with the following very different beliefs.[21]
- People's productivity is enhanced when working for an arousing purpose (teleological).

- A person's inner drive (intrinsic motivation) is a deeper motivator than someone else's push (extrinsic motivation).
- People function best when moving from their own unique strengths, talents, interests, and possibilities (strength centered).
- People have a desire to belong and to contribute to a larger community.
- People are better motivated in an environment that values cooperation and collaboration over competition.
- People are putting their total self into the relationship when they are growing holistically.

B. The behavior cannot change until the attitude changes. The negative attitudes are directly related to the excuses you may have adopted to avoid the imagined failures. Recognize some of your safeguarding strategies. Some examples are depression, distancing, blaming yourself or others, guilt, assuming the worst, criticizing, indecisiveness, alienation, detouring with sideshows, self-elevation, and hostility.

C. Choose a present life situation or two that you have handled successfully. Debrief your successes with someone or with yourself by identifying the positive components by name (see Table A10.1 in Appendix). It is important that you recognize these feelings in yourself so you can use them to outgrow your old self-doubts and replace them with these positive counterparts.

D. Choose some other life challenges that are persistently difficult, use the B = S → R formula to see if you may have acquired fears or negative habits of mind from prior obstacles that prevent you from adopting new attitudes. Now, put yourself into the process of experiences using the B = S → YOU → R formula. What choices are you willing to make to create conditions for change? What would it be like to be at your best one day if you were to be successful with the same challenges? What are some of the assets from C that you can use to meet new challenges?

Tool #3

Birth Order

Rationale

Each child is born into a family position that determines the individual's interacting behaviors within the family and, later, characteristic attitudes toward life tasks, life goals, and life styles. The development of these characteristics is generally based on the child's creative endeavor to overcome inferior feelings and the responses from parents, siblings, and others significant to the child's early life decisions and behaviors. Comparing one's biological birth order and psychological birth order yields viable information about the individual as well as his/her relationships with others in the family, work, or community.

Objectives

1. To investigate the biological and psychological birth order of an individual
2. To use the information in conjunction with the family constellation for lifestyle assessment
3. To apply Objectives 1 and 2 in a group or parent-education setting

Suggested Reading

- Chapter 6
- Eckstein, D., & Kern, R. (2002). *Psychological fingerprints: Lifestyle assessment and interventions* (5th ed.). Dubuque, IA: Kendall/Hunt.

Instructions

A. Collect individual birth order information with the following questions:
   - When you were growing up, who were the members of your family?
   - Do you consider yourself to be an oldest, second, middle, youngest, or only child?
   - What did you like about being the _____ child in your family?
   - Draw a family diagram as the example in the case of Rachel (see Chapter 6, Figure 6.1).
B. Gather insight about early childhood experiences to help determine psychological birth order: gender, childhood illness/disabilities of siblings, loss (miscarriages or deaths), extended family who lived with the family, divorce, remarriage, adoption, age differences between siblings, sibling competition, stepfamily factors, and parental attitudes.
C. Make guesses about the individual general attitude toward self and others. Allow the individual to agree or correct your description of him or her.
D. If in a group:
   - Assign small groups by birth order (firstborn, middle child, last born, and only child) and have them share their experience growing up being in the position they were.

- Ask the members to describe/stereotype their siblings by birth order.
- Ask the firstborn to add to the descriptions given by others,

E If for parent education, have the parents express their experiences growing up and their observation of their children.

Tool #4

Change in Harmony

Rationale

Harmony is a social/spiritual ideal that finds expression in many cultures and also in Individual Psychology. In Eastern thought, the unity of life lies in the belief that all things are formed with the energy of opposites of yin and yang. To be in harmony is to move forward with the flow of change, and the nature of how each of the opposites mutually compensate and produce each other cyclically and constantly. Individual Psychology collaborates with this value system, recognizing that we are only parts of the whole and that the ultimate protection and provision for our survival is not by competition or comparison but by cooperation and contribution when we interrelate to others, society, nature, and the universe.

Objectives

1. To see individual development as life movement (from inadequacy to fulfillment) in a circular, reciprocal fashion as expressed in the Taoist/naturalistic worldview.
2. To conceptualize how Individual Psychology collaborates with various value systems, facilitating the understanding and cultivation of harmony as ideal mental health.

Suggested Reading

- Chapters 1, 7, 8, and 9.
- Carlson, J., Kurato, W. T., Ng, K., Ruiz, E., & Yang, J. (2004). A multicultural discussion about personality development. *The Family Journal, 12*, 111–121.

Instructions

A. Become acquainted with the eight directions of life situations in Figure 10.3 that models the Chinese *Ba Gua* (eight trigrams) of the Taoist Book of Change. The eight directions represent the use of our energy as a response to the universe. Name your own goals

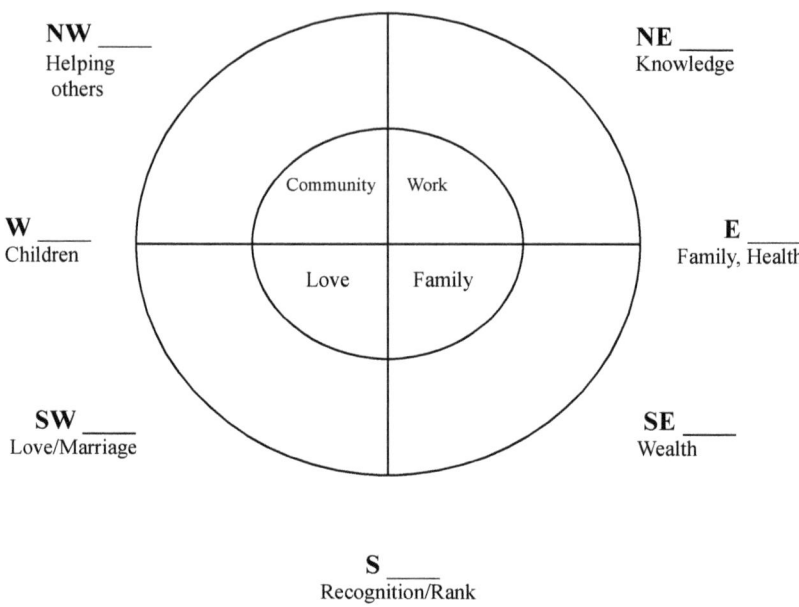

Figure 10.3 Balancing eight directions of change.

that reflect some of life demands (e.g., work/education, love, family, and community).

B. Position yourself in each diameter that connects a pair of the oppositional directions. What directions are you heading toward in the present? Is your circle evolving on all sides outward to a new and larger circle? Or, is your circle lopsided? Stagnated?

C. According to Chinese beliefs, the interconnectedness of the polarized life goals is best achieved by the harmonious balance of yin and yang forces. The manifestation of yang and yin is often described in pairs of concepts that are interdependent and complimentary. Record the life goal and directions of your life movement from Figure 10.3 to Table 10.3. Examine the balance of your energy uses and ask whether you need more yang attitudes or yin attitudes. For example, the life direction of NW (community service) requires one to give and serve using much yang energy. To achieve a balance, one needs to acquire life attitudes of SW (ensure one is grounded at home life) of receiving and rest.

Table 10.3 Life Goal, Direction of Change, and Balance Worksheet

Your Life Goals as Shown in Figure 10.3	Directions of Change	Balance Y/N	Example of Paired Yang and Yin Attitudes
	≡≡ (S) ≡ (N)		Maleness–Femaleness Day (Sun)–Night (Moon) Positive–Negative Intelligence–Wisdom Strength–Endurance Construction–Instruction Giving–Receiving Loving–Being loved Developing–Preserving Knowledge–Mystery
	≡≡ (E) ≡ (W)		
	≡ (SW) ≡≡ (NE)		
	≡≡ (SE) ≡ (NW)		

Note: The yang life force is represented by a solid line and yin, the dashed line. To balance the yang and yin energies is to utilize attitudes opposite of one's life direction in one's thoughts, feelings, and actions.

D. To be in harmony is to partake in the reconciliation of the opposites by joining the cosmic movement, often expressed as the wind and the water. To experience more harmony, in what areas of your life can you rely more on the yin wisdom, and in what areas, the yang strengths?

E. For Individual Psychology, the only means for solutions to the immediate problems of life that face the individual is to develop the courage to cooperate. On the other hand, for the purpose of social evolution, we must have the courage to contribute—a willingness to consider the welfare of others in our own personal striving for overcoming and perfection. If cooperation and contribution coincide with the yin and yang worldview, what plan of action could you take to move toward a healthier state of social living?

Tool #5

CHARACTERistics: Directed Reflection

Rationale

Character is related to the concept of self-respect. Self-respect, according to Adler, is "the feeling that one is a worthwhile human being in spite of one's faults and imperfections." We have an everyday opportunity to reflect the underlying character components of individuals we encounter and thereby reinforce the life choices that they are making. Directed reflection is a tool that allows courage facilitators to identify and affirm that the individuals are doing their best regardless of the objective conditions.

Objectives

1. To draw out and help develop character in others using the technique of directed reflection.
2. To practice the use of the 36 "character"istics or components that help define one's character in Table A10.2 in Appendix. These serve as the traits or qualities that can be directly reflected back to the individual in response to his/her "success" report.

Suggested Reading

Chapter 8

Instructions

A. Risk making educated guesses when you hear the trait or quality that is behind the person's words about his/her or others' success stories.
B. Try to "hear" the following responses and take notice of the differences:
   - How did you feel about that?
   - You must feel good about how that turned out for you.
   - It feels really good inside when *you realize that you are capable of handling things for yourself.*
C. "Catch" their character when occurring: As the individuals relate their stories, respond to their telling with appropriate timing, sincerity, and the directed reflections from the 36 components of character from Table A10.2.
D. If the individuals do not immediately recall any successes, open interaction with the following statements or questions: Tell me about one of your wins or successes. Tell me what you accomplished lately. Have you done something new that you've never done before? or What kind of positive risks have you taken? Then, get set to listen and focus on the character component. If the person's first response doesn't seem to lead anywhere, then an appropriate response might be: And how was that for you?

Sample Dialogue

In this example, a girl in her junior year of high school is reporting what might be termed a negative success. However, even in some of the sadness about losing a relationship, there are opportunities to directly reflect the underlying positive elements of character that made it possible for her to end the relationship.

Girl: I finally broke up with my boyfriend last night. You know, he was pretty abusive to me.

Adult: As much as that may hurt right now, you sound pretty confident about what you did. [Confidence]

Girl: I was kind of scared for a long time but I made up my mind to do it and now it's done.

Adult: So, you overcame your fear and took a big step. [Freedom from fear/anxiety]

Girl: It was, especially for me; I don't like to cause trouble.

Adult: You'd rather keep the peace if you can, but now you know you can take charge like this yourself! [Power and control]

Girl: I deserve better, he always put me down and told me I was stupid.

Adult: And you have more worth and value than that. [Equality]

Girl: Duhhhhh! Of course I do!

Adult: And now you are feeling really in control of the situation. [Independence]

Girl: Yeah. He wants to make up but I'm not interested anymore.

Tool #6

Constructive Ambivalence

Rationale

Our presenting problem is often influenced by a more significant issue or personality pattern. As often is the case, ambivalence is at the core of a particular problem and ambivalence often creates distress. To facilitate the courage of self-affirmation, the technique of motivational interviewing is useful in examining and resolving ambivalence. The person-centered yet directive approach encourages "free mindedness," while discouraging the individual from the "either/or," "yes, but," or double mindedness.

Objective

1. To examine and resolve ambivalence through the use of a person-centered, directive approach.
2. To facilitate the individual experiencing ambivalence to develop forward movement with a yes attitude.

Suggested Reading

- Chapters 1 and 8
- Rollnick, S., & Miller, W. R. (1995). What is motivational interviewing? *Behavioral and Cognitive Psychotherapy, 23,* 325–334.

Instructions

A. Use a person-centered approach to build rapport and trust by seeking the person's frame of reference and expressing acceptance and affirmation.
B. Through reflective listening, encourage the person to articulate the nature of the ambivalence.
C. Assist the person in clearly understanding the argument for change.
D. Counselor is directive in helping the person to examine and resolve the ambivalence.

Sample Dialogue

Robert is a 23-year-old U.S. Marine. He has come to counseling at the request of his parents who are concerned about his drinking. He admits to occasional heavy drinking, defined by the client as 8–10 drinks per drinking occasion, but states that happens infrequently (a couple times a month). He also states he is very close to his squad (eight other Marines) and they do everything together—they are closer than family. Robert has completed two combat tours and soon has to make a decision about leaving the Marine Corps. This decision is causing him a great amount of stress.

Mark: Thank you so much for coming in today. What would you like to talk about?
Robert: Well, my parents think I have a drinking problem, so I agreed to see you to talk about my drinking.
Mark: You would like to talk about your drinking.
Robert: Yes, sometimes I drink a lot, like maybe a six-pack or two over an evening. I don't do this often, but last weekend I drank 18 beers on a Saturday afternoon and evening.
Mark: Eighteen beers.
Robert: Yeah, that was a lot, but I have this big decision to make and I was just tired of dealing with it. I wanted to escape and I kind of did.
Mark: Big decision.
Robert: Yeah, I'm on leave right now and when I get back to my base the Marine Corps needs to know whether I'm going to stay in or get out. I have made up my mind, but it is hard. I love the Marine Corps. I became a man in the Marine Corps and love those guys. I've been in combat with some of them twice and we saw and did some stuff that no one should ever have to do or see. It was horrific, but they were there for me and I was there for them and now I have made the decision to leave and I feel like that decision is the right one, but it is killing me inside. It's like turning my back on my family. But I can't stay in knowing I might have to go back again. I'm not scared.

	I would die in a heartbeat for my squad members. That is not it. It is the whole war is so messed up. You end up killing the wrong people, innocent people, and no one cares. You are just doing your job, but no one knows what that job is. It changes day to day. It is ugly, confusing, and good people are dying. I no longer want to be a part of the chaos, and now it is my choice and I have made that choice, but it is so hard. I know it is the right thing to do, but when I tell Gunny [his immediate boss] and my squad members it will be hard, so hard. I don't want to do it.
Mark:	So let me see if I understand correctly. Your time in the Marine Corps is just about up and even though you love the Marine Corps and particularly your squad members, you know you need to leave and you most certainly do not want to face the chaos of combat again—too many innocent people are dying—and you know the decision is the right one, but sharing your decision with your Marine Corps "family" is killing you on the inside.
Robert:	That is right. It is killing me on the inside.
Mark:	Tell me more about how you feel this is the right decision.
Robert:	I was a kid when I left for boot camp; I did not know anything about life. Now, 4 years later I want to live. I want to make a difference. Before I never thought about college. I thought college was just more high school, but now I want to be an educated person. Learning is exciting to me. I want to learn as much as I can while I am young so I can be a better person, a more complete person. In Iraq, my friends and I were all the same; we joined the Marine Corps because we had nothing better to do. Now I have many better things to do.
Mark:	Sounds like you feel that you have grown up while in the Marine Corps and you are excited about getting on with your life and going to school.
Robert:	Yes! I am very excited.
Mark:	But then there is Gunny and your Marine family …
Robert:	I know. I love them and it will be hard leaving that. We are so close and I am certain I will never be as close to any group of people again, as I am to them. I will miss that terribly.
Mark:	It sounds as though you really know what you want, so I'm wondering what is the real issue?
Robert:	What do you mean?
Mark:	I hear your excitement about moving on and you have a plan, and yet I'm seeing you struggling with the decision and drinking a whole lot to avoid the stress of the decision, so what does all that mean to you?

Robert: It means it is a tough decision and in a way I feel that I am being selfish and letting the Corps down; they trained me. I'm experienced and now I'm turning my back on them.
Mark: Sounds like it is real important to you not to let others down.
Robert: Yeah, I suppose.
Mark: Even to the point that what others think influences what you do.
Robert: Yeah, I think my actions have often been based on pleasing others.
Mark: What do you think about that?
Robert: I never want to let others down.
Mark: And how about letting yourself down?
Robert: I have done that plenty of times.
Mark: So, it seems to me that your decision to leave the Marine Corps is pleasing to you, but not pleasing to others and that is the problem.
Robert: Yes, I guess you are right.
Mark: So, what is more important to you: Doing what you know in your heart and mind is the right thing to do for you, or doing what others want you to do?
Robert: I guess it is that simple.
Mark: It seems to be.

Tool #7

Courage Assessment

Rationale

Courage has many allied characters that allow us to evaluate risk, acquire skills, and solve problems. In the presence of fear, true courage requires a careful evaluation of the situation and is mutually informed by a person's feeling of compassion and the expression of confidence. The individual's displayed behaviors and perceived confidence are both expressions of compensation or striving. Social usefulness and a sense of balance are criteria of good and bad compensations. To Adler, courage is a precondition to real cooperation by which we may move from the useless side to the useful side of adjustment to face life tasks, to risk mistakes, and to feel the sense of belonging. A lack of courage, in contrast, breeds feelings of inferiority, pessimism, avoidance, and misbehaviors.

Objectives
1. To investigate the individual's attitudes toward oneself and others from the aspects of over- or undercompensation tendencies.
2. To investigate the individual's fear from the aspects of his/her disjunctive and conjunctive feelings.

3. To assess the individual's courage level from the aspects of confidence and socially useful attitudes toward oneself and others.

Suggested Reading
- Chapters 1, 7, and 10

Instructions

A. While listening to the individual's sharing of his/her ways of meeting life challenges/problems or a plan of action, assess whether the individual may lean on bad compensation, which refers to our tendency to overcompensate or undercompensate in one or all life task areas. Good compensation is our choice of socially useful activities that transform our perceived liabilities to assets such as social responsibility, closer contact with humanity, acceptance and conquest of difficulties, and social courage.

B. Gather more information on how the individual may experience disjunctive feelings or conjunctive feelings.

C. Guess the attitudes the individual has toward himself or herself and others in terms of self-interest (socially uselessness) or social interest (socially usefulness).

D. Use the worksheet in Table 10.4 to develop an overall sketch of the person's life attitudes toward work, love, friendship/family/community, and guess his/her courage and confidence level (see Figure 10.1 for socially useless and socially useful attitudes).

Table 10.4 Aspects of Courage Worksheet

	Aspects of Courage	Fear (Disjunctive Feelings, Socially Useless Attitudes)	
		Self	The Other
Cognitive/Evaluative Attitudes	Overcompensation		
	Undercompensation		
	Balanced with practical wisdom	Confidence (Conjunctive Feelings, Socially Useful Attitudes)	
		Self	The Other

Note: Examples of *disjunctive feelings* are: sad, dejected, disappointed, glum, lazy, hostile, depressed, nervous, blue, fearful, timid, hateful, spiteful, apathetic, anxious, resistant, numb, jealous, envious. *Conjunctive feelings* include love, admirable, like, hope, happy, pleased, glad, enthusiastic, interested, curious, confident, toward, accepting, grateful.

Tool #8

Consultation With Parents and Teachers

Rationale

Problem solving at home and in the classroom with children who misbehave is a mission possible for parents and teachers. Courageous confrontation and conflict resolution with authenticity and mutual respect could yield a joyful outcome for all. Teachers and parents can model and create relationships of equals with children and teens. Problems are opportunities for parents and teachers to search for solutions with the child that will have longtime effects on the development of the individual and his or her relationships with others.

Objectives

1. To provide a step-by-step conversational script for parents and teachers who encounter problematic situations with the children at home or in the classroom.
2. To support parents and teachers with practical techniques (goal disclosure and encouragement) when the going gets tough.

Suggested Reading

- Dinkmeyer, D., Jr., & Carlson, J. (2001). *Consultation: Creating school-based interventions* (2nd ed.). Philadelphia: Taylor & Francis.
- Dreikurs, R., Grunwald, B. B., & Pepper, F. C. (1982). *Maintaining sanity in the classroom* (2nd ed.). New York: Harper & Row.
- Dreikurs, R., & Soltz, V. (1964). Children: The challenge. New York: Hawthorn.
- Grunwald, B. B., & McAbee, H. V. (1985). *Guiding the family: Practical counseling techniques.* Muncie, IN: Accelerated Development Inc.

Instructions

A. Establish the tone
   Take time to establish rapport and create a relationship of equals. Discuss privacy and confidentiality, if needed. Confirm that this is an educational process and not a witch hunt or other blame-oriented activity. The search is for solutions in an open and honest exchange of ideas. Be sure to obtain an understanding of how this is a problem for the teacher or parent.

B. Get a specific description of the problem
   - Can you give me a specific example of when he or she was a problem *for you*? Maybe something that happened in the last day or so.
   - What specifically did the student say or do? If I were watching, what would I have seen?
   - What happened then?
   - How did you feel when that was going on? Did you feel mad, sad, glad, or scared, or a combination of those?
   - Then what happened? What did he or she say or do then?
C. Obtain a second example (see Step 2)
D. Patterns of transaction
   Classroom version:
   - There are some typical things that go on in classrooms. If we can talk about some of these, maybe I can get some idea of what goes on for (name the student).
   - Tell me about the morning routine. How does _____ go about coming into the room each day?
   - Give me some idea of how _____ goes about meeting responsibilities in the classroom? Does he/she have jobs to do? How well does he/she go about them?
   - What is _____'s behavior like in the lunchroom? On the playground?
   - When there is work to do, how does _____ spend his/her time?
   - How does _____ get along with the other children?
   - What happens when it is time to go home?

   Family version:
   - There are some typical challenges that occur nearly every day in the life of a family.
   - Tell me how the morning routine usually goes.
   - How about completing chores and responsibilities around the house?
   - Tell me about how meal time goes.
   - Describe how _____ goes about getting homework done.
   - How does _____ get along with the brother and sisters?
   - What happens at bedtime? (Or, what happens about getting home on time?)
E. Focus on the parents/teachers
   Set aside the child's behavior concerns for a moment and focus on the parents' and teachers' strengths and personal ideals using the In Store: Eleven Seven (Tool #15). Apply the techniques of directed reflection (Tool #5). Observe the values parents and teachers have about home and school and the possibilities of their over- or

underuse of their strengths when solving the conflict with the child. Refer to the Most Memorable Moment tool (Tool #18) for more options.

F. Identify the goal of misbehavior (if needed)
Share the goal disclosure tool with the parents/teachers and have them guess the children's goal of misbehavior. Practice with them the use of the Goal Disclosure: "The Could It Be's" (Tool #12) with the children.

G. Develop tentative solutions
Focus on one problem at a time. Offer concrete, workable options. Remind that the work is for improvement, not perfection. Avoid telling the person what to do. You might ask some of the following questions: Have you thought about …? What would happen if you …? Would you be willing to consider …?

H. Go around
What was helpful or useful today?

Tool #9

E-5 Group Session Guide

Rationale

People are socially embedded, self-determining, and creative. All behaviors serve the purpose of social significance. Individuals choose to use, underuse, or overuse their assets, strengths, resources, and creative abilities. The movement from a "felt minus" to a "perceived plus" can be best accomplished through a sense of social equality coupled with empathy, encouragement, and education. There are at least six pathways to understand oneself and others: early memories, family constellation, childhood challenges, day and night dreams, childhood changes, and story.

Objectives

1. To empower others and oneself through the identification and helpful utilization of personal assets, strengths, contributions, and connections.
2. To maximize the individuals' courage to meet the challenges of living in an atmosphere characterized by equality, empathy, encouragement, and education.

Suggested Reading

- Chapters 6, 8, and 10

Instructions

Follow the script of the processes:

> [ ]: for additional use with the second through the next-to-the-last sessions.
> { }: for additional use with the last session.
>
> A. Welcome and introductions
> "Welcome to the E-5 Group."
> "Please tell us your first name and your reason or reasons for being here."
> ["Please, remind us again of your name and your expectations for this group."]
> {"Welcome to the closing celebration of our E-5 Group."}
> B. Purpose
> "The purpose of this group is to empower self and others by identifying strengths, abilities, and creativity through the practice of equality, empathy, encouragement, and education."
> {"How has this been for each of you?" (Take a few moments to go around the group and have each member respond.)}
> C. Guidelines
> - The guidelines for the E-5 Group are based on the principles of respect, routine, rules, rights, and responsibilities.
> - Respect for others and self ensures equality in interactions through balancing kindness and firmness.
> - Routine provides consistency and predictability thus enhancing creativity.
> - Rules provide guidelines for expected conduct and communication and confidentiality.
> - Rights include listening with empathy and speaking without interruption.
> - Responsibility to self, others, and the environment provides for communicating, contributing, and cooperating for the good of all participants.
>
> (Make a 5R poster to put on the wall for younger children.)
> {"We have followed guidelines for the E-5 Group based on the principles of respect, routine, rules, rights, and responsibilities. In what ways have we maintained this focus in our group?" (Take a few moments to go around the group and have each member respond.)}
> D. Processing
> - "At each meeting of this group, one participant will share information about himself or herself from any two of the following categories."

- Early memories—A specific memory of an event from your life that occurred before age 10.
- Family constellation—Information about you and your family and how you found your place in the family.
- Childhood challenges—Any medical, behavioral, neighborhood, or school problems that you experienced growing up.
- Daydreams or night dreams—Images while awake and asleep.
- Childhood changes—Any shifts in your family, home, or school that may have had an impact on you.
- Story—A slice of life, an event, or situation that you recall from any time in your life.

- [Process since last session. To the volunteer from last time: "How have you used the information about your strengths since the last time we met?"
- Pause, to the other members of the group: "What have you noticed about the strengths in yourself or others since the last time we met? Who will start?"
- After group feedback exchange, "At this meeting, one of you will share information from any two of the following categories: early memories, family constellation, childhood challenges, daydreams or night dreams, childhood changes, and story.]

{Process for the last session}
- Expectations:
  - What were your expectations for this group when it started?
  - How, if at all, did your expectations change during the group?
  - How were your expectations met or not met?
  - What contributed to your expectations being met or unmet?
- Empowerment:
  - What new decisions have you made?
  - How have you utilized your creativity?
  - What new choices have you made?

{For the last session, skip Steps E–M and go to Step N.}

E. Volunteering
"Who will volunteer to share?"

F. Instructions to the other participants
"As you listen to _____ share his or her early memory, family constellation information, childhood challenges, daydreams and night dreams, childhood changes, and story (a slice of life),

please identify and record as many strengths, contributions, and connections as you hear _____expressing."
G. Instructions to the volunteer
"What information have you chosen to share?" (Note to the group leader: Depending on the two categories selected, please read the appropriate sections below.)
- Early memories: "When you are sharing an early memory, think as far back as you can. What specific event or moment do you remember or recall? In the memory, what or whom did you see? What or whom did you hear? What or who was moving? What smells do you recall? What tastes do you recall?"
- Family constellation: "When you are sharing information about your family constellation, please answer the following questions: When you were growing up, who were the members of your family? When you were growing up who lived with you? Do you consider yourself to be an oldest, second, middle, youngest, or only child? What was that like being the _____ child in your family? Of all your family members, who was the most like you? How was he/she like you?"
- Childhood challenges: "When you share about childhood challenges, consider any medical, behavioral, or school problems that you experienced as a child. What or who was helpful in addressing the challenge? What did you decide about the challenge?"
- Daydreams and night dreams: "When you share a daydream or night dream, recall all the sights, sounds, movements, tastes, and smells that were part of your dream."
- Childhood changes: "What changes occurred in your family, home, school, or neighborhood when you were growing up? How were you affected by these changes? What decisions do you recall making as a result of these changes?"
- Story (a slice of life): "Please tell a specific story from your life. State your age at the time of the story. Describe in as much detail as possible the people, places, and things in the story."
H. Listening and listing by group members
"As you share your information with us, we will each be writing a list of the strengths, contributions, and connections that we hear."
I. Upon completion of the sharing of information
"Now that _____ has completed sharing his/her information, what are some of the strengths, contributions, and connections that you heard?"

"Who will compile the written list for _____? We need someone to write the list on newsprint and someone else to make a list on a tablet."

J. Sharing the list with the volunteer
"Please read the list of strengths, contributions, and connections to _____."
Pause. "What was it like for you when you shared the list with _____?" Pause.

K. Processing the strengths, contributions, and connections
To the volunteer: "How was it for you when we identified some of your assets, strengths, contributions, and connections?"
Pause. "Look over the list. What you would modify or add?" Pause.
"Of the items on the list, which ones seem to be most relevant? Of those, please select five to seven that seem to stand out to you."
Pause. "How do things go for you when you utilize your strengths, assets, and connections in a way that is useful to yourself and others?"
Pause. "What happens when you underutilize your strengths, assets, and connections?"
Pause. "What happens when you overutilize your strengths, assets, and connections?"
Pause. "Is there a place in your life right now where you might use your strengths to lead you in a new direction? Or help you meet a situation that has been a challenge for you?"
Pause. "How would that be for you?"
Pause. "How might you be overusing your strengths? How might you be underusing your strengths?"
Pause. "What might work better for you?"
Pause. "How might you make some adjustments during the coming week to improve things for you?"

L. Closing
To the rest of the group: "During the next week, observe the strengths, contributions, and connections of the people with whom you come in contact."

M. Go around
"What was helpful or useful about having been a part of this group today/tonight? Who will start?"

N. Closing of the last session (select one of the following activities)

O. Affirmation coupons
This activity involves each of the group members writing special affirmations for one another. Duplicate sufficient copies of the affirmation coupons (Figure 10.4). Give each group member as many copies of the coupons as there are members in the group

```
┌─────────────────────────────────────────────┐
│  A SPECIAL AFFIRMATION FOR:_____ │
│  ··········································  │
│         AFFIRMATION COUPON                   │
│  ··········································  │
│   You are hereby entitled to fully appreciate, without qualification, the │
│   specially created affirmation noted on the reverse side of this coupon. │
│                                              │
│              Signed: _____ │
└─────────────────────────────────────────────┘
```

Figure 10.4 Affirmation coupon.

(including the group leaders). Ask the participants to write an affirmation for everyone in the group. Some examples include:
- I'm glad you were here because …
- I appreciated your …
- I value your …
- I smile inside when …
- I feel relaxed (warm, happy, up) when you …
- You do a really good job with …
- I admire …
- You are entitled to …

When the coupons are written, ask the group members to fold each coupon in half and staple it together. When the group has completed the coupons, take time to allow the members to mill and exchange their coupons. Instruct the group members to save the coupons and open them at the rate of one per day or as the need for affirmation arises. When all coupons are shared, ask the group to return to the circle for the closing reading.

P. Nontangible gift certificates

This activity is quite similar to the affirmation coupons, however, it involves the giving on nontangible gifts to each group member. In this case, duplicate sufficient copies of the "gift certificates" (Figure 10.5) so each person has enough for each member and the group leaders. Suggest that they complete these so each one reflects a specific wish for the individual to whom they are being given. Gifts should be personalized for each recipient so that one person doesn't just give the same gift to everyone. These should be nontangibles and more than one word. For example, one gift might be to wish one all success in a career endeavor or exploration. Another might be to wish someone the gift of a very special relationship that he/she is seeking. When the individual members have completed their certificates, allow time to mill and exchange

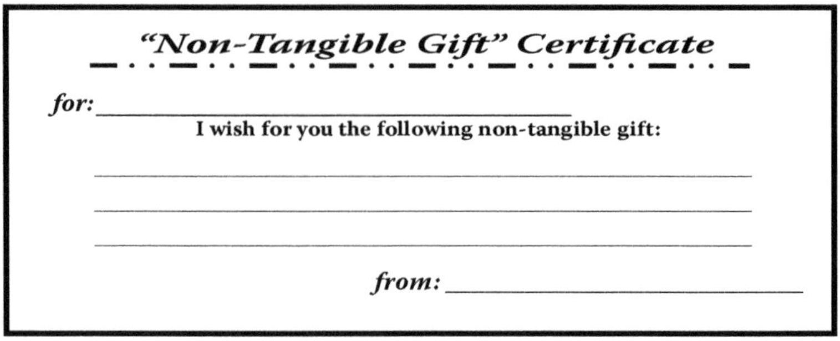

"Non-Tangible Gift" Certificate

for:_____

I wish for you the following non-tangible gift:

_____
_____
_____

from: _____

Figure 10.5 Nontangible gift certificate.

gifts. When done, ask the group to return to the circle for the closing reading.

Q. Final reading: Read "Life Is Choice" and end the session

Life Is Choice

Life is choice …
Even though colored by perceptions of who I am,
and expectations of others.
I am shaped and governed by
what I believe …
how it is
that the world should treat me,
and how I expect to fit in.

Life is choice …
I am filled with a limitless array
of options …
which can only be narrowed
by the self-constructed barriers
I elect to place in the way.

Life is choice …
Allowing for lessons
And hope for the future.
Granting each moment
the potential for fully experiencing the present.

Life is choice …
Filled with an endless array
of opportunities
for doing my best;

Knowing that living requires
the "courage to be imperfect."

Life is choice ...
Portrayed in a rainbow
of individuality;
Displayed by all who are part of,
and yet apart from,
those who people my world.

Life is choice.
from the past

—AL MILLIREN

Tool #10

En-COURAGE-ment

Rationale

When defined using the root meaning of *courage*, encouragement is the process of giving courage to another. Encouragement communicates a heartfelt emotional experience that translates to cognitive decisions. The discouraged may have an excessive desire to seek approval and please authority, assuming that they will only be worthwhile when they are better than others. They believe that they are unable to cope with life effectively and may attempt to achieve significance and belonging based on faulty goals that produce negative behaviors and outcomes. Encouragement is the essential tool for the individual to challenge his or her misdirected goals and to bring change in a realistic way. It is through encouragement that the facilitator *gives courage*, empowering the individual to see a new direction and take action. The Adlerian concepts and tactics of encouragement have been widely applied in educational, familial, therapeutic, and organizational relationships and settings.

Objectives

1. To recognize ways that bring discouragement.
2. To recognize the roadblocks of communication that turn people off.
3. To develop the motivational conditions necessary for encouragement.

Suggested Reading
- Chapters 1 and 10.
- Dinkmeyer, D., & Eckstein, D. (1996). *Leadership by encouragement* (Trade ed.). Boca Raton, FL: CRC Press.
- Losoncy, L. E. (2000). *Turning people on: How to be an encouraging person*. Sanford, FL: InSync Communications LLC and InSync Press.

Instructions
A. It is said that half the job of encouragement lies in avoiding discouragement. Pay attention to our self-talk and our conversation with others and see if you can catch the following discouraging attitudes in yourself or others.
   - Overambition/setting high expectations or standards
   - Focusing on mistakes to motivate
   - Comparing one [student] to another [students]
   - Making pessimistic interpretations
   - Dominating by being too helpful
B. Use the 12 roadblocks of communication to spot whether you or others communicate with these discouraging tendencies (Table A10.3).
C. Recognize that encouragement is more of an attitude than a technique. We can only be encouraging when we are not seeking private goals of superiority or utilizing safeguards to disguise our feelings of inadequacy. If we did not grow up with a positive experience at home and in schools, we must seek every possibility to cultivate in ourselves an encouraging orientation by the following principles. We can learn to be capable of giving courage to ourselves and others, and to enhance belongingness and connection (come-unite).
   - Focus on effort or improvement, not outcomes
   - Focus on strengths and assets
   - Focus on constructive building/learning, not blaming
   - Separate the deed from the doer (as we accept the doer as he/she is, we could disagree with his/her behaviors or decisions)
   - Practice mutual respect
   - Share decision making
   - Remain open to differences
   - Practice democracy and equality
   - Have the courage to participate and cooperate
   - Know the difference between praise (based on judgment and evaluation) and encouragement (nonjudgmental unconditional positive regard)

Tool #11

Family Constellation in the Workplace

Rationale

Each individual works in his/her unique style. This style originated in one's early family experience and becomes the perceived "rules" for social living by which the individual approaches the problems of work/school in constellation to coworkers/classmates. The Disney characters of Winnie-the-Pooh, Rabbit, Tigger, and Eeyore can be used to identify strengths and stress responses to assist the individual in better understanding self and others in work relationships.

Objectives

1. To investigate the individual work attitudes and collective work atmosphere.
2. To use the information in conjunction with the family constellation techniques to assess styles of cooperation and contribution of the individuals at work or in the classroom: strengths, assets, and resources.

Suggested Reading

- Chapters 4, 6, and 10
- Kortman, K., & Eckstein, D. (2004). Winnie-the-Pooh: A "honey-jar" for me and for you. *The Family Journal*, 12(1), 67–77.
- Milliren, A., & Harris, K. (2006). Work style assessment: A Socratic dialogue from the 100 Aker Wood. *Illinois Counseling Association Journal*, 154(1), 4–16.
- Milliren, A., Yang, J., Wingett, W., & Boender, J. (2008). A place called home. *The Journal of Individual Psychology*, 64(1), 81–95.

Instructions

A. The Home Page can be used effectively with both individuals and groups. Have the individual or group members fill out the worksheet responding to each of the questions and collect family constellation information as in Tool #13.
B. Use Disney characters to describe how one thinks, feels, and acts. Each character has its moments of strengths, or overused or underused attitudes (see Table 10.5).

Table 10.5 Strength and Stress Responses of Pooh Bear and Friends

Pooh Characters	Strength	Stress Response
Winnie-the-Pooh	Harmony, sensitive, caring, warm, giving	Overadapt, overplease, self-defeating
Tigger	Connection, spontaneous, playful, witty, energetic, fun	Blame others, make excuses, become disruptive
Rabbit	Production, logical, systematic, organized	Bossy, demanding, perfectionist
Eeyore	Status quo, enjoy being alone, likes independence, good at routine tasks, insightful, reflective	Withdraw, misunderstood, complex

C. What to look for
- Psychological patterns: Guess what the person would say about the following; guess the person's strengths: *I am, Others are, The world is, Therefore.*
- Translation of life style to work style: *I am* as if I am the manager or employee. *Others are* as if they are coworkers. *The world is* as if it is the work place.

D. Describe the work atmosphere by observing the general patterns of strengths and stress responses of their workers.

Tool #12

Goal Disclosure: The "Could It Be's"

Rationale

Rudolf Dreikurs originated the concept of the four immediate goals of misbehavior as a means for understanding the child's private logic. These goals—attention seeking, power, revenge, and assumed inadequacy—serve to identify the child's mistaken notion of how he or she can achieve a sense of belonging within the group. Disclosing the goals to the child is useful in that, even though the child might choose not to change the behavior, it is like Adler's concept of "spitting in one's soup." Even though one chooses to continue to eat it, the soup will not taste nearly the same.

Objectives

1. To guess the hidden reason for a child's misbehavior.
2. To guess and disclose the goals of the child's behavior to the child.
3. To obtain confirmation through either agreement or disagreement or a recognition reflex by the child.

Suggested Reading
- Chapter 6
- Bettner, B. L., & Lew, A. (1996). *Raising kids who can.* Newton Center, MA: Connections Press.
- Grunwald, B. B., & McAbee, H. V. (1985). *Guiding the family: Practical counseling techniques.* Muncie, IN: Accelerated Development Inc.

Instructions

Each goal is presented in the form of a "guess" followed by a specific reference to each one of the four goals, that is, Could it be that you do (this and so; a summation of the behavior) in order to (a characterization of the mistaken goal)?

A. If you wish to go through a process of clarifying the goal or purpose of the misbehavior, ask the child, "Do you know why you chose to do (identify the misbehavior)"?
B. If the child responds affirmatively, allow him/her time to explain what he/she thinks is the reason (purpose).
C. If the child does not know, or if the response is not focused on the goals of misbehavior, respond by saying, "I have some ideas about that, too. Would you like to know what I think? Would you be willing to listen?"
D. If the child's answer is no, it is important to respect the child's decision.
E. If the child's answer is yes, proceed to ask the following questions, one at a time, noting the recognition reflex as it occurs. This series of could it be's must be asked in an objective manner, without judgment or accusation. The questions are designed solely for the disclosure of goals or purposes and provide for an indirect interpretation of the misbehavior. Consequently, all four questions must be asked in order to avoid jumping to conclusions about the purposes of the misbehavior.
   - Could it be that you believe that I have not given you enough attention? (Or, Could it be that you want me/others to spend more time with you? Or, Could it be that you want to feel special? Or, Could it be that you want to keep me/your teacher busy with you?) The goal here is that of *attention getting.*
   - Could it be that you want your own way and to show everyone that you are in charge? (Or, Could it be that you can do what you want and no one can stop you?) In this case, the goal is that of *power.*
   - Could it be you want to hurt others as much as you feel hurt yourself? (Or, Could it be you want to hurt your teacher and

the other children in your class? Or, Could it be you want to get even with …?) Goal of *revenge*.
- Could it be that you want to be left alone? (Or, Could it be that you think you are not smart and don't want anyone to know?) Goal of *assumed inadequacy*.

F. The "hidden reason" technique: One method of reaching a resistant child is through the "hidden reason" technique. When children say or do something that is out of the ordinary, you can guess at what is in their mind, that is, their reason for what they are doing. This is not the psychological reason but rather the one that they formed in their mind, in their own words. This technique is not easy to learn, but it can be very effective and highly reliable. If no is said to your guess, then you are wrong. If they say maybe, then you are close. When you guess correctly, they compulsively say yes. The hidden reason may be disclosed to the child in a manner similar to disclosing the four goals but with the use of different questions, which are presented next:[22]
- Could it be that you feel insignificant unless you are the best in whatever you do?
- Could it be that you feel rejected unless everybody likes you?
- Could it be that you feel that you must never make a mistake?
- Could it be that you feel that you are trying your best and people show no appreciation?
- Could it be that you want to be better than _____?
- Could it be that you want to make me feel guilty and sorry for what I did to you?
- Could it be that you do not care about the price you will have to pay for making me (him/her) feel this way?
- Could it be that you want to show me how much smarter you are than me?
- Could it be that you feel superior to me when you put me in a position in which I do not know what to do with you and I feel helpless?
- Could it be that you are not talking in order to frustrate me (and others) and make me feel helpless and defeated?
- Could it be that you are willing to do anything in order to feel like a big shot?
- Could it be that you want people to feel sorry for you and give in to you?
- Could it be that you use sickness in order to have a legitimate excuse for not living up to your responsibilities?

- Could it be that you believe that as a minor you cannot be punished for stealing or destroying other people's property?
- Could it be that you are very pleased with yourself when you make other people suffer or feel foolish?

Some others that seem to show up from time to time:
- Could it be that you have to feel successful at all costs in order to prove yourself?
- Could it be that you try so hard so that others cannot outdo you?
- Could it be that you think you should be taken care of and live the easy life?
- Could it be that you feel the world owes it to you and you shouldn't have to work to get it?
- Could it be that you feel you have to outdo all the others and show them who is best?
- Could it be that you hesitate a little in life just to be certain that you won't make a foolish mistake?

Note: There is no harm in guessing, because if you guess incorrectly, it is merely shrugged off. In the moment that you guess correctly, the child feels understood and changes from being hostile and resistant to being cooperative. This again forms the beginning of a working relationship in which children can receive help in changing some of their mistaken ideas. It is also important to recognize that individuals are not usually aware of their hidden reason, but in the moment during which you have guessed correctly, suddenly they become clearly aware of the validity of the guess.

Tool #13
Home Page

Rationale

An important area of psychological investigation is found in the atmosphere that existed in one's early family experience. During early childhood, it is the family atmosphere, established in the home and presented by the parents in their own interactions as well as in interactions with and around the children, that offers the standards or "rules" for social living. Each person interprets these parental messages in his or her own way, thus, family atmosphere is not a direct determiner of one's personality. However, it contributes heavily to the development of life style. Since children interpret the messages received according to their experience of the events taking place in the home, it is important to understand how they perceived their place in the home and family, and therefore understand their basic beliefs governing their "life plan."

Objectives

1. To access the individual's assets, strengths, resources, and private logic.
2. To ascertain elements of the life style (the cognitive map) of an individual.

Suggested Reading

- Chapters 6 and 10
- Milliren, A., Yang, J., Wingett, W., & Boender, J. (2008). A place called home. *The Journal of Individual Psychology*, 64(1), 81–95.

Instructions

A. The Home Page (Figure 10.6) can be used effectively with individuals and groups. Have the client or group members fill out the worksheet responding to each of the questions.
B. Once completed, the client's responses are explored using a process of respectfully curious inquiry (RCI).
C. Respectfully curious inquiry is a conversational technique about the individual's life journey. It is designed to discover where the individual has been, what is currently happening for him/her, and where the individual would like to be. As this exploration progresses, observations of the client's behavior are connected to a developing understanding of the client's logic. With this process, the client is assisted in bringing his/her beliefs to awareness. There are seven basic characteristics or FLAVERS of effective RCI.

F = Focusing on what it is the client wants and arrives at mutually agreed upon goals.
L = Listening attentively, empathetically, and reflectively.
A = Assessing client's strengths, resilience, and social interest.
V = Validating client resources and "character"istics encouraging client growth.
E = Engaging in the humor that abounds in the ironies of social living.
R = Replacing information gathering (factophilia) with appropriate clarification, creative intuition, imaginative empathy, and stochastic questions.
S = Socratic dialoguing (What? Who? Where? When? How?) that serves as the key element of the RCI process.

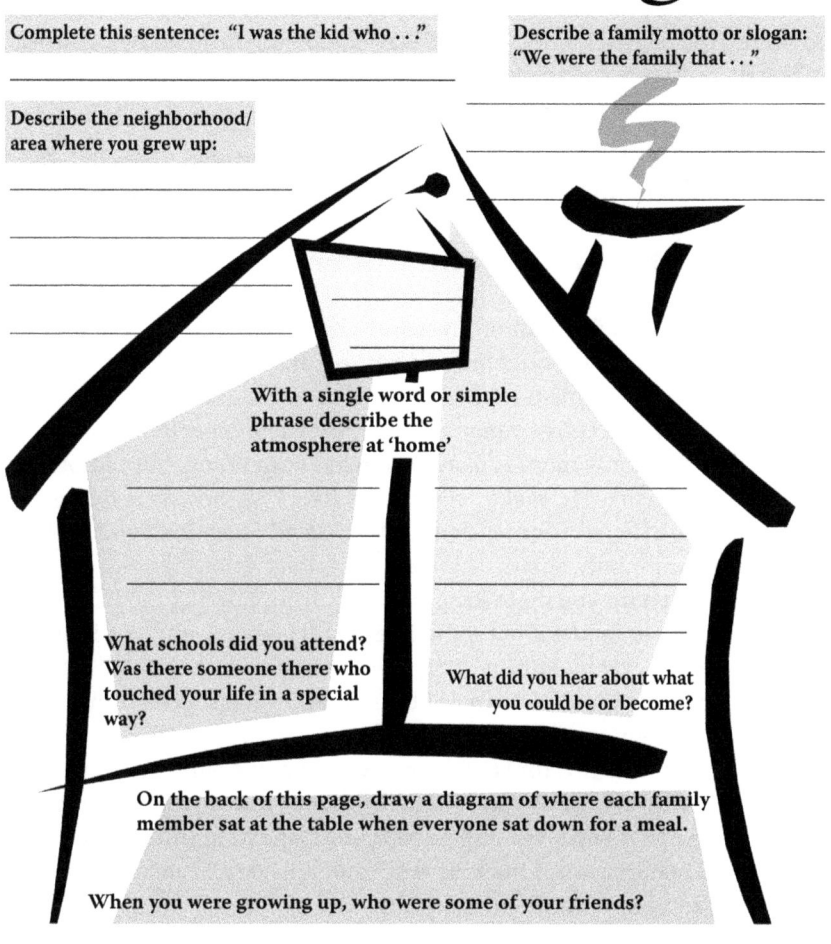

Figure 10.6 "Home" page.

D. Adler would tell us that one's lifestyle values are evident in everything the person does or says. Therefore, any information clients provide us can offer clues to their private logic. Because our target is to gain an understanding of the individual's life style and to help them achieve an awareness of how they go about it, our questions tend to revolve around building awareness and stimulating action.

Sample Dialogue

The following dialogue occurred following Steph's response to the question, "What did you hear about what you could become?" Although she was seeing the counselor because she was not feeling fulfilled by her work, she began to discover that a lot of her dissatisfaction resulted from feeling that she could never please her father.

Steph: I was always told I could be anything I wanted to be. But, they never liked the fact that I wanted to be a teacher just like they both were. They seemed to think that I should want to be better than what they were.

Counselor: How was that for you?

Steph: I always felt a lot of pressure. That I wasn't good enough. If I had an A, I should have had an A+. It seems like I was always a disappointment to them.

Counselor: So, you feel like you just can't meet their expectations.

Steph: I think my mom is okay with what I am doing, but I know my dad isn't. He makes comments like, "So, how is it living the high life on your teacher's salary." And I just don't answer him but it really hurts.

Counselor: What do you do to keep that hurt from hurting too bad?

Steph: I try to ignore it but sometimes I still go home and cry. I know I will never make him happy. I wish just once he would tell me he is proud of me. Sometimes I try so hard … it just doesn't make any difference.

Counselor: How has this impacted your relationships outside the home?

Steph: With my friends and their children, I always try to help them see that whatever they choose, the important thing is that they are happy. And the kids at school, I just try to encourage them and point out their strengths.

Counselor: So, in a way, as much as you find your situation with your dad to be difficult, it has helped you to be more positive and encouraging with others.

Steph: Oh yeah, I guess that is the good side to it all.

One of Steph's major assets is that she seeks equality among people. (Discussion that occurred later in this interview confirmed the fact that it was important to Steph for people to communicate that they valued one another. This was also an area of concern for her in her classroom where she placed a lot of emphasis on the students caring for one another.) Steph also understands how to avoid conflict, is sensitive to others, and wants to please. Most of all, she wants to be and also be viewed as an encourager.

Tool #14
Hope Is a Choice

Rationale

We live in a troubled world and we often work with individuals who struggle for meaning and spiritual direction. Hope, like courage, can produce endurance and encouragement for us in the face of fear and despair. Hope is a way of thinking and believing that is goal directed that produces routes to desired goals with the motivation to use those routes. It is when we are most vulnerable and powerless we are given the most profound opportunities to risk believing that things will get better. Even in the most despairing of times each of us possess the power of choice. Facilitating hope in and of itself creates the opportunity for positive personal change.[23]

Objectives

1. To develop the understanding that hope is both a cognitive and emotional concept that allows one to move toward one's goal.
2. To facilitate the person in need of hope to locate and enhance his/her motivation.
3. To facilitate the development of a plan that will be actively carried out.
4. To facilitate the self-encouragement skills.

Suggested Reading

- Chapter 9

Instructions

A. Identify a situation where the individual feels discouraged or experiences losses. Help the person to express emotional, behavioral, or perceptional concerns.
B. Assist the individual in a reason for change.
C. Allow the individual to hold conflicting views.
D. Use encouragement to increase the individual's desire for change.
E. Conduct strength assessment using the invitational conversation guide (Tool #1) or the In Store: Eleven Seven tools (Tool #15).
F. Once the desire exists, assist the individual in understanding how best to enact the change by developing a plan.
G. Identify lifestyle themes (or life attitudes) that present challenges to the individual's implementation of the plan using early recollection or family constellation (Table 10.6, Hope Worksheet #1-2).

Table 10.6 Hope Worksheet #1-2

Situation of Concern	Ideal Goal Desired	Plan or Strategies
Personal information	Life Tasks Work— Love— Friendship— Family— Community— Self— Universe—	Family constellation— Early recollections—
Psychological pattern	I am— Others are— The world is— God is or life is—	Therefore— Strengths— Challenges—
Options, opportunities, directions[a]	I have— I am— I can— I will—	Others have— Others are— Others can— Others will—
Self-encouragement	Replace disjunctive emotions with conjunctive feelings (Chapter 8)	Family motto— Spiritual affirmation— (See Table A10.4, Worksheet #2-2)

[a] The instruction of options, opportunities, directions contributed by Wes Wingett, personal communication.

H. Identify disjunctive emotions related to the decision to change or not to change.
I. Reinforce hope by facilitating self-encouragement using a family motto or scriptures (Table A10.4, Hope Worksheet #2-2).

Tool #15

In Store: Eleven Seven

Rationale

Courage facilitators work with the assets, strengths, and resources the individual brings to the change experience. At the heart of a helping relationship is the individual's cooperation and participation in the change processes. The seven starters and eleven Socratic-style questions are developed to emulate Adler's creative style of inquiry. "Good" questions are the what, who, where, when, and how kind of questions. The question why is never asked unless it really means "For what purpose?" Creative opportunities are in store for use by which the facilitators can pull the right thread and allow for an increasingly deeper depth of communication between two equals.

Objectives

1. To access the individual's assets, strengths, resources, and private logic.
2. To ascertain elements of the life style (the cognitive map) of an individual.

Suggested Reading

- Chapter 10
- Wingett, W., & Milliren, A. (2004). Lost? Stuck? An Adlerian technique for understanding the individual's psychological movement. *Journal of Individual Psychology, 60*(3), 265–276.

Instructions

A. Eleven questions: The following 11 Socratic-style questions are valuable in the process of information gathering with the self and others.
   - The one-word question—Howazzitforu? This is our tongue-in-cheek approach to emphasizing that we often only need a single, basic question available to us. How was it for you? How is it for you? What is that like for you? What was that like for you?

- Consideration of one's choices—Many times it is important to indirectly point out to a client that they had a choice about some aspect in life. Of all the possibilities, what brought you to _____? Of all the choices available to you, how did you decide on _____? What is it about _____ that draws you to it?
- Feelings, feelings, feelings, feelings—Particularly when working with younger clients and adolescents, it is helpful to provide a framework for the identification of feelings. To simply ask, How do you feel about that? may yield nothing more than I don't know. We prefer to say something like: When you consider that situation (When you think about what was going on, or When you look back on that), are you mad, sad, glad, or scared, … or a combination of those? You might follow the person's response with: When you are feeling _____, what is that like for you? Where in your body do you experience your feeling of _____?
- The snapshot—Borrowed from the process of exploring early recollections, the most vivid moment is a significant part of almost all stories. We basically like to ask: Like in a picture or a snapshot of that event, what is it that stands out for you?
- Making connections—Many times people may bring up some decision or belief that they held in the past. These often arise from a discussion of an early memory or recollection and it is our practice to bring that into the present for the person. By asking, How does that connect for you now? or How does that play out for you in your life right now? We can show our clients that they are conducting their lives based on decisions made when they were in elementary school, for example.
- Decisions, decisions—Similar to helping people realize they had a choice about what to think and do, asking about the decision they might have made as a response to some event in their life can provide some insight into present beliefs. Most of the time these will relate to one of the life tasks—whether it be friends, family or work—and these decisions often take place during adolescence. Do you recall the decision you made about that when it was going on? Do you remember what thoughts you had when that was happening? What led you to that conclusion?
- Outcomes: If I do; if I don't—So many times we focus on life as if we have no choice: I must go home; I have to fix dinner; I should be studying. When we hear our clients talking about the demands they make on themselves, we can ask: What

would happen if you didn't do that? What happens when you don't do that? What would happen if you did? What happens when you do?
- Evaluation—Similar to the "what if you do, what if you don't" questions, there are times when we deliberately want the person to evaluate a behavior or belief. Quite simply, the question follows this form: What makes _____ so important (special, necessary, tempting, etc.) for you?
- What would I see?—Simply for clarification of some part of the person's story, we might ask: If I were watching, what would I see happening? or What would I have seen happening? What would it look like? Under the unusual circumstances when a person does not easily access visual information, we might ask instead: Will you tell me more about it? Can you describe that in more detail? What are some examples?
- Goal setting—An important element of the therapeutic process is to be on the same page with our clients. In fact, one of the major mistakes made by beginning counselors/therapists is to not set goals with their clients. By simply asking, "How did you hope I might be helpful to you today?" we are able to go a long way in establishing mutual goals. Other questions include: How do you think I might be able to help you here today? How might we best use our time together today? and How has what we have been discussing been useful for you today?
- "The Question" of questions—Since Adler formulated "The Question" and Dreikurs brought it to our attention, "The Question" has appeared in the Adlerian literature (as well as that of a number of other approaches to counseling and therapy) under a variety of names. Quite simply, Adler would ask his clients, "What would you be like if you were well?" Often referred to as the "Miracle Question," it can serve to provide the counselor/therapist with an idea of what it is that that the client is avoiding. We find success with the question in this form: If I possessed a magic power that could make everything change for you just the way you'd like it to be, how would things be different for you?

B. Seven story starters: The following are seven story starters that are inviting for individuals to open doors allowing us into their world. Many times an individual opens a lot of doors and we don't always know which one is the best one to pursue. We pick one of the doors and save the rest for later. Usually, if the door is

important and we don't follow it right away, the client will bring us back there in some other way.
- Bicycle (roller skate, swim, skateboard, piano)—We initiate this starter with the question: Do you know how to ride a bike? If we don't get a response to the affirmative, we ask for one of the other activities listed. If the person indicates a yes, we follow-up with: Tell me about the first time when you learned to ride? These stories often parallel the way in which the person goes about learning something new. As we identify a person's approach to learning, we find clues as to how we can go about effectively working with them (see the sample dialogue).
- Groceries—Grocery shopping is one of those basic activities of life that almost everyone faces. It is one of a number of simple challenges of living for which each of us develops a strategy or routine. We ask the starter question in this manner: What store do you go to when you do your major grocery shopping? The responses are quite variable. We would use a similar question to ask about store Y and store Z. In the ensuing discussion we would discover the person's values that may relate to a view of life in general.
- Birth position—True to the tradition of Adlerian psychology, we have to explore the person's birth position. When operating in a time-limited counseling/therapy situation, we don't always take the time to do a full family genogram. What we want to do, though, is to discover the person's view of the world from their particular place in the birth order. We simply ask: What is your birth position? Were you an only child? First? Second? Middle? Last? Once we have a response, we follow that with: What was being a _____ child like for you? From here on, it depends on the person's response and we select the ensuing questions that allow us to "pull that thread."
- Lost, stuck—The purpose of the lost or stuck story is to assist the person in moving from lost to found or from stuck to free. It is best to use this starter if the person indicates a feeling of being lost (I'm just lost in a fog about what to do) or stuck (I feel stuck in this relationship and don't know where to go next). However, it is sometimes useful just to open dialogue with an invitation such as: "Tell me about a time in your life when you were lost. Maybe you were traveling and could not find your way home. Maybe you were lost trying to find an address or you were lost in a shopping mall." Or, "Tell me about a time in your life when you were stuck in the snow or sand or mud." We typically get a story from the person

that provides an outline of his or her unique problem-solving strategy. Again, our Socratic-style questions will depend on the nature of the person's response.
- Home—When you think about a place you call home, can you give me one word that best describes it?
- Name—On occasion, this story starter can yield some major depth in a discussion with a client. We have had individuals talk about how proud they were to be named after someone. We have had others discuss that they thought they had a kiddie name. Some say they were special because of how their name was picked or that they were terribly disappointed to have the name they had. We begin by asking: Do you know how you got your name? If the answer is no, ask the person to make up a story. Do you know what your name means? If not, again they can be asked to make something up. What do you like (or dislike) about the name you have? What name would you choose if you were to change it?
- Personal encourager—As you were growing up, was there a person that believed in you? Who was that person? What were the things that he or she would say or do? How did you know they believed in you? Not everyone has a personal encourager, but quite often we find there is at least one person that was a source of support and encouragement.

Sample Dialogue

Client: I remember watching all of the other kids on their bikes and wishing I could be out there with them. When my brother came home, I asked him to help me learn.
Counselor: How did that go for you?
Client: He told me he would run along with me and hold on to the back of the bike if he thought I was going to fall.
Counselor: How was that for you?
Client: Well, our driveway kind of went downhill so I was doing pretty well pedaling and balancing. But, then, I realized that he wasn't even back there running behind me. I turned my head to look for him and ran into the bushes! I had no idea how to stop.
Counselor: So, as you think about that, were you feeling mad, sad, glad, or scared, or some combination of those?
Client: I was really mad at first 'cause he lied to me. But then I realized that I had been riding—on the first try! So I got excited about it. I walked my bike back to the top of the driveway and got on and tried it again. I realized that I really didn't need him. I could do things on my own!

As this story unfolds, we discover that the client may need to find someone to help her early on when learning something new. However, once she gets started, she pretty much proceeds on her own. She has kind of a dependent independence. With further questioning, we discover that this is her approach to life and when she is too dependent or too independent, or when she is not dependent or independent enough, she has difficulty with some of the challenges of living. This was identified as a goal for her counseling sessions and the counselor worked with her to find a balance.

Tool #16

Lifestyle Interview: Variations

Rationale

Lifestyle assessment is an effective way of understanding one's self and others. In the lifestyle assessment, information about early family and life experiences can be gathered via a psychometric measurement, such as BASIS-A, or simply by interviews. A lifestyle interview reveals a sketch of the person, the themes and patterns of the person's beliefs and convictions, his/her attitudes toward their self and others, as well as his/her approaches toward meeting the demands of life.

Objectives

1. To provide a guideline of a brief lifestyle interview with creative modifications.
2. To demonstrate the processes of lifestyle self-assessment.

Suggested Reading

- Chapter 10
- Bass, M. L., Curlette, W. L., Kern, R. M., & McWilliams, A. E., Jr. (2006). Social interest: A meta-analysis of a multidimensional construct. In S. Slavik & J. Carlson (Eds.), *Readings in the theory of individual psychology* (pp. 123–150). New York: Routledge/Taylor & Francis Group.
- Walton, F. X. (1998). Use of the most memorable observation as a technique for understanding choice of parenting style. *The Journal of Individual Psychology, 54*, 487–494.
- Walton, F. X. (1996). *Questions for brief life style analysis.* Paper presented at University of Texas Permian Basin Spring Counseling Workshop, Odessa, TX.

Instructions
- A. Walton suggests five questions for a brief lifestyle interview:
  - Complete the statement: I was the kid who always …
  - Which sibling did you think was most different from you when you were a child? How? If the person is an only child, ask: How were you different from the other kids?
  - When you were a child, what did you think was most positive about your mother/father? Was there anything you rejected about Mom and Dad?
  - Unforgettable or most memorable observations: When you were growing up, can you recall any conclusions you made about life such as "when I get to be an adult, I certainly will always …" or "I will never let this happen in my family or in my life"?
  - Finally, obtain two early memories (recollections): What was the earliest specific incident you can recall? (Record these in the present tense in the precise words of the individual.) What moment was the most vivid? What feeling is connected with the incident?
- B. Conduct a lifestyle interview with yourself with Walton's five questions. Write down what you have learned about yourself.
- C. Adlerians suggest that we look for feelings and recurrent themes such as whether the person is alone or with others, active or passive, cooperative or competitive, and the kind of relationships with others at home or school. We also look for how these feelings might relate to things that happen in his/her life at the present time. (When was last time when you had these feelings?)
- D. Make a lifestyle assessment with yourself (or others) using the following Socratic question scripts.

   [Initial instruction]
   "Here's what I am going to do while we talk. I am going to start to write a list … I am going to listen for your assets and strengths (or, the things you already do well). As I listen, I am going to write down some of things you might be using or able to use in some of the challenges you have. About work, maybe, or home, or with family or friends … So, can we just talk for a while?"
   Birth position:
   - Let's begin our exploration with your birth position. How many brothers and sisters did you have?
   - How was that for you?
   - What was the competition between you like?

- Was there anything else about being the youngest (oldest, middle, or only) child that comes to mind?
- So, what was your conclusion to that?

I was the kid who:
- While you were growing up, did you have any special nicknames? Or were you known in any special way? Sort of like "I was the kid who …"
- Can you think of other examples of this in your life?

School experience:
- On a typical day, how do you use your time?
- Think back to your first few years of school. What was it like for you when you were in kindergarten or first or second grade?

First regular-paying job:
- Since we were talking about work earlier, I've been wondering, what was your first regular-paying job?
- What did you like most about that job?
- Was there anything else about the job?
- Was there any sort of downside to that job?

Groceries:
- So, in terms of groceries, what store do you prefer to shop?
- In addition to the unique items, what else attracts you there?
- What I am interested in is how you go about solving a common challenge of everyday living. Shopping is a routine challenge of day-to-day living. How do you approach it?

Other questions:
- Do your recall any kind of a decision you made because of that incident?
- I'm just wondering, now, as you were growing up, was there a person that believed in you?
- What was that like for you?

Four feelings:
- When you look back on that time, were you feeling mad, sad, glad, or scared, or a combination of those?
- So when you take in all of that, do you feel mad, sad, glad or scared, or a combination of those?

Strength summary:
- Well, thanks. Let's summarize, then, with a list of strengths from today's conversation, talk about your goal, and see how all of these elements can come together to maybe be of some help to you.

Tool #17

Lost or Stuck?

Rationale

Lost or stuck is a strategy designed to understand and assess individual psychological movement relative to problem solving. Individual Psychology is a psychology of movement. It is through this movement that the individual expresses his/her unique orientation to oneself, others, and the world. The individual feels lost or stuck because of some situation or experience has occurred for which one is ill prepared to cope. Every individual possesses all the internal resources that are needed for coping with the problems of living. Although these resources may be unknown to the individual or thought to be unavailable, each one of us has a strategy or set of strategies for problem solving. The purpose of lost or stuck is to help a client identify a unique and creative problem-solving approach and ultimately move from lost to found or from stuck to free.

Objectives

1. To recognize personal problem-solving strategies.
2. To modify the strategies when warranted.
3. To apply personal problem-solving strategies to current challenges.

Suggested Reading

- Chapter 8
- Wingett, W., & Milliren, A. (2004). Lost? Stuck? An Adlerian technique for understanding the individual's psychological movement. *Journal of Individual Psychology, 60,* 265–276.

Instructions

A. Identification of the individual's problem-solving approach. Listen for the keywords *lost* or *stuck* as the client describes the current problematic situation. Many times when individuals describe the situations that brought them into counseling, they will use the words *lost* or *stuck* as a way to conceptualize the problem. For example, "I'm lost. I don't know where to turn" or "I am lost in my relationship with my spouse." Other examples include, "I have tried everything and I always end up stuck in the same old rut" or "I am stuck in this mess and don't see any way out!"

B. Elicit from the individual a time in the past when he or she was lost or stuck with an invitation such as, "Tell me about a time in your life when you were lost while traveling or you were lost and could not find your way home. Maybe you were lost trying to find an address or you were lost in a shopping mall." Or, "Tell me about a time in your life when you were stuck in the snow or sand or mud." The client will then begin to share a story that will provide an outline of his or her unique problem-solving strategy.

C. Define the components of the individual's problem-solving approach that have been successful in the past. When reviewing with the individual how he or she found the way out of the problem or became unstuck, the counselor/therapist listens for cognitive, affective, and behavioral components of the individual's problem-solving process. For example, when the individual realized the he or she was lost or stuck, how did he or she think and feel and act? When the individual began to take the initial steps toward problem solving, how did he or she think and feel and act? When the individual had solved the problem, how did he or she think or feel or act? What choices did the individual make that may have precipitated the initial problematic situation? What preventative steps can be taken or have been taken since the first incident? Were people involved in the initial problem and, if so, what people?

D. Apply appropriate and effective components of the problem-solving approach to the current problem. What kind of "self-talk" is warranted? How do you want to feel before, during, and after the resolution of the situation? What actions will you take that will be rational, intelligent, sensitive to yourself and others, and effective and efficient? How will other people be involved in the problem-solving process? What will be done to prevent problems from occurring in the future?

E. Assess the extent to which the revised strategy moves the client toward an enhanced level of social interest while at the same time solving the problem.

Sample Dialogue: The Snowstorm

The following is an example of the strategy as it was employed in a recent counseling interview:

Counselor: Tell me about a time in your life when you were lost or stuck. You may have been lost trying to find a place, or lost in a mall, or stuck in the sand or mud or snow.

Client: Well, it was before I was married and I was still living at home. I was driving home from work after a bad snowstorm and I thought I could make it home. Well, I was a few miles from home and I started to slide off the road and I ended up in the ditch and I couldn't move the car.

Counselor: And then what did you do?

Client: Well, I sat there for a while feeling stupid, and then I decided I had better do something before it got dark. I bundled up and started walking toward a farm place that I saw.

Counselor: And then what?

Client: I got to the farm place and saw a light on in the house and walked up to the back door and knocked on it.

Counselor: And what were you thinking?

Client: I thought "There is a light on, and I'll bet there are people in the house that might help me out of my ditch dilemma."

Counselor: And then what happened?

Client: An older couple came to the door and invited me into the house. I told them my story and warmed up. The husband and I took one of his tractors down to my car and we pulled the car out of the ditch. I offered to pay him, but he wouldn't take anything but a thank you. I proceeded home slowly and thankfully.

Counselor: Let me see if I understand the situation. You were unmarried, living at home. You were driving home after a snowstorm and you slid into a ditch. You sat there for a while and then you bundled up and walked up to a farmhouse and knocked on the door. A couple answered the door, invited you to warm up, listened to your story, and offered to help. You and the helpful husband pulled your car out of the ditch, you offered to pay him, he refused, and you proceeded cautiously and thankfully home.

Client: Yes, that's it. That's how it happened.

Counselor: And that's how you solved the problem. Now, let's examine the problem-solving process that you utilized from beginning to end.

Client: Sounds good to me.

Counselor: First you realized that you had a problem and did some negative self-talk.

Client: Yes, I reminded myself of my stupidity and replayed some lectures about driving too fast in the snow, and not having snow tires, and taking unnecessary chances.

Counselor: After you surveyed the situation, you decided to bundle up and walk toward the farmhouse. How did you make that decision?

Client: Well, I thought I could probably stay in the car and wait for someone to find me, or I could walk to the farmhouse that was about a half mile away. It was not freezing cold and I had some extra clothes in the car and I thought there was probably enough daylight left to easily make it to the farm place.

Counselor: And what were you thinking as you approached the farm place and saw the lights on in the house?

Client: I was thinking that I hoped people were there, and that they would be Midwestern farm folks who would probably help me if they could.

Counselor: And you knocked on the door?

Client: Uh-huh. The husband and wife answered and invited me in to warm up. I told them my story and asked for help.

Counselor: How was it for you to ask for help?

Client: A little scary. However, I thought they would probably help if they could. And they did.

Counselor: And you worked together to pull the car out of the ditch, and you offered to pay him and he refused, and you went on your way. So, the steps that you utilized in solving the problem were: (1) surveying the situation for possible options, (2) identifying sources of help, (3) asking for help from people that you did not know, (4) offering payment and verbal thanks to your helper, and (5) proceeding cautiously toward your destination.

Client: Yes, that is what I did. I never broke it down into steps like that before.

Counselor: What would happen if you applied those same five steps to your current problematic situation?

Client: I don't know for sure, but I am willing to give it a try.

This example demonstrates the use of the strategy to identify an individual's personal problem-solving style. This particular individual's problem-solving style will be an effective tool for her in solving future problems that she may encounter, provided that "farmhouses" are available to her. It is clear that she is able to ask for help; it is not so clear what her strategy is if no one is available to hear the request or if the request for help is denied. Although she is able to use her strategy in the current situation, the counselor/therapist may wish to explore with her what she could do when help is not readily available.

Tool #18
Most Memorable Moment

Rationale

The most memorable observation was designed by Walton for use with parents. It is a technique that employs autobiographical memory in the process of understanding the belief system of parents as it relates to the choice of parenting style. Given the selective nature of memory, the observation of the most memorable moment reveals the parents' private logic as it pertains to parenting. With modifications, this technique can be applied to teachers about teaching and to others about other life tasks.

Objectives

1. To help the individual see mistaken thinking that contributes to difficulties at home.
2. To ask parents about observations made about life in his/her family during early adolescence.
3. To help determine what it was that seemed important about life in the family.
4. To apply the understanding of how the parents' beliefs may be generalized to help or hinder the use of more effective parenting techniques.

Suggested Reading

- Walton, F. X. (1996). *An overview of a systematic approach to Adlerian family counseling.* Paper presented at University of Texas Permian Basin Spring Counseling Workshop, Odessa, TX.
- Walton, F. X. (1998). Use of the most memorable observation as a technique for understanding choice of parenting style. *Journal of Individual Psychology, 54*(4), 487–494.

Instructions

A. First obtain information about the family constellation and the presenting problems.
B. Ask the questions: Sometimes in our early teenage years, or even in late preteen years, it seems very common for each of us to look around our family life and draw a conclusion about some aspect of life that appears to be important. Sometimes it is positive, "I really like this aspect of life in our family. When I get to be an adult I'd like it to be just this way in my own family." Often it is negative, "I don't like this at all. This is really distasteful. When I

get to be an adult I am going to do everything I can to keep this from occurring in my family." What was it for you? As you think of life in your family about age 11, 12, 13, or so, what conclusion do you think you drew? It may have been positive, it may have been negative, or it may have been both.
C. Help parents see how they may have one or more of the following types of compensations:
- Overemphasizes the likelihood of an occurrence of a situation the parent guards against.
- Overemphasizes the negative influence of such a situation, if it should occur.
- Underestimates their ability to deal with the situation in an effective problem-solving way if it should occur.
D. Help parents modify parenting techniques based on the new understanding
- Encourage parents by pointing out that the same style that takes us to our successes also leads us to our difficulties.
- Find specific examples that the parents are overemphasizing the likelihood of the occurrence of the situation that is guarded against.
- Help parents develop a repertoire of techniques to deal with the challenging situation with a focus on wining the cooperation of children and adolescents.
E. This same procedure can be adjusted for use with teachers: When you were thinking about teaching and planning to have a classroom of your own, what were some of the things that you were absolutely going to make sure happened? Or, didn't happen?

Sample Dialogue

When asked the most memorable observation questions, Scott replied:

> As the firstborn child in the family, I had to keep up with their expectations. I had to be good in all that I did but could not have what I wanted. My father did not have much education and could not provide enough for the family. My parents fought all the time and they finally divorced when I was in college. I thought to myself that I never would subject my children to the pains of poverty and divorce.

> The influence of overcompensation regarding Scott could be that he could be a perfectionist in his role of father and provider for his family. His desire to guard against being a failure later translated into his hardworking ethic as well as his protective yet highly demanding style of parenting with his children.

Tool #19

Recollecting Early Memories

Rationale

Recollections are not reports of experiences. The individual recalls the experience as if it were occurring at the moment. The memories exist for the individual as little life lessons kept available as guides for decision making about the challenges of living. It is the interpretation of these selected events that the individual carries as reminders of the goals and limits for participation in life. The active recollecting activity reveals the individual's perception about the self, others, and the world, as well as ethical convictions and plans of action.

Objectives

1. To provide conversational guides of collecting early school recollections.
2. To provide conversational guides of collecting early career recollections.
3. To collect early memories that may be applied to understand the individual's perceptions of school, work, and home.

Suggested Reading

- Chapters 4, 6, and 10
- Milliren, A. P., & Wingett, W. (2005, January). *Socratic questioning: The art of precision guess work*. Workshop presented at Chicago Adlerian Society, Chicago, IL.

Instructions

A. For general early recollection: Record as much detail as possible of two early recollections of early memories. An early recollection of an early memory is a specific event occurring in early childhood.
B. School days

- When you recall kindergarten through second grade, what did you like best about the school day? Consider the school day to include the time from leaving home before school to returning home after school.
- What I liked best about the school day was …
- Three to five things I liked about this particular part of the school day included …

- Use the summary form (Table 10.7) to develop a personal profile of strengths.
- Use the profile to help teachers, parents, and students develop an understanding of their own beliefs and use the assets and strengths for problem resolution at home or in school. Use a transitional question such as, "How could you use some of the strengths to meet a situation that has been a challenge for you?"

C. Early career recollections
- Relax and think back to the earliest memory that you have that contains the idea of a career or job. This could include your parents' careers, or any early memory that you believe relates to career. Try to focus on a specific early memory, and immerse yourself in the details. Write this memory down.
- Experience the specific elements of the memory, including the emotions and physical sensations that accompany it. Write these down as detailed as possible.
- Develop a photograph of the most salient part or scene in the memory and describe it along with one emotional work that explains the affect of the photo scene.
- Take a moment to look over your earlier career recollection. Try to identify the fictive thoughts of partial truth that are evident in your early recollections. Use the following examples as a guideline. Write down your thoughts.
  - Overgeneralization. For example: People are hostile.
  - False or impossible goals of security. For example: I have to please everybody.
  - Misperception of life and life's demands. For example: Life is so hard.
  - Minimization or denial of one's worth. For example: I'm stupid.
  - Faulty values. For example: Be first even if you have to climb over others.

D. Recollections of the future
- Recall your childhood fantasies. What would you have become if the dream came true?
- What did you hear others say about what you could be or become?

E. Some techniques for use in interpreting early recollections
- The headline techniques. Consider the early memory as a short newspaper article. Write a headline that is a statement about the essence of the story, a logical abstraction. Sometimes it is

helpful to begin such headlines with one or more of the following beginnings: Life is …, People are …, I am….
- How is the problem solved?
- Does the client go forth, withdraw?
- Alone, with others?
- Pampering?
- Give, take?
- People in memory are prototypes. *Father* may mean "men" or "authority figures," and probably does not mean the father in the individual's present world. Look for the individual's view of role of men and women.
- What does the individual's view as circumstances that place one up or down.
- How are emotions used?
- What is happiness or unhappiness to the individual?
- Does he/she do for? Is he/she done to?
- Does he/she confirm, question, accept, feel powerless, rebel?
- Is rebellion open or secret?
- Does he/she try to improve the situation or is some other motive more dominant?
- Look at the issue of control. Who or what controls the situation? Does he/she seem to guard against life going out of control?
- Does he/she attend carefully to details? (A vocational clue as well as a statement about the psychological situation he/she finds most appealing.)
- Is he/she a doer or an observer?
- Birth of a sibling may suggest sibling rivalry or dethronement. (The individual's action in memory may suggest the course he/she followed after the sibling arrived.)
- First school experience may show how we view and hand the world "out there."
- What obstacles do life or people present to the client?
- Memories of misdeeds often suggest the type of behavior we are determined to avoid.
- What constitutes success and failure to the individual? What is the private world with which the individual operates? Remember that the conviction that shows up in early memories contributes to the individual's personal set of rules for living.

Table 10.7 Summary of Early Recollections and School Days

Assets and Strengths	Indicators	Assets and Strengths	Indicators
Multiple Intelligences			
Word	Number	Body	Picture
Music	Nature	Self	People
Life Tasks			
Work/play			
Self-care/ self-confidence			
Family/friends/ community			
Intimate relationships			
Spirituality/ philosophical values			

Tool #20

Trust Only the Movement

Rationale

Alfred Adler believed that individuals move from a "felt minus" to a "perceived plus" with their creative power. Dreikurs identified four goals of misbehaviors: attention, power, revenge, and the display of inadequacy. Subsequently, the four goals are expressions of all forms of a felt minus. To develop courage with the discouraged individual who misbehaves is to go beyond the behaviors and redirect the individual to move from felt minus feelings to perceived plus thoughts.

Objectives

1. To recognize the connection between a felt minus feeling and the goals of misbehaviors.
2. To engage and encourage the development of perceived plus thoughts that can be implied in an action plan.

Suggested Reading

- Chapter 6
- Milliren, A., Clemmer, F., Wingett, W., & Testerment, T. (2006). The movement from "felt minus" to "perceived plus": Understanding Adler's concept of inferiority. In S. Slavik & J. Carlson (Eds.), *Readings in the theory of individual psychology* (pp. 351–363). New York: Routledge/Taylor & Francis Group.

Instructions

A. Listen carefully to what the individual is saying through his/her misbehaviors. Look for felt minus statements/thoughts.
B. Identify the goal of a misbehavior using Table 10.8. Use Figure 10.1 to assess the direction of the individual's life movement.
C. Help the individual develop the perceived plus statements.
D. Assess the level of discouragement, fear, or felt minus thoughts.
E. Use the eleven questions and seven story starters (Tool #15) to conduct a strength assessment.

Table 10.8 From Felt Minus to Perceived Plus

Goals of Misbehaviors	Felt Minus	Perceived Plus
Attention	I want other people to notice me.	I notice and encourage the useful behavior of others.
Power	I want to show others that nobody can boss me around or tell me what to do.	I can work with others to solve problems that are helpful to the world.
Revenge	I want to hurt others like I have been hurt.	I know when and how to empathize with others.
Display of inadequacy	I have given up on myself and want others to leave me alone.	I can encourage myself and accept encouragement from others.

```
------0---------1---------2---------3---------4---------5---------6---------7---------8------
Felt minus                                                                   Perceived plus
```

> **Motivation**
> On the scale from 1 to 8 (+/−): Choose a couple of situations or relationships that have been challenging for you. Where are you now? What would it take for you to move one or two spaces?

___

Figure 10.7 Motivation scale. (*Source*: Adapted from Milliren, A. P., & Wingett, W. (2005, January). *Socratic questioning: The art of precision guess work*. Workshop presented at Chicago Adlerian Society, Chicago, IL.

F. Encourage the use of the strengths to develop yes attitudes that will guide the movement.

G. Pay attention to the overuse or underuse of the strengths (e.g., overcompensation or undercompensation. Describe the individual using the life attitudes in Figure 10.1.

H. Follow the steps of the "Motivation Scale" (Figure 10.7). With encouragement, help develop an action plan by which the individual can progress toward the stated perceived plus attitudes.

Tool #21

Ups, Downs, and Side by Sides: Relationships of Equals

Rationale

Relationships can go beyond being merely facilitative. They are augmentative. To augment is to increase, enlarge, and expand. Positive relationships can only flourish in a positive, encouraging atmosphere. At any rate, there seems to be a scale that ranges from paternalistic or maternal, to manipulative or possibly coercive, to facilitative, to augmentative, and to synergic mutuality of growth. The relationship scale describes the stages of a relationship from the desire to control or impose limitations (either directly or indirectly) on the behavior of the other, to one being the catalyst for the other's growth, and to a relationship of equals. All relationships have the dimension of horizontalness. They are relationships of equals where we can cooperate, collaborate, and work side by side.

Objectives

1. To use the relationship scale to help understand the problems and promises of what partners in a relationship can bring to each other.
2. To seek understanding of how a partner can behave so that she/he provides *conditions* wherein another person's growth can occur.

Suggested Reading

- Chapter 5
- Milliren, A. (in press). Relationships: Musings on the ups, downs, and the side-by-sides. In D. Eckstein (Ed.), *Relationship repair: Activities for counselors working with couples*. EI Cajon, CA: National Science Press.

Instructions

A. Have each individual locate where she/he thinks the stage of the relationship is on the following relationship scale. Use the self-narratives to help the assessment (see Table 10.9).

Paternal/maternal	Manipulative/coercive	Facilitative	Augmentative	Synergetic/mutual
*	*	*	*	*

B. How could each partner orient his/her behavior so that it serves to maintain or enhance the self-esteem of the other person?

Table 10.9 Stages of Relationships

Stages	Personal Narrations
Paternal/maternal	The difficulty in this idea, for me, is that the efforts are directed toward the other person and, although noble, may deny any process of mutuality of growth. Plus, there might still be some subtle manipulative activity involved.
Manipulative/coercive	How do I get him/her to be/do the things I want? As much as I think I am in control, the other person is always in the position of having the power of no.
Facilitative	The focus of control is on myself. I am willing to function as a catalyst for the other's growth—more or less as a partner in the other's life journey.
Augmentative	I am only capable of growing myself ... and, in doing so, others may discover the growth process through mine. Thus, I am only able to *augment* another's growth and can never *make* it happen.
Synergic/mutual growth	The word *synergistic* keeps coming back, the idea of a cooperative endeavor. If I grow, you grow.

C. By being who they are, how can the partners work to activate, stimulate, and validate the *resources* of each individual?
D. How can the couple each strive to maintain an atmosphere of acceptance and openness so that risking, trusting, and loving can be stimulated?
E. How can the couple work to remain *present centered* to be receptive to the *contemporaneous* experience of myself, the other person, and the situation?
F. How can each partner work to practice the *courage to be imperfect* knowing that he/she will not always be able to live up to these expectations?
G. If I act as if I can relate to others as equals, I will, in fact, be able to do so.

Tool #22

Walk the Line

Rationale

Belonging, mastery, independence, and generosity are identified as four foundations for self-worth for Native Americans. The circle is a symbol for the wheel of life. Every direction and every path is to be honored and walked. All lessons from walking the paths are equal and each spoke of the wheel is a pathway to truth, peace, and harmony.

Objectives

1. To develop self-understanding using the framework of the Native American circle of courage.
2. To see the interrelationship between the attitudes toward a spirit of belonging and the goals for growth Native Americans recognize through the problems we encounter waking the paths.
3. To apply the circle of courage to alcoholic recovery as an example of implications.

Suggested Reading

- Chapter 9
- Brendtro, L., Brokenleg, M., & Bockern, S. V. (1992). *Reclaiming youth at risk: Our hope for the future.* Bloomington, IN: National Educational Service.

The Art of Facilitating Courage • 197

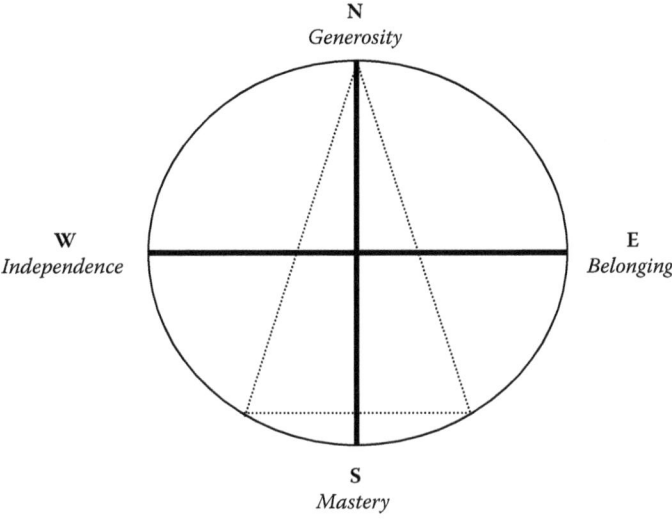

Figure 10.8 Circle of courage. Modeled after the Circle of Courage. Artist: George Blue Bird.

Instructions
  A. Become acquainted with Figure 10.8 (also see Table 10.10) that models the Native American circle of courage with the italic descriptors for the directions of north, south, west, and east.
  B. Imagine that you are walking on the paths from south to north and from east to west, what problems do you encounter?
  C. What opportunities these problems present?
  D. What goals of growth could you draw from these observations?
  E. A triangle enclosed within a circle has been a symbol for Alcoholics Anonymous (A.A.) for decades. The circle stands for the whole world of A.A., and the triangle stands for A.A.'s Three Legacies of Recovery, Unity, and Service. Instead of being isolated in the problems alcoholism brings to the individual, one can find freedom by recognizing the community feeling that exists through unconditional acceptance and help from others as well as extending one's service to the needy. Use Steps A, B, C, and D to facilitate the alcoholic recovery process.

Table 10.10 Problems as Opportunities

Goal	Problems	Strengths
Belonging	Alienation	Attachment
	Distrust	Trust
	Withdrawal	Warmth
	Detachment	Friendship
	Antagonism	Cooperation
	Exclusion	Acceptance
Independence	Irresponsibility	Autonomy
	Undependability	Responsibility
	Rebelliousness	Assertiveness
	Easily misled	Self-confidence
	Recklessness	Self-control
	Helplessness	Optimism
Generosity	Selfishness	Altruism
	Disrespect	Respect
	Indifference	Kindness
	Rancor	Empathy
	Vengeance	Forgiveness
	Emptiness	Purpose
Mastery	Incompetence	Achievement
	Inadequacy	Talent
	Disinterest	Concentration
	Confusion	Comprehension
	Chaos	Organization
	Defeat	Coping

Source: Adapted from Brendtro, L., Brokenleg, M., & Bockern S. V. (1992). *Reclaiming youth at risk: Our hope for the future.* Bloomington, IN: National Educational Service.

Appendix

Table A10.1 Replacing Negative Attitudes with Positive Attitudes

Relief—Replaces *painful feelings of pressure, tension, stress, and anxiety*. These negative feelings arise from your:
- Feelings of hopelessness
- Fear of failure
- Fear of experiencing undeserved success
- Feelings of victimization where no victimization was intended
- Impotent rage that you can't do anything about and has no place to go
- Anger at yourself for being angry, which is an unacceptable state of mind
- Pressure, tension, and stress of your old way of moving through life on the basis of inappropriate attitudes that makes your progress harder than it needs to be

Positive control—Replaces (a) *feeling out of control*, and (b) *controlling in negative, destructive ways*:
- Of the situation
- Of yourself
- Of your life

Identity—Replaces playing the roles of other people's terms such as *the pleaser, the super responsible child, the rebel*, and so on.
- On your own terms, not someone else's script
- Not a role that you have been playing since childhood
- "I know who I am. I am the one who just did that homework!"

Maturity—Replaces *feeling immature*.
- I am a grown-up now. I am doing grown-up things that need to be done.
- I am not playing a role from childhood.

Belonging—Replaces *feelings of unbelonging*.
- I am a member in good standing of the human race.
- I belong to myself.
- I belong wherever I happen to be.

Security—Replaces *insecurity*.
- My security is not in material things or other people.
- My security is not in phony idealism.
- I am secure within myself.
- There is a self here to be secure within.

(continued on next page)

Table A10.1 (continued) Replacing Negative Attitudes with Positive Attitudes

Trust—Replaces *distrust of oneself and others.*
- I can trust my fellow members of the human race. I don't have to trust them perfectly. I don't have to predict betrayal of my trust and then find a way to prevent it. (That is negative control.)
- I can trust myself in spite of my faults and imperfections. If I make a mistake, I can learn from it. I won't make it again.

Equality—Replaces *feeling inferior, not good enough.*
- I am no more and no less human than anyone else.
- I don't have to prove I am equal. There is nothing to prove.
- I don't have to overcompensate. It only makes things worse. It's a self-inflicted good intention to relieve the pain of my inferiority. I don't need it anymore.

Liberation—Replaces *feeling trapped.*
- I am liberated from my childhood fears.
- I am liberated from my childhood misconceptions about people, life, and myself.
- I have liberated myself from my old, mistaken attitudes. I had the courage to do my homework.
- No one else can liberate me. I will continue to liberate myself.

Independence—Replaces *feeling dependent.*
- I am competent to live my life on my own terms.
- I am free to cooperate with my fellow human beings in an interdependent relationship of equals.
- I can trust my own judgment.
- I can validate my own successes.

Accomplishment—Replaces *I can't win for losing.*
- I did it! I made it happen in the real world.
- I didn't do it perfectly, I did it well enough.

Success—Replaces *feelings of failure.*
- I can succeed after all.
- I deserve to succeed. I earned it.
- I am not driven to succeed, I am free to succeed.
- I succeed not because I have to prove myself. I succeed because it is in me to do so.

Confidence—Replaces *self-doubt.*
- I did it once, I can do it again. It's not that hard.
- I have earned the right to trust my judgment and feel confident within myself.

Courage—Replaces *discouragement.*
- Courage is the willingness to take a risk.
- I took the risk. I had the courage.

(continued on next page)

Table A10.1 (continued) Replacing Negative Attitudes with Positive Attitudes

- I know that if I don't succeed, it will hurt. But it won't hurt as much as it did when I was a child. It won't be the end of the world. I won't take it personally.
- I didn't wait for the courage to come. I went ahead and did it anyway. The courage came afterward.

Appropriate responsibility—Replaces *too much responsibility or too little.*
- I didn't assume too much responsibility.
- I didn't cop-out either.
- I assumed appropriate responsibility for myself.
- I am choosing to allow other persons the same privilege.
- I am prepared to share responsibility with them as an equal.

The power of choice—Replaces reacting to situations out of *old attitudes and roles.*
- I am not powerless and out of control. I have the power of choice. I chose to do my homework.
- I used my adult judgment to make that choice. It wasn't a perfect choice. It didn't have to be. It was good enough. It got the job done.

Trust in judgment—Replaces *doubt about judgment.*
- I decided to do my homework. That was a pretty good decision.
- I can trust my judgment. It isn't perfect, it is good enough. If I make a mistake, I can learn from it.
- I am using my judgment to tell me which risks are worth taking.

Good enough—Replaces *feelings of inferiority.*
- Good enough is as good as I am right now.
- I don't have to be any better than that. If I am better still tomorrow, that is all right, too.

Proactive—Replaces *reactive.*
- I am operating independently on a realistic basis.
- I am not against anyone; I am for me on an appropriate basis.
- I am using my judgment to tell me which positive actions to take in my own behalf.

More energy available—My energy isn't bound up in *self-anger* and *self-contempt* anymore.
- I am not fighting myself to a standstill anymore.
- I am not using my energy to battle negative attitudes and emotions that shouldn't be there in the first place.
- When my energies are liberated from the control of these old attitudes, I feel liberated, free to take life as it comes and do the best I can with it.
- I deserve to use this new energy in useful, productive ways that will make me happy.

(continued on next page)

Table A10.1 (continued) Replacing Negative Attitudes with Positive Attitudes

Forgiveness—Replaces *resentment.*
- I am free now to forgive others by choosing to let go of my anger at them.
- It's not for them; it's for me!
- They don't have to know I've forgiven them. It's my choice to tell them or not.
- In letting go of my anger, I am relieving the pain of my depression, anxiety, frustration, obsessive thinking, and self-doubt.
- I am outgrowing my role as the victim, the suffering martyr, and the Marlboro Man with no feelings from the neck up or down.
- I am replacing them with a mature identity, with adult judgment.

Meaning—Replaces *meaninglessness.*
- I have replaced my feelings of meaninglessness (inferiority, worthlessness, unbelonging, inferiority, and all the other components of self-contempt) with the meaning I have chosen to give my life.
- I have stopped living on other people's terms and started living on responsible, appropriate terms of my own.
- I am freeing myself to take life as it comes and do the best I can with it.

Social interest—Replaces *self-centeredness.*
- Now that I belong to the human race as a member in good standing, I am free to have an appropriate regard for the well-being of my fellow citizens on this planet.
- I am not a do-gooder or a champion of the underdog. I am free to assume appropriate responsibility for doing what I can do to make life better instead of worse.
- I have replaced my self-serving good intentions with the real intention to do for others what reality requires me to do.
- I am not required to do it perfectly, just well enough to get the job done.
- I am not the prisoner of my misperceptions about people, the world, or myself. My old attitudes have gotten out of the way. I can see reality more clearly for what it is. I understand what it requires me to do. I feel adequately prepared to do it.

Peace of mind—Replaces *turmoil, anxiety, and chaos.*
- I am at peace with myself.
- I am free to be at peace with others in the present.
- I can let down my guard. It wasn't preventing anything anyway.
- I can take it when it comes.

Source: Based on Messer's activity "Debriefing Homework," personal communication.

Table A10.2 Components of Character and Examples of Directed Reflections

Acceptance of unpleasant reality—To do the best with what comes one's way.	You're feeling good about handling all the stuff that has been coming along. You must feel pretty solid about hanging in there even though things have been difficult for you. Despite all that's come down on you, you must feel really good about how you are handling things. So, you're feeling pretty capable. You made the best of a crummy situation. That's got to make you feel really good. You've learned to make lemonade very well.
Accomplishment—To know that one achieved and that it was good enough.	You did it! You made it happen in the real world. Even though it didn't come out perfectly, it is nice to know that it was good enough as it was. It must give you a really proud feeling to have done your best and know that it was good enough. Wow! You really did it! You knew you could!
Approachability—To be available to others who may seek them out.	I've noticed how you show a real concern for others. It must make you feel good when others seek you out. You have a nice manner that draws people to you. That must really make you feel good about yourself. It feels good to know you are a good friend. When you are there for them like that you must feel pretty strong and dependable.
Appropriate anger—Can express legitimate anger in mature/responsible ways.	It's really great when you are able to express your anger appropriately. You're feeling pretty proud of yourself for being able to tell them why you were angry about their decision. I see you were able to really convert your anger into positive energy. It must be great to have accomplished all you got done. You must feel pretty level-headed right now. You expressed your concerns in a calm and effective manner. It must feel good for you to express your grievance to them without getting all out of sorts.
Appropriate responsibility—Assumes level of responsibility appropriate to the situation.	You handled that really nicely and still let them be responsible for themselves. How good is that for you? You took responsibility for your part and that was enough for now.

(continued on next page)

Table A10.2 (continued) Components of Character and Examples of Directed Reflections

	It feels good for you to be able to take responsibility without having to take over. You feel good about contributing just enough.
Belonging—Feeling that one is a member in good standing in the human race.	You feel good about being able to be a part of things. It's nice to feel that you fit in and belong. There's a good feeling in feeling that you are included and that you belong. It feels good to belong. You know you have a right to be here just as much as anyone else.
Confidence—Feeling prepared to cope with the positives and negatives that life offers.	You did it! You can do it again when you need to. It feels good to know you can handle whatever comes your way. There's a powerful feeling to know you can succeed. There's a powerful feeling to know you can handle things.
Counting one's blessings—To recognize and appreciate one's blessings.	It's great knowing that you can focus on what is going right for you. You must really feel on top of things knowing you have a knack for appreciating what you have going for you. You may have felt a little down for a while but now you know you can focus on what is going well for you. You feel good about yourself that you can see and appreciate the good things about your life.
Courage—Knowing which risks need to be taken and those that do not.	You took the risk and had the courage to see what would happen. You know what risks are worth taking and which aren't. That must make you feel really courageous—to do what needed to be done and not worry about it. It can be a little scary at times and still you weren't afraid to try. You're feeling very courageous to make good decisions even though you know it won't be easy.
Courage to succeed—To be able to risk success and tolerate a successful outcome.	You're feeling pretty successful right now. Giving things a try takes being willing to risk doing something and that is exactly what you did. You must feel pretty courageous when you try something new without knowing how it will turn out. When you take a risk like that it feels pretty good to have everything go okay.

(continued on next page)

Table A10.2 (continued) Components of Character and Examples of Directed Reflections

	You've got to be proud of yourself for sticking to it and trying again. You did it! And now you can enjoy that success.
Equality—Behaving as an equal, feeling neither inferior nor superior to others.	It's like you are no more or no less than anyone else. There's a good feeling that comes from not having to prove that you are equal to others.
Identity—To be one's own person and have flexibility in one's relationships.	It's great when you don't feel like you have to play a role anymore. It's great being able to operate on your own terms and not someone else's. It's a good feeling when you can act on being yourself. It feels so good to be able to just be yourself.
In touch with reality—To perceive the world objectively and appropriately.	You are right on target with your view of the world and it makes everything have more sense. I'm sure it feels pretty good to realize that your plan was impossible but you have put together an even better alternative one.
Independence—Free from a dependence on others to validate their existence.	You're feeling good about really being free to make your own decisions. Right now you are feeling pretty independent—you are living life on your own terms. It's a good feeling that you can validate your own successes.
Intellectual self-respect—To feel smart enough in the moment.	It's just really nice to know that you are smart enough to handle the situation. You feel confident about your abilities to handle something new. That's a great sense of self-respect for you. Now you know that you know what you need to know.
Less vulnerable to temptation—No need to resort to mischief or self-destructive behavior.	It's nice just being yourself for who you are, not for what others want you to be. It feels like you are strong when you make smart choices in difficult situations. You've got to be feeling on top of the world. You're not needing to create mischief in order to be noticed. Doesn't it make you feel really powerful? You know you have a choice and can choose the best action for yourself.

(continued on next page)

Table A10.2 (continued) Components of Character and Examples of Directed Reflections

	It's so neat to be in charge of yourself. You didn't need to push their buttons because you fixed your own.
Liberation—Neither rebel nor victim but can solve problems constructively.	It's great not being trapped in your old beliefs about people (or things). It's freeing when you just do the best you can do.
Living in the present—To be able to function in the real world right now.	There's a nice feeling when you are able to move ahead and make things happen. You didn't just sit around waiting for the perfect time, you did it right now.
Lovability—Able to love and be loved.	What you did just then was like giving yourself a hug for being okay. I'm sure that is a really secure feeling to be comfortable enough with yourself to love and be loved. It's an awesome feeling to have someone out there love you and you can freely love him or her back. It just feels good to open your heart and let the love flow out and back.
Maturity—Being at an appropriate stage of development for one's age.	You're feeling pretty grown-up now when you make good decisions for yourself. It's an important part of growing up to feel as capable as you do right now. It feels good to be able to meet your own needs without relying on others.
Positive regard—Free to have a positive regard for fellow human beings.	You are approaching others as equals—no more or less than you see in yourself. Isn't it just great to believe in the human race and spirit? You seem to understand other's viewpoints and respect their right to their opinion. That's got to be a great feeling. When you see the good in others it creates a pretty nice feeling inside for you.
Power and control—To be able to make positive things happen.	You're feeling pretty proud of yourself. You did well and were in control of the situation at the same time. Wow! You must be feeling really in charge of things. You were in control of yourself and could make things better for everyone. That has got to be powerful for you. You made a difference and it was good for everyone.

(continued on next page)

Table A10.2 (continued) Components of Character and Examples of Directed Reflections

Power of choice—Can make choices and live with the consequences of the choices.	You chose to do what you needed to do and live with the outcome. That must make you feel pretty capable. That must be a powerful feeling to be aware of the consequences of your actions and to accept the outcomes. You feel good about the choices you made. When you discover that you have choices and can choose your own actions, you feel pretty much in control of yourself and your life.
Relief—From the pressure, tension, and stress of having to prove one's worth.	It's nice to know you can just be your own person. It's a great feeling of relief to just know that you are enough. It's great to know you are okay just the way you are. You must be really relieved. You don't have to put up a façade to prove who you are anymore.
Relief from guilt—Feeling active remorse and able to make restitution when needed.	It feels like a good space to be in—you can fix the situation and then move on without worrying about it anymore. You should be feeling pretty guilt-free—you made a mistake but were able to fix it and then move on. It's sad knowing you can't take it back, and you are willing to apologize for what was said and get on with your life. You feel relieved to have made amends and be responsible for your actions. It feels good to be able to forgive yourself. You can choose to fix it or forget it and know that it will be all right.
Relief from fear and anxiety—To have a positive view of the future and take life as it comes.	That must be pretty good for you. You can make things happen as they come and have a good outlook about it. You feel good that you handled it appropriately without just reacting. You're taking life as it comes and handling it. You are feeling very resourceful. You have the tools to handle whatever comes your way without the worry.
Security—To be comfortable in one's ability to cope with the ups and downs of life.	You're feeling pretty okay just within yourself and your ability to handle it. That makes you feel pretty secure in yourself, accepting life's challenges as they come and know you will cope.

(continued on next page)

Table A10.2 (continued) Components of Character and Examples of Directed Reflections

Securing cooperation—To be able to work in an atmosphere of mutual respect with others.	That seems to be a positive thing going for you—getting others to pull together to do what needs to be done. It must be a great feeling to realize that you've participated in helping your team (group) work well together. It feels great to be a part of family activities and projects.
Self-acceptance—Feeling good enough as one is. "I am a worthwhile human being in spite of my faults and imperfections."	As good as you are right now—that's good enough. You feel just okay as you are and that is good enough. You didn't have to be any better than that and it felt all right to you.
Self-respect—Able to live with others as equals and positively contribute to one's community.	You got a good thing going for you right now, a give-and-take respect for others and what you can contribute. That's got to make you pretty comfortable—to see your value and worth as well as everyone else's. You must feel pretty good about the way you are able to treat others equally. You feel pretty satisfied with yourself. You know who you are, where you're going, and how to help others along the way.
Serenity—At peace with oneself and free to be at peace with one's neighbors.	It is a really comfortable feeling when you don't have to keep up your guard. It's a nice feeling of peace of mind. You feel comfortable enough just in being yourself.
Success—Possesses the feeling to be free to succeed and to be successful.	You accomplished what you set out to do. You feel free to succeed in your own way without having to prove yourself.
Tolerance of pain or disappointment—Accepts life as it comes without despairing.	Even when you were having a bad day (time), your optimism seems to come shining through. I've been watching you smile in the face of adversity. It must be a really good feeling to take things just as they come. Even though you are feeling sad right now, it is good to know you tried your best and you can do it again if you wish. Even though you were disappointed, you knew how to roll with the punches.

(continued on next page)

Table A10.2 (continued) Components of Character and Examples of Directed Reflections

Trust—Trusting oneself while discriminating those worthy of trust.	It's an okay feeling to be able to trust other people. You feel disappointed but even when they let you down, you can make other decisions.
Trust in one's judgment—Open to learning from experience.	So you decided to do the homework and it turned out to be a good decision. You now know that it is okay to trust your judgment.
Unselfish—Having the freedom to give of oneself to others.	Your compassion for others must give you a great feeling of being okay in yourself. There's a nice feeling that comes from sharing experiences—it has really helped some of the group members. It feels good to give without expecting anything in return. That's really enjoyable for you—to give of yourself when you want and let others enjoy your gifts.

Sources: Components of character based on Messer, M. (1995). *The components of our character* (pp. 29–40). Anger Institute: Chicago, IL. Examples of directed reflections based on Milliren, A., Messer, M. H., and Reeves, J. (n.d.). *"Reflections" on character*. Unpublished manuscript.

Table A10.3 Twelve Roadblocks to Communication

Roadblock	Sample Expressions
1. **Ordering, directing, commanding**—Telling the other to do something, giving an order or a command.	I don't care what the other parents do, you have to do the yard work. Don't talk to your mother like that! Now you go back up there and play with Ginny and Joyce! Stop complaining! Nonverbal: physically putting child in his room
2. **Warning, threatening, promising**—Telling the other what consequences will occur if he/she does something, or carrying out the consequences (rewarding or punishing).	If you do that, you'll be sorry! One more statement like that and you'll leave the room! You'd better not do that if you know what's good for you! If you're a good boy, Santa Claus will come. If you calm down, I'll listen to you. Nonverbal: spanking, rewarding
3. **Moralizing, preaching, shoulds and oughts**—Invoking vague outside authority as accepted truth.	You shouldn't act like that. You ought to do this. Children are supposed to respect their elders.
4. **Advising, giving solutions or suggestions**—Telling others how to solve a problem, giving advice or suggestions, providing answers or solutions.	Why don't you ask both Ginny and Joyce to play down here? Just wait a couple of years before deciding on college. I suggest you talk to your teachers about that. Go make friends with some other girls.
5. **Teaching, lecturing, giving logical arguments**—Trying to influence the other with facts, counterarguments, logic, information, or your own opinion.	College can be the most wonderful experience you'll ever have. Children must learn how to get along with one another. Let's look at the facts about college graduates. If kids learn to take responsibility around the house, they'll grow up to be responsible adults. Look at it this way—your mother needs help around the house. When I was your age, I had twice as much to do as you.

(continued on next page)

Table A10.3 (continued) Twelve Roadblocks to Communication

Roadblock	Sample Expressions
6. **Judging, criticizing, disagreeing, blaming**—Making a negative judgment or evaluation of the other.	You're not thinking clearly. That's an immature point of view. You're very wrong about that. I couldn't disagree with you more.
7. **Praising, agreeing**—Offering a positive evaluation or judgment, agreeing.	Well, I think you are pretty. You have the ability to do well. I think you're right. I agree with you. You've always been a good student. We've always been proud of you.
8. **Name-calling, labeling, stereotyping**—Making the other feel foolish, putting the other into a category, shaming the other.	You're a spoiled brat. Look here, Mr. Smarty. You're acting like a wild animal. Okay, little baby.
9. **Interpreting, analyzing, diagnosing**—Telling others what their motives are or analyzing why they are doing or saying something; communicating that you have them figured out or have them diagnosed.	You're just jealous of Ginny. You're saying that to bug me. You really don't believe that at all. You feel that way because you're not doing well in school.
10. **Reassuring, sympathizing, consoling, supporting**—Trying to make others feel better, talking them out of their feelings, trying to make their feelings go away, denying the strength of their feelings.	You'll feel different tomorrow. All kids go through this sometime. Don't worry, things'll work out. You could be an excellent student, with your potential. I used to think that, too. I know, school can be pretty boring sometimes. You usually get along with other kids very well.

(continued on next page)

Table A10.3 (continued) Twelve Roadblocks to Communication

Roadblock	Sample Expressions
11. **Probing, questioning, interrogating**—Trying to find reasons, motives, causes; searching for more information to help you solve the problem.	When did you start feeling this way? Why do you suppose you hate school? Do the kids ever tell you why they don't want to play with you? How many other kids have you talked to about the work they have to do? Who put that idea into your head? What will you do if you don't go to college?"
12. **Withdrawing, distracting, sarcasm, humoring, diverting, indirection**—Trying to get others away from the problem; withdrawing from the problem yourself; distracting others, kidding them out of it, pushing the problem aside.	Just forget about it. Let's not talk about it at the table. Come on. Let's talk about something more pleasant. How's it going with your basketball? Why don't you try burning the school building down? We've been through all this before.

Source: L. E. Losoncy, personal communication.

Table A10.4 Hope Worksheet #2-2

Disjunctive Feelings	Family Motto or Scriptural Affirmation
Example: I could not see anyway forward.	After darkness, there is light.
	"But those who hope in the Lord will renew their strength. They will soar on wings like eagles; they will run and not grow weary, they will walk and not be faint." (Isaiah 40:31, NIV).
The following contains numerous scriptural affirmations that may be copied, enlarged, and attached to index cards for individuals to use to counteract disjunctive feelings in response to life difficulties. These verses may also be used as a Q-Sort activity, where they are sorted by themes or categories.[a]	
"God hath not given us a spirit of fear, but of power, and of love, and of a sound mind." (2 Timothy 1:7, KJV)	"But those who hope in the Lord will renew their strength. They will soar on wings like eagles; they will run and not grow weary, they will walk and not be faint." (Isaiah 40:31, NIV)
"Cast all your anxiety on him because he cares for you." (1 Peter 5:7, NIV)	"I can do all things through Christ who strengthens me." (Philippians 4:13, NKJV)
"Who shall separate us from the love of Christ? Shall trouble or hardship or persecution or famine or nakedness or danger or sword? … No, in all these things we are more than conquerors through him who loved us." (Romans 8:35, 37, NIV)	"For I am convinced that neither death nor life, neither angels nor demons, neither the present nor the future, nor any powers, neither height nor depth, nor anything else in all creation, will be able to separate us from the love of God that is in Christ Jesus our Lord." (Romans 8:38–39, NIV)
"The Spirit of the Sovereign Lord is on me, because the Lord has anointed me to preach good news to the poor. He has sent me to bind up the brokenhearted, to proclaim freedom for the captives, and release for the prisoners." (Isaiah 61:1, NIV)	"This then is how we know that we belong to the truth, and how we set our hearts at rest in his presence whenever our hearts condemn us. For God is greater than our hearts, … if our hearts do not condemn us, we have confidence before God and receive from him anything we ask …" (1 John 3:19–21, NIV)
"The thief does not come except to steal, and to kill, and to destroy. I have come that they may have life, and that they may have it more abundantly." (John 10:10, NKJV)	"Be self-controlled and alert. Your enemy the devil prowls around like a roaring lion looking for someone to devour. Resist him, standing firm in the faith …" (1 Peter 5:8–9, NIV)

(continued on next page)

Table A10.4 (continued) Hope Worksheet #2-2

Disjunctive Feelings	Family Motto or Scriptural Affirmation
"And by his stripes we are healed." (Isaiah 53:5, NKJV)	"'Not by might nor by power, but by my Spirit,' says the Lord Almighty." (Zechariah 4:6, NIV)
"So do not fear, for I am with you; do not be dismayed, for I am your God. I will strengthen you and help you; I will uphold you with my righteous right hand." (Isaiah 41:10, NIV)	"No weapon forged against you will prevail, and you will refute every tongue that accuses you. This is the heritage of the servants of the Lord …" (Isaiah 54:17, NIV)
"But those who hope in the Lord will renew their strength. They will soar on wings like eagles; they will run and not grow weary, they will walk and not be faint." (Isaiah 40:31, NIV)	"Some trust in chariots and some in horses, but we trust in the name of the Lord our God. They are brought to their knees and fall, but we rise up and stand firm." (Psalms 20:7, NIV)

Note: KJV = King James Version; NIV = New International Version; NKJV = New King James Version.

[a] The scripture affirmation proportion of Hope Worksheet #2-2 was adapted from Sori, C., & McKinney, L. (2005). Free at last! Using scriptural affirmation to replace self-defeating thoughts. In K. B. Helmeke & C. F. Sori (Eds.), *The therapist's notebook for integrating spirituality in counseling: Homework, handouts, and activities for use in psychotherapy* (pp. 223–234). New York: Haworth Press.

Epilogue

> A bruised reed he will not break, and
> a smoldering wick he will not snuff out …
>
> —**Matthew 12:20**[1]

The idea of writing this handbook was sparked by an epiphany Julia experienced on a snowy morning three years ago: We live in a problematic and discouraging world and what we need is courage.

Just as we were finishing this book, we witnessed a transformational moment in American history. America elected its first African American president; a truly unlikely candidate considering his humble upbringing and this nation's racist tendencies and history of oppression. In a time of global doubts and fears, Americans demonstrated their courage to imagine, believe, and change. President Barack Obama in his acceptance speech recaptured the nation's true strength that comes from "the enduring power of our ideals; democracy, liberty, opportunity and unyielding hope." Faced with a long and challenging journey ahead, he called out to each of us to work harder and not only look after ourselves but to look after each other. *Yes, we can!*

Such community feeling and the "yes" attitude is exactly the answer to apathy and hostility. The genesis of our belonging is our longing to be part of the whole. Courage is our being and longing fulfilled in action. Courage brings its allied strengths to life as we labor to meet face-to-face all of the demands of living in the interest of ourselves and others. A good life, or happiness, is not something we own. It is a state of well-being when our deepest longing is answered with our courage to accept what is and to participate by acting as if what we are doing is making a difference.

We continue to marvel at how Individual Psychology, the psychology of courage, helps us to have access to the transcultural ancient wisdom for modern problems. Pragmatically, with its commonsense approach, Individual Psychology offers doable ways to achieve true mental health at home, in schools, at work, and in the community.

We are glad we have had the opportunity to introduce you to Alfred Adler whose work has been influential in our lives. He has brought to us meaning and understanding of how the world is and how we need to be in it. We hope you find this handbook useful and timeless in your own journey toward self-enhancement and care for others.

Notes

Preface

1. Adler (1931/2003).
2. Dreikurs (1971/1994, p. xii).
3. The loss of community value is directly linked to the consequences of the ambiguity and ambivalence of American individualism. See Bellah, Madsen, Sullivan, Swider, and Tipton (1985).
4. May (1977, p. 7).
5. Adler in Stein (n.d.).
6. "For Adler, we need to construct a society which stresses education for harmonious group life by encouraging the development of 'social interest.'" This quote from the editors of *Superiority and Social Interest* (Adler, 1979, p. 15) was in recognition of the increasing appreciation that Adler offered a theory of positive mental health.
7. Glasser (2005) recognized that Adler's counseling model is in line with the public mental health model that stresses the role of education and improvement of mental health. The traditional mental health model is flawed with prestige and misdiagnosis, and is pathology based. Glasser advocated that mental health professionals (i.e., psychiatrists, clinical psychologists, social workers, and counselors) replace the medical model with the public mental health model.

   Adler's criterion for mental health is social interest. Maslow noted that social interest is the only available word that describes

mental health that is "the flavor of the feelings for mankind expressed by self-actualizing subjects. They have for human beings in general a deep feeling of identification, sympathy, and affection in spite of occasional anger, impatience, or disgust. … They have a genuine desire to help the human race. It is as if they were all members of a single family." See note 6, p. 15.
8. Blagen (2008). Also see "Community Feeling at Work: The Courage of Recovery" section of Chapter 7.
9. Adler originally called sex the intimacy between two individuals of opposite gender. See Chapter 5 for discussions about same-gender and transgender love.
10. The narratives and reflections were mostly obtained through interviews we conducted, recorded, and transcribed over a period of 2 years both in and outside of America. In our interviews we basically used Socratic questions and early recollection to access the individuals' perception of their work, love, friends, and family living.

Chapter 1

1. Two examples of laypersons' definitions of courage from Phillips (2004).
2. Decades ago a philosopher, Herbert Gardiner Lord (1918) wrote a book with a similar title, *The Psychology of Courage*. His book had a special focus on training soldiers for courage. It is only recently that the movement of positive psychology has taken an interest in courage as a virtue and attempted to contribute to our understanding of courage via empirical and scientific measures. Also see Evans and White (1981) and Putnam (1997).
3. W. I. Miller (2000).
4. R. May (1975, p. 3).
5. Moran (1987). Based on his wartime experiences, Moran, the doctor of Winston Churchill, observed in his book, *Anatomy of Courage*, that fear precedes the birth of courage and the use of courage in soldiers.
6. Becker (1997).
7. Editors Ansbacher and Ansbacher (Adler, 1979, p. 8) noted the similarity between existential psychology and Individual Psychology. They credited Adler for his influence on existentialist and humanistic psychological theorists such as Satire, Maslow, May, and Frankl who were explicit regarding the linage from Adler. They wrote that existential psychology is known to be in the system of Adlerian psychology in that it "sees man as a unique being,

fundamentally concerned with the meaning of his existence and with plans and projects to solve his existential programs."

R. May (1977) equated anxiety to Adler's concept of inferior feeling. The word *feeling* means one's subjective attitude toward one's weaknesses. "Turning specifically to anxiety, Adler asks: What purpose does it serve? For the anxious individual himself, anxiety serves the purpose of blocking further activity; it is a cue to retreat to previous states of security. Hence it serves as a motivation for evading decisions and responsibility. But even more frequently emphasized by Adler is the function of anxiety as a weapon of aggression, a means of dominating others" (p. 155). In his philosophical interpretation of anxiety, May traced back to Spinoza (1632–1677) that "fear is essentially a subjective problem—that is, a matter of one's state of mind, or attitudes" (p. 27).
8. Adler (2006a, p. 38).
9. Dixon and Strano's (2006) notes on the differences among inferiority, inferiority feelings, and inferiority complex.
10. Definition given by Milliren, Clemmer, Wingett, and Testerment (2006, p. 357).

> A key concept in Individual Psychology: the complex of the personal philosophy, beliefs and characteristic approach to life of individuals, and the unifying feature of their personality. The life style represents the creative response to early experiences of individuals which in turn influence all their perceptions of themselves and the world, and thus their emotions, motives and actions. (Adler, 1931, p. 239)

> Adler (1979, p. 69) observed the patterns of how we creatively use our experiences of social living and discussed the differing styles we use in approaching these challenges. He wrote about basic attitudes such as optimism, pessimism, aggressive types, and defenders (Adler, 1927/1992). Adler also wrote about the four temperament types: sanguine, choleric, melancholic, and phlegmatic. These were later replaced by four types of social-interest activities: the socially useful, the ruling type, the getting type, and the avoiding type (Adler, 1956). However, Adler was opposed to labeling people and so he only offered various typologies as a way to teach about a variety of life styles. Contemporary followers of Adler have since posited more themes of life style.

11. Carlson, Watts, and Maniacci (2006, p. 44).
12. Alder (1979, p. 52).
13. Wolfe (1932/1957, p. 110).
14. Adler (1956, p. 159).
15. Dreikurs (1989, p. 29).

16. Yearley (1990). Courage is never a virtue by itself. For example, universal to Confucianism and Platonic teachings, wisdom and passion precede courage so that the three virtues bring not only harmony to one's soul but also justice to the commonweal (see Chapter 7).

    The Confucius teaching of the three virtues—reason, passion, and courage—has an exact counterpart in the basic plan of Plato's *Republic* where harmony is achieved by the courage to cooperate by every human being who has three souls that correspond to the three classes of citizens within the state: the rational (wisdom, thinking), the spirited (willing, courage), and the appetitive (feeling, moderation). We speculate that with further investigation, there may be a relationship between the three Confucian virtues, Plato's virtues, and the characters in the *Wizard of Oz* (i.e., the Scarecrow for thinking, the Cowardly Lion for courage, and the Tin Man for feelings).
17. See note 14, p. 305.
18. *The Analects 17.23* by Confucius (BC 551–479).
19. Adler (1979, p. 275).
20. Way (1962). Adler was repeatedly compared to Confucius by Adlerians (McGee, Huber, & Carter, 1983, p. 238). Adler was regarded as the Confucius of the West in the introductory essay by Mairet to Adler's *The Science of Living* in 1929.
21. Peterson and Seligman (2004, p. 29). Oddly, some authors of positive psychology have found that courage is missing, either explicitly or thematically implied, in the eastern traditions of Confucianism, Taoism, and Buddhism (Dahlsgaard, Peterson, & Seligman, 2005, p. 205). Instead, courage has a different meaning and is manifested as an integral aspect in these traditions, which is discussed in Chapters 7, 8, and 9. Also see note 7, Chapter 2.
22. See note 14. "Much of our view of the enhancement of the self-esteem as the guiding fiction is included in Nietzsche's 'will to power' and 'will to seem'" (p. 111). To Adler, this will to power is equivalent to the striving for perfection, a compensatory force inherent in us to overcome our inferior feeling. The concept behind the expressions of power or perfection is *overcoming* (p. 114). The will to power is a guiding fiction that is originated in our safeguarding tendency. Our self-boundedness (*Ichgebundenheit*) can only be compensated, however, by our desires to contribute to others. In Chapter 9, we will revisit the concept of the will to power in its spiritual–existential root that means *the will to more life*. Also see Chapter 9, note 13.

23. See note 12, p. 60.
24. See note 3.
25. See note 16.
26. Lin (1937/1996, 1959), Eckstein and Cooke (2005).
27. Bazzano (2006) believes, along with Adler, that we are moving toward a postmodern perspective on ethics. Common sense is the ideal complement to the transcendental wisdom associated in Zen Buddhism. "Being with is not enough. We need to be for" (p. 8). The Taoist concepts illuminate the existential courage embedded in the Adlerian belief: What is, is.
28. See note 12, p. 275. Adler's psychological postulation and the theist views of spirituality are not comparable with the fundamental difference, in that for Adler, God is human idea; for Christians God is revealed. "For Adler, the meaning of life is the experience of fellowship and the courage for it … Furthermore, while Christianity unreservedly endorses the call for encouragement, it holds that there can be no courage for life without faith in God" (Jahn in Adler, 1979, p. 273).

    They need not be at odd with each other, nevertheless, as they converge in the interest of understanding the person in relation to the world. According to Adler, social interest is salvation to human community just as the gift of grace is to the faith community. In Individual Psychology, the individual is placed in the center of the world striving toward the community. The goal of a community is to "strengthen the weak, to support the falling, and to heal the erring." Adler was concerned about the interconnectedness of the brotherly love and the common weal, the man–earth relationship.

    "The overpowering goal of Adler is his conception of the brotherhood of man. For the theologian the earth is God's creation and man is God's creature. From this view the brotherhood of man is the eternal ideal of mankind" (Jhan in Adler, 1979, p. 274).
29. Milliren, Evans, and Newbauer (2006, p. 109).

Chapter 2

1. Adler (1964, p. 79).
2. Adler (1956, p. 134).
3. Adler (1979, p. 40). Social interest as an aptitude and ability can be best observed in the attitudes we display when we acquire a new life skill. The value of training is illustrated in the following quote by Adler:

> What do you first do when you learn to swim? You make mistakes, do you not? And what happens? You make other mistakes, and when you have made all the mistakes you possibly can without drowning—and some of them many times over—what do you find? That you can swim? Well life is just the same as learning to swim! Do not be afraid of making mistakes, for there is no other way of learning how to live! (http://thinkexist.com/quotes/alfred_adler/)

4. Dreikurs (1989, p. 8). Dreikurs elaborated on this dilemma in depth:

> Adler found an answer to this perplexing problem of contradictory social demands, expressed on one hand by existing conditions and on the other by the ideal human society which a person with fully developed social interest will have in mind. Adler advised to look at each problem "*sub speci aeternitatis*," i.e., from the viewpoint of eternity. Doing so, one can conceive of the basic rules of social living, detached from the overwhelming demands and mistaken perspectives imposed upon us by situations and by our own fears, anxieties, distorted approaches, and goals. The ideal expression of social interest is the ability to play the game with existing demands for cooperation and to help the group to which one belongs in its evolution closer toward a perfect form of social living. This implies progress without creating unnecessary antagonism, which can and does inhibit progress more than it stimulates it.

5. See note 3, pp. 135 and 256.
6. See note 3, p. 136.
7. In Adler's (1979) view:

> … only the individual who is prepared for social cooperation can solve the social problems that life imposes. By this we mean that there should exist a certain degree of contact feeling—of striving for cooperation—in the law of movement of the individual. Where it is lacking we meet with failures. I have already shown that this inclination for cooperation and social achievement has not been properly developed in children who feel insecure. Insecure children build a life style which shows a lack of social interest, because an insecure individual is always more concerned with himself than with others. He cannot get away from himself. (p. 90; also see Preface, note 7)

Adler's thoughts on normal development in relation to social interest as in this quote communicated a profound love that we interrelate to the spiritual concept of agape and the Confucius pragmatic idea of commonweal *ren* in this book. See the discussions on global humanity in the Preface and notes 21 and 28 of Chapter 1.

8. See note 4, p. 6. According to Dreikurs:

> Readiness to cooperate, which is one of the characteristics of a good comrade, is tested most rigorously in the difficult situations. Most people are perfectly willing to cooperate so long as everything is to their liking. It is much more difficult to remain a good comrade in an uncongenial situation. If the tie which binds a man to a group is weak, he will easily break away as soon as anything he does not like happens. The stronger his feeling of membership, the more surely will he remain loyal to the group, even when he cannot enforce his own wishes. We never find conditions which entirely conform to our wishes in any human relationship, be it friendship, the family, love or work. Sooner or later, therefore, we are bound to become involved in critical situations, and the way we behave then will show whether we are community minded or not.

9. Adler (1931/2003, p. 20).
10. One's ability to contribute in the interest of others or being the brother's keeper is related to the life task of getting along with the universe and the task of keen keeping (see Sonstegard and Bitter, 2004, p. 79) that we will elaborate on in the psychological and spiritual contexts of the courage to belong in Chapters 8 and 9.
11. See note 4, p. 9. Emphasizing the abilities of cooperation and contribution as basic elements of the social interest, Adler indicated that "each individual has to make an adjustment to two social levels which oppose each other. Fulfilling the social tasks which confront us means we are not meeting not only the acute obligations presented to us by the needs by the group around us, but also the needs for improvement and social development" (Dreikurs, 1989, p. 8).
12. See note 4, p. 8. Dreikurs described the necessity for the individual to make an adjustment on the two different social levels:

> Even if one were capable of fulfilling completely the demands of the social order and the surrounding people—an impossible task in itself because of contradictory demands by various people and groups—he could still fail in his social adjustment if the need for improvement were neglected. A person may be for all practical purposes socially well adjusted, working efficiently in his job, being a good husband and father, and participating in the social activities of community; still he fails in his social obligations if he is opposed to change, progress and improvement. On the other hand, a person who is interested only in the necessary changes and, therefore, neglects and defies the immediate demands of his social environment is obviously socially maladjusted.

13. Andreas and Andreas (1989, p. 38).
14. See note 2, p. 138.

    The feeling for the *Gemeinschaft* is wider than the term "society" suggests. It embraces a sense of relatedness, not only to the human community, but to the whole of life, and is therefore the highest expression of Adler's concept of totality. It means the human being's sense of himself as a part of the unity of existence in contrast to the fear of standing in the cosmos as a single unrelated organism. We sometimes see examples of this sense of kinship with all that exists in the work of great artists, like that of Beethoven, in the recognition of oneness, and in the love, sympathy, and desire for combination with life which music such as his so often expresses. (Way, 1962, pp. 201–202)

15. See note 2, p. 156.
16. See note 3, p. 305.
17. In Adler (1979, pp. 14–16), Ansbacher and Ansbacher give an account of Adler's theory as the theory of positive mental health and social interest as the criterion of mental health that influenced the later development of humanistic psychology and the self-actualization concept studied by Maslow.

Chapter 3

1. Adler in Stein (n.d.).
2. Adler in Brett (1931/2003, pp. 18–19).
3. Dreikurs (1989, p. 5).
4. Way (1962, pp. 206–207). Often, man can be a problem to himself since, as Way noted, "Outward adaptation is therefore no criterion in itself. One may be outwardly successful, yet a failure in one's own eyes; conversely, one may be a failure from the world's point of view, yet sufficiently content in oneself" (p. 207). Thus "it would be difficult to conceive of a society in which some form of adaptation along these lines would not be demanded of the individual. But the character and the extent of the adaptation required will, of course, vary with every generation and with every alteration in the structure of society" (p. 206).
5. Dreikurs and Mosak (in Mosak 1977b, c, and d) offered two additional life tasks in an attempt to more adequately describe the demands of human living. They postulate a fourth life task as the necessity of the individual to learn how to get along with himself, how to deal with himself. The fifth life task relates to the problem of man establishing himself in relationship to the universe.

6. Sonstegard and Bitter (2004).
7. Mosak (1977a, p. 108).
8. See note 6.
9. Wolfe (1932/1957).
10. See note 4, pp. 206–207.
11. See note 13 of Chapter 1 and related discussions on compensation, overcompensation, and undercompensation.
12. Adler (1931/2003, pp. 18–19).

Chapter 4

1. Wolfe (1932/1957, p. 203).
2. Partially based on S. Osipow (personal communication, 1987).
3. The use of "drop in" to a career field was inspired by Steve Jobs in his commencement speech delivered at Stanford University on June 12, 2005. Jobs is the CEO of Apple and former CEO of Pixar Studios.

   If I had never dropped out, I would have never dropped in on this calligraphy class, and personal computers might not have the wonderful typography that they do. Of course it was impossible to connect the dots looking forward when I was in college. But it was very, very clear looking backwards ten years later. ... Again, you can't connect the dots looking forward; you can only connect them looking backwards. So you have to trust that the dots will somehow connect in your future. You have to trust in something—your gut, destiny, life, karma, whatever. This approach has never let me down, and it has made all the difference in my life.

4. Adler (1979).
5. Palmer (1999).
6. Interviews from Yang (1992).
7. Suprina and Lingle (2008, p. 201).
8. Hall (1976, p. 201). For more readings on protean career orientation, please refer to Hall (1986, 2002), Hall and Mirvis (1996), Hall and Moss (1998).
9. The "Protean Man" refers to Lifton's analysis of the contemporary personality as continually changing its identity. Proteus, in the Greek myth, was unable to not change his shape unless seized and chained. He had to respond to his inner drive of change and to reflect the environment. The Protean Man who has no idea of "where I belonged and no idea of my self" (in May, 1977) best describes the modern anxiety we experience and the changing world we live in. According to May, we respond to this anxiety by

a process of numbing: an emotional withdrawal in which people who can do nothing else, dull their sensitivities, and cut off their awareness of threat.
10. Hall and Mirvis (1996, p. 21).
11. Stoltz (2006).
12. The concepts of personal traits as a "success formula," life themes, vocational personality, and career adaptability are major components of the career construction theory by Savickas (2005). Socratic questions in Dialogue Box 4.5 are examples of his creative modification of early recollection techniques that can be used in counseling for career construction by focusing on the individual's career stories.
13. Losoncy (2004). Encouragement is an attitude that is equal to the totality of our beliefs, emotions, and actions. Simply put, encouragement is about the art of giving courage (see more discussion on encouragement in Chapter 10).
14. According to Yang and Waller (2005), there are five ways for this to occur: curiosity, persistence, flexibility, optimism, and risk taking. These skills would assist us in learning how to deal with our thoughts, feelings, and behaviors as we become more comfortable with our self in the face of the hurdles and barriers of work life. Also see Mitchell, Levin, and Krumboltz (1999).
15. Bloch and Richmond (2007).
16. M. Agenlian, personal communication, April 2005.
17. Clint and Lucy's career situations were first discussed in Sandberg and Yang (2006).
18. Some of these questions were presented in 2007 at the women's retreat at Association for Counselor Education and Supervision, Columbus, Ohio.
19. Gibran (1923, p. 25).

Chapter 5

1. In his book *The Four Loves* (1960/1988), Lewis explicitly says that his definition of friendship is narrower than mere companionship; friendship in his sense only exists if there is something for the friendship to be about. To Lewis, eros is distinct from sexuality, which Lewis calls Venus, although he does spend time discussing sexual activity and its spiritual significance. He warns against the danger of elevating eros to the status of a god, but he also praises it as an indifferent appreciation of the beloved as opposed to any pleasure that can be obtained from them.

2. Beecher and Beecher (1966, p. 91).
3. Wolfe (1932/1957).
4. See note 2, p. 106.
5. See note 3, p. 324.
6. See note 3, p. 318.
7. Based on Beecher and Beecher (1966) and Wolfe (1932/1957).
8. Dreikurs (1971, p. 123).
9. Adler (1931/2003, p. 231).
10. Mansager (2008).
11. S. Dermer, personal communication, September 2008.
12. Suprina and Lingle (2008).
13. See note 3, p. 324. Also, according to Adler, "Love and marriage are essential to human cooperation—not just a cooperation for the welfare of two persons, but cooperation for the welfare of humanity as well" (p. 219).
14. Fromm (1956/2006).
15. The NIV Topical Study Bible, New International Version (1989).
16. Butler (2000).
17. See notes 1 and 7.
18. See note 7, p. 198.

Chapter 6

1. Adler (1931/2003, p. 117).
2. Beecher and Beecher (1966, p. 210).
3. Lewis (1960/1988).
4. Dreikurs (1971, p. 65; 1989, p. 6).
5. Grunwald and McAbee (1985, p. 69).
6. Mosak (1977a, p. 198).
7. Adler (2006a, p. 37).
8. Synthesized from Dreikurs and Soltz (1964) and Dinkmeyer and Carlson (2001).
9. Adler (2006b, p. 243).
10. Johansen (2006, p. 239).
11. Adler (1956).
12. Based on Ansbacher (2006, p. 262). The attention getting goal fits all four quadrants; the goals of power and revenge also fit socially useless active and socially useless passive. The purpose of Figure 6.2 is to illustrate how the two dimensions intersect.
13. G. Smith, personal communication, December 2007.
14. Nelson, Erwin, Brock, and Hughes (2002).
15. Wolfe (1932/1957, p. 231).

Chapter 7

1. Sonstegard and Bitter (2004, p. 79).
2. Zeig (2009).
3. Chang (2004), Yang (1991).
4. Suprina and Lingle (2008).
5. An interview with Jack Lawson by Diller (1999, p. 167).
6. The problematic social dynamics can be organized into five major categories. The first common problem is our failure to see others as equals. Neither dominance nor submission wins us genuine respect in our relationships as they reflect the same inadequacies and fears that elicit our need to control, resent, or withdraw when the disjunctive feelings are present. Second, the natural superior position our tradition gives to males, parents, or authority figures in a hierarchical system is confronted with the individual's needs for respect and inner freedom. Third, we are deeply but differently influenced by the social demands of class, prestige, and wealth. We knowingly or unknowingly compete and fight to achieve our own sense of importance and superiority according to these externally valued expectations. Fourth, we are mistaken with the need to be good or right according to these cultural norms. The moralistic and righteous arguments impede mutual understanding and respect in relationships, as others may feel defeated, subdued, or inadequate. Last, we often fail to recognize that behavioral problems are not the cause but the result of relationship conflicts.
7. Dreikurs (1971, p. 177).
8. See note 6, pp. 9–11.
9. See note 6, p. 10. Also see Dreikurs (1970) and Terner and Pew (1978).
10. See note 6, p. 67.
11. See note 6, xiii.
12. Our approach to social equality in Individual Psychology is rather different from the popular concept of social justice that is based on John Rawls's *A Theory of Justice* (2005), which emphasizes the equitable distribution of rights, obligation, goods, power, and resources. In Individual Psychology, equality pertains to the problems of the individual and the problems of the society: "the strife for an egalitarian society expresses man's desire for social harmony" (see note 6, p. 188).
13. Way (1962).
14. Confucius, *The Record of Rites*, Book 9 (BC 551–479).
15. Cleary (1989), Yang and Milliren (2004).
16. See note 7, p. 35.

17. Adler in Stein and Edwards (1998, p. 285).
18. Palmer in W. R. Miller (1999).
19. Dreikurs (1971, p. 222).
20. Blagen (2008). This writing is exerted from the manuscript *The Best Kept Secret: Adler's Influence on A.A.*
21. *Alcoholics Anonymous* (1976, p. 17 and 60). The quotes we use in this book are from A.A. are from the original text of this publication. Archival evidence shows us that Bill Wilson was the primary author in consultation with Dr. Robert Holbrook and the original 100 members of A.A. It is noteworthy that thoughts and expressions of A.A. strikingly resemble Individual Psychology concepts as this quote expresses the vitality and primal value of community feeling for the addicted person.
22. See note 21. The 12 steps are a set of principles that if practiced seem to lift the obsession to drink and more important, perhaps, assist the individual in seeking and contributing to social interest. The 12 traditions apply to the life of the fellowship itself. Following are the twelfth step and the first tradition:
    Step 12: Having had a spiritual awakening as the result of these steps, we tried to carry this message to alcoholics, and to practice these principles in all of our affairs.
    Tradition 1: Each member of Alcoholics Anonymous is but a small part of a great whole. Alcoholics Anonymous must continue to live or most of us will surely die. Hence our common welfare comes first. But individual welfare follows close afterward.
23. Cheever (2004). Bill Wilson was always seeking his mother's console and even when he was one of the most trusted and recognizable leaders in American culture. His mother was physically not present in his life from age 11 and yet their correspondence via mail was close and continued throughout his adult years.
24. See note 23, p. 172.

Chapter 8

1. In Yang (1998).
2. Sonstegard and Bitter (2004, p. 8).
3. Adler (1927/1992, p. 156).
4. Wolfe (1932/1957, p. 198).
5. See note 2, pp. 80 and 100.
6. See note 3.
7. Suprina and Lingle (2008).
8. Yang (1992).

9. Mosak (1977c, pp. 105–106).
10. Dreikurs in Messer (2001).
11. Milliren, Evans, and Newbauer (2006, p. 109).
12. Dreikurs (1971, p. 52).
13. Dewey (1984, p. 188).
14. See note 3.
15. See note 12, p. 29.
16. Dreikurs (1989, p. 67). According to Lombard, Melchior, Murphy, and Brinkerhoff (2006, p. 209), neurotic style is a direct derivative of the formulation of one's life style that is faulty in its expression or movement toward a goal. This view explains the Adlerian stance on neurosis as a way of living, not a deficit. They stated that "the concept of neurosis is no longer included as a diagnostic category in the DSM–IV classification system (American Psychiatric Association [APA], 1994). This absence suggests it is less of a discrete disorder, and more a general problem of behavior (p. 210)."
17. This is a brief highlight of behavioral examples discussed in the classical Adlerian literature such as Adler (see note 3), Wolfe (1932/1957) and Dreikurs (1971).
18. Wolfe (1932/1957, pp. 259–260).
19. See note 18. For a synopsis of Wolfe's writing on evasion of reality as the fundamental dynamics of neurotic behavior see pp. 272–280.
20. See Serenity Prayer in Chapter 9.
21 May (1983, p. 27). The concept of self-affirmation as courage gives the spiritual context to our striving and overcoming. See Chapter 9, notes 5 and 14.
22. May (1977, p. 392).
23. Gomes (1952/2000, xxi). Also see Chapter 9, note 21.
24. Krakauer (1996, p. 56).
25. See note 24, p. 189. Capitalization by Chris McCandless. The following is a passage from Tolstoy's "Family Happiness" highlighted by McCandless several weeks before he died (p. 169):

> I have lived through much, and now I think I have found what is needed for happiness. A quiet scheduled life in the country, with the possibility of being useful to people to whom it is easy to do good, and who are not accustomed to have it done to them; then work which one hopes may be of some use; then rest, nature books, love for one's neighbor—such is my idea of happiness. And then, on top of all that, you for a mate, and children, perhaps—what more can the heart of a man desire?

26. Walton (1996b).

Chapter 9

1. Mosak (1977d, pp. 109–112).
2. Adler did not elaborate on the ontology of the creative power although he alluded to the use of creative power as the fourth question of life (Adler 2006a, p. 36). His position of the creative power is the human urge to overcome, from which we speculate that many of our spiritual attitudes originate. Stone (2006, p. 103) stated that "When Adler used the word, *creative*, he meant a constructive and ingenious means that humans employ in devising for themselves a subjective view of the self, the world and how they should act."
3. Both Kant and Vaihinger's "as if" philosophy influenced the individual psychology of Alfred Adler in his postulation of fictional finalism (Stone, 2008). Our misbehaviors are the results of the distorted as ifs that are only for self-preservation. On the contrary, with healthy mindedness (i.e., social interest), when one acts as if it would bring the desired outcome from the future to the present, one has hope. When one acts as if with beliefs, one has faith. Also see note 22.
4. Mansager (2003, p. 65).
5. Adler (1979, p. 32). The interrelatedness of the individual striving for perfection, psychological movement, human adaptation, development, and evolution is further described by Adler as the following:

   > But it is certain that our concept of life as development can no longer be doubted. Thereby movement is ascertained at the same time, movement toward self-preservation, procreation, contact with the surrounding world, victorious contact in order not to perish. We must take our point of departure from this path of development, of a continuous active adaptation to the demands of the external world, if we want to understand in which direction life moves.

   The thought of human striving has it root in existential philosophy. Furtmuller (1979) noted that contemporary followers of Spinoza and Nietzsche were present in Adler's circle and Adler's thoughts were deeply connected to Spinoza's thoughts of ethics and the existential thoughts on striving and will to power. Spinoza called the striving toward self-preservation or self-affirmation itself "power" implying the *overcoming* of something that, at least potentially, threatens or denies the self (Tillich, 2000, p. 20). See Chapter 1, note 22, and Chapter 8, note 21.
6. See note 4, p. 66.

7. McBrien, 2004, p. 413. Adler wrote: "Social interest ... means feeling with the whole, *sub speice aeternitatis*, under aspect of eternity."
8. Based on Yang and Drabik (2006). Existentially, suffering, according to Frankl (1946/1984), is the loss of meaning and purpose. Buddhists believe that living is suffering. Suffering is inescapable with the inevitability of birth, aging, disease, and death. Suffering is caused by desire and attachment. The root resolution to human problems is detachment. The only way to eliminate suffering is for one to eliminate his/her desire and attachment by following the true path of correct thought, speech, actions, livelihood, understanding, meditative effort, mindfulness and concentration."

    To the Taoist, to possess the fullness of living means to be in perfect harmony with one's original nature and to have the complementary opposites at work. Suffering is present when the harmony is absent. To overcome suffering, the best way is our action through inaction as happiness will return naturally by the reciprocating life force.
9. Lewis (1940/1996). From the Christian perspective, suffering is deeply connected to divine grace. In Lewis's reasoning, the ultimate good for man is in consciously surrendering oneself to God, which entails a complete commitment to approach God in love, with total openness, vulnerability, and trust. Without suffering in one's life, man would not, perhaps could not, turn toward God with utter faith, remaining instead, focused on one's own goals, desires, and worries of the world. Suffering, thus, is given to man by God out of love, so that man might be made perfect through surrender.
10. Mosak, Brown, and Boldt (1994).
11. See note 5, p. 31.
12. Adler (1931/2003, pp. 57–58).
13. It would be a mistake to simply regard "power" as the goal of self-ideal, the goal of superiority, and the goal of overpowering others. See note 5 for Spinoza's view on striving and overcoming as documented by Tillich (1952/2000). Also see our discussion of self-affirmation and ambivalence in Chapter 8 and Chapter 1, note 22. Bazzano (2006) believes that Adler's contribution to ethics in psychology, although started from a Kantian approach, was atypically reconciled to Nietzsche's notion of the will to power. We believe that the will to power in the context of Individual Psychology is related to the creative power in our innate longing for perfection and the resultant overcoming.

    Adlerians' uses of will to power, however, were rather disconcerted. It was often referred to as the guiding fiction of personal power of the individual. Adler used the term as characteristic of the neurotic. For example, Adler stated, "*We wish to point out the absolute primacy of the will to power, a guiding fiction* which asserts itself the more forcibly and is developed the earlier, often precipitously, the stronger the inferiority feeling of the organically inferior child comes to the foreground" (Adler, 1956, p. 111).

14. Tillich (1952/2000, p. 32). Also see Chapter 8, note 21.
15. Weatherhead as quoted in Savage and Nicholl (2003, p. 55).
16. Adler (1979, pp. 305–306). "Individual Psychology wants to train fellow men; it must therefore prove its fellowship in its dealing with the erring. Only in this spirit can the erring individual be won for cooperation; only in this way is it possible to give him a clear understanding of his mistaken style of life. The healing process must begin with winning the erring human child for cooperation."
17. Lewis (1961/1976, pp. 42–44). Yang (2009) observing the grief of the divorced and the widowed, wrote: "In the midst of grief and suffering, there appears a connection to a deeper understanding and longing: I want to be whole again. Hidden in the feeling of deprivation is truly the desiring for the wholeness. I began to wonder, is it possible that our grief of death is only a reflection in the mirror of the life we are longing for."
18. Gomes (1952/2000, xxi).
19. W. R. Miller (1999) pointed out that to accept means to take, seize, or catch according to its Middle English root.
20. Beecher and Beecher (1966, p. 125).
21. See note 14, p. 156. Tillich stated: "The polarity of participation and individualization determines the special character of the courage to be ... If both poles are accepted and transcended the relation to being itself has the character of faith." Also see note 5 and Chapter 8, note 23.
22. See note 3. Within the framework of positive psychology, hope is described together with optimism and future mindedness as family of strengths that represent a positive stance toward the future (Seligman, 2002, pp. 156–157). Other definitions and constructs of hope include the concept that hope can only exist in the face of despair as a way of coping; hope is a concept that allows an individual movement toward a goal; and hope is a way of thinking and believing that is goal directed and produces routes to desired goals with the motivation to use those routes. Hope is both a cognition and an emotion. Having a sense of hope is in the affective domain, and yet acting on hope requires motivation and a plan that is actively carried out (Blagen & Yang, 2008). Also see Snyder (1994, 2000), Snyder and Lopez (2000), and Godfrey (1987).

23. Lewis as quoted in Yang (2009).
24. Virginia Tech Convocation [Producer]. (2007, April 17).
25. Templeton (1999). Agape, which originated in Christian spirituality, has been regarded as the underlying principle found in most world religions. For example, the passage of "You shall love your neighbor as yourself" in Matthew 22:39 parallels the Confucian teaching "love your enemies," or to "love without thought of return."
26. Beecher and Beecher (1966, p. 96).
27. Watts (1992, 1996, 2000).
28. 1 Corinthians 13:4–8. The NIV Topical Study Bible, New International Version (1989).
29. W. I. Miller (2000).
30. See notes 3, 22, and 29.
31. Serenity prayer used in Alcoholics Anonymous and in 12-step programs.

Chapter 10

1. Cheever (2004, p. 43). A passage from a letter Bill Wilson wrote to his boyhood and lifetime best friend, Mark Whalon, in 1951.
2. As this book is intended for both professional facilitators as well as those who are interested in self-enhancement and helping others, we have chosen to use the term *courage facilitators* to represent the readership of Part III of the book.
3. Sonstegard and Bitter (2004). Facilitators who are capable of self-help are outgoing, self-confident, relaxed, firm, and responsible (Manaster & Corsini, 1982, p. 154). The facilitator would possess the traits of an ideal Adlerian as the following (based on Sonstegard, Dreikurs, & Bitter, 1983).
    - Emotionally—Strong, warm, friendly, caring, courageous, good-humored, and positive.
    - Behaviorally—Quick, alert, paces properly, competent.
    - Cognitively—Knowledgeable, intuitive, clear thinking, keen.
4. See note 3. The authors recounted the background and development of *The Question*: "Adler used to ask his clients, 'What would you be like if you were well?' Dreikurs adapted what came to be known in Adlerian circles as 'The Question' in the following manner: 'What would you be doing if you didn't have these symptoms or problems?' or 'How would your life be different if you didn't have these symptoms or problems?' (p. 70).
5. Milliren and Wingett (2004).
6. See note 3, p. 78. This question was originally designed by Powers and Griffith to elicit personal goals in counseling process.

7. In discouragement, we see an individual's style of life coming up short on courage and social feeling. Adlerians believe that discouragement (or lack of courage), more or less, provides safeguards for our fictive self-esteem that only seeks to reach a hidden goal of perfection. The creative power enables individuals to escape life's demands by the manifested symptoms, excuses, aggression, distance seeking, anxiety, or exclusion tendency (Adler, 1956). Dreikurs observed four goals in discouraged children and their behaviors: attention seeking, power contest, hurting back as hurt is perceived, and withdrawal from tasks where failures are expected.

    Adler (as quoted in Stein & Edwards, n.d.) stated:

    > All symptoms of neuroses and psychoses are forms of expression of discouragement. Every improvement comes about solely from encouraging the sufferer. Every physician and every school of neurology is effective only to the extent that they succeed in giving encouragement. Occasionally, a layman can succeed in this also. It is practiced deliberately only by Individual Psychology.

8. Based on note 3, pp. 77–79. Questions of work and the first question of "to be" were by Losoncy (2004); second question on "to be" was by Palmer (1999); and questions on spiritual belonging was by W. R. Miller (1999, p. 189).
9. Lingg and Wilborn (1992, p. 65).
10. Milliren, Evans, and Newbauer (2006, p. 116). Similarly, Carns and Carns (1998) reviewed the literature on encouragement and found that encouragement can be defined as a set of skills, a condition of becoming, and a process of facilitating an outcome. The definition of encouragement is challenging because it is, "partially what one does and partially what one does not do" (Azoulay as quoted in Cheston, 2000, p. 298). To Carlson, Watts, and Maniacci (2006) encouragement is both an attitude and a way of being with others that is also part of our lifestyle development.
11. Dinkmeyer and Losoncy in Cheston (2000). Eckstein (2006), in his discussion of encouragement, stated, "Many philosophers and psychologists contend that there are only two basic human emotions: love and fear. Encouragement communicates caring and movement toward others (love); conversely, discouragement often results in lowered self-esteem and alienation from others (fear)."

    Eckstein's approach of relating encouragement to the "quiet power" and the Rogerian "actualizing tendency" suggests the possibility that encouragement is conceptually connected to the existential concept of the will to power, and the Taoist "feminine" (yin) side of courage. Thought of encouragement as "the ability to perceive a spark of divinity in others and then to act as a mirror that reflects that goodness to them "provides a spiritual connotation of courage being a virtue that, when realized, mutually cultivates other virtues or characteristics in relationships." Also see Dinkmeyer and Eckstein (1996).

12. The presentation of socially useful and socially useless attitudes in the form of conceptual oppositional pairs are apparent in Adlerian literature such as Adler (1927/1992) and Beecher and Beecher (1966).
13. See note 3.
14. See note 10.
15. Miller (2000). See discussions in Chapter 9 about agape love as the common denominator of social interest and humanistic conditions of change.
16. See note 3, pp. 69 and 71.
17. See note 3 for the assessment of life tasks, early recollection, and family constellation. Also see Adler (1931/2003) about dreams.
18. Adler (1956, p. 329) indicated that only by guessing can we see the individual's movement as the individual is not aware of how he or she sees or resolve problems and overcome of difficulties. Adler also referred to this "guessing" of intuition as a gift of an artist:

    > Each individual always manifests himself as unique, be it thinking, speaking, or acting. We are always dealing with individual nuances and variations. It is partly due to the abstractness and limitations of language that the speaker, reader, and listener must have discovered the realm between the words in order to gain a true understanding of and the proper contact with the partner. (p. 194)

19. Prochaska and DiClemente (1982).
20. For comprehensive account of Adlerian techniques in counseling and psychotherapy, see Carlson and Slavik (1997).
21. The $B = \{S \rightarrow R\}$ and $B = \{S \rightarrow YOU \rightarrow R\}$ formula are based on Losoncy, L. E. (2004).
22. Excerpted from Dreikurs, R., Grunwald, B. B., & Pepper, F. C. (1982). *Maintaining sanity in the classroom* (2nd ed., pp. 30–31). New York: Harper & Row.
23. This activity is contributed by Mark Blagen based on Blagen, M. T., & Yang, J. (2009).

Epilogue

1. The NIV Topical Study Bible, New International Version. (1989).

References

Adler, A. (1956). *The Individual Psychology of Alfred Adler: A systematic presentation in selections from his writings* (H. L. Ansbacher & R. R. Ansbacher, Eds.). New York: Harper & Rowe.
Adler, A. (1964). *Social interest: A challenge to mankind.* New York: Capricorn Books.
Adler, A. (1979). *Superiority and social interest: A collection of later writings* (3rd rev. ed., H. L. Ansbacher & R. R. Ansbacher, Eds.). New York: Norton.
Adler, A. (1927/1992). *Understanding human nature.* Chatham, NY: Oneworld Publications. (Original work published 1927)
Adler, A. (2003). Critical Considerations on the meaning of life. In H. T. Stein (Ed.) & G. L. Liebenau (Trans.), *The collected clinical works of Alfred Adler* (Vol. 5, pp. 176). Bellingham, WA: Classical Adlerian Translation Project. (Original work published in 1924)
Adler, A. (2003). *The meaning of life.* In H. T. Stein (Ed.) & G. L. Liebenau (Trans.), *The collected clinical works of Alfred Adler*, Vol. 5, (p. 176). Bellingham, WA: Classical Adlerian Translation Project. (Original work published 1931)
Adler, A. (2006a). Fundamentals of individual psychology. In S. Slavik & J. Carlson (Eds.), *Readings in the theory of Individual Psychology* (pp. 33–43). New York: Routledge/Taylor & Francis Group.
Adler, A. (2006b). How the child selects his symptoms. In S. Slavik & J. Carlson (Eds.), *Readings in the theory of Individual Psychology* (pp. 243–255). New York: Routledge/Taylor & Francis Group.
Alcoholics Anonymous (3rd ed.). (1976). New York: Alcoholics Anonymous World Services.
Andreas, C., & Andreas, S. (1989). *Heart of the mind.* Boulder, CO: Real People Press.
Ansbacher, H. L. (2006). The relationship of Dreikurs' four goals of children's disturbing behavior to Adler's social interest–activity typology. In S. Slavik & J. Carlson (Eds.), *Readings in the theory of Individual Psychology* (pp. 257–264). New York: Routledge/Taylor & Francis Group.

Bass, M. L., Curlette, W. L., Kern, R. M., & McWilliams, A. E., Jr. (2006). Social interest: A meta-analysis of a multidimensional construct. In S. Slavik & J. Carlson (Eds.), *Readings in the theory of Individual Psychology* (pp. 123–150). New York: Routledge/Taylor & Francis Group.

Bazzano, M. (2006, May). *Who is the other? Social interest and interdependence in Adler and Zen Buddhism*. Paper presented at North American Society of Adlerian Psychology Conference, Chicago.

Becker, G. D. (1997). *The gift of fear and other survival signals that protects us from violence*. New York: Dell.

Beecher, W., & Beecher, M. (1966). *Beyond success and failure*. Marina del Rey, CA: DeVoss & Company.

Beecher, W., & Beecher, M. (1981). *The sin of obedience*. Richardson, TX: The Beecher Foundation.

Beecher, W., & Beecher, M. (1983). *Parents on the run*. Marina del Rey, CA: DeVoss & Company.

Bellah, R., Madsen, R., Sullivan, W. M., Swider, A., & Tipton, S. M. (1985). *Habits of the heart: Individualism and commitment in American life*. Los Angeles: University of California Press.

Brendtro, L., Brokenleg, M., & Bockern S. V. (1992). *Reclaiming youth at risk: Our hope for the future*. Bloomington, IN: National Educational Service.

Bettner, B. L., & Lew, A. (1996). *Raising kids who can*. Newton Center, MA: Connections Press.

Blagen, M. (2008). *The best kept secret: Adler's influence on A.A.* Manuscript in preparation.

Blagen, M. T. and Yang, J. (2009, April 18). Courage and hope as factors for client change: Important cultural implications and spiritual considerations. Retrieved from American Counseling Association Website: http://counselingoutfitters.com/vistas/vistas08/Blagen.htm

Bloch, D. P., & Richmond, L. (2007). *Soul work: Finding the work you love, loving the work you have*. Palo Alto, CA: Davies-Black Publishing.

Blustein, D. L. (2006). *The psychology of working. A new perspective for career development, counseling, and public policy*. Mahwah, NJ: Lawrence Erlbaum Associates.

Butler, L. H. (2000). *A loving home caring for African American marriage and families*. Cleveland, OH: The Pilgrim Press.

Careles, R. A., Darby, L., & Cacciapaglia, H. M. (2007). Using motivational interviewing as a supplement to obesity treatment: A stepped-care approach. *Health Psychology, 26*, 369–374.

Carlson, J., Kurato, W. T., Ng, K., Ruiz, E., & Yang, J. (2004). A multicultural discussion about personality development. *The Family Journal, 12*, 111–121.

Carlson, J., & Slavik, S. (Eds.). (1997). *Techniques in Adlerian psychology*. New York: Taylor & Francis.

Carlson, J., Watts, R., & Maniacci, M. (2006). *Adlerian therapy: Theory and practice*. Washington, DC: American Psychological Association Books.

Carns, M. R., & Carns, A. W. (1998). A review of the professional literature concerning the consistency of the definition and application of Adlerian encouragement. *The Journal of Individual Psychology, 5*, 72–89.

Chang, I. (2004). *The Chinese in America: A narrative history*. New York: Penguin.

Cheever, S. (2004). *My name is Bill: Bill Wilson—His life and the creation of Alcoholic Anonymous.* New York: Simon & Schuster.
Cheston, S. E. (2000). Spirituality of encouragement. *The Journal of Individual Psychology, 56,* 296–304.
Cleary, T. (1989). *The book of balance and harmony.* San Francisco: North Point.
Dahlsgaard, K., Peterson, C., & Seligman, M. E .P. (2005). Sacred virtue: The convergence of valued human strengths across culture and history. *Review of General Psychology, 9,* 203–213.
Dewey, E. A. (1984). The use and misuse of emotions: Individual psychology. *Journal of Adlerian Theory, Research, and Practice, 40,* 184–195.
Diller, J. V. (1999). Cultural diversity. A primer for the human services. New York: Brooks/Cole.
Dinkmeyer, D., Jr., & Carlson, J. (2001). *Consultation: Creating school-based interventions* (2nd ed.). Philadelphia: Taylor & Francis.
Dinkmeyer, D., & Eckstein, D. (1996). *Leadership by encouragement* (Trade ed.). Boca Raton, FL: CRC Press.
Dixon, P. N., & Strano, D. A. (2006). The measurement of inferiority: A review and directions for scale development. In S. Slavik & J. Carlson (Eds.), *Readings in the theory of Individual Psychology* (pp. 365–373). New York: Routledge/Taylor & Francis Group.
Dreikurs, R. (1958). *The challenge of parenthood* (3rd ed.). New York: Duell, Sloan, & Pearce.
Dreikurs, R. (1970). The courage to be imperfect. In Alfred Adler Institute (Ed.), *Articles of supplementary reading for parents* (pp. 17–25). Chicago: Alfred Adler Institute.
Dreikurs, R. (1971). *Social equality: The challenge of today.* Chicago: Adler School of Professional Psychology.
Dreikurs, R. (1989). *Fundamentals of Adlerian psychology.* New York: Greenberg.
Dreikurs, R., Grunwald, B. B., & Pepper, F. C. (1982). *Maintaining sanity in the classroom* (2nd ed.). New York: Harper & Row.
Dreikurs, R., & Soltz, V. (1964). *Children: The challenge.* New York: Hawthorn.
Eckstein, D. (2006). *Four directions and the seven methods of encouragement.* Workshop delivered at Governors State University, University Park, Illinois.
Eckstein, D. (in press). *Relationship repair: Activities for counselors working with couples.* El Cajon, CA: National Science Press.
Eckstein, D., & Cooke, P. (2005). The seven methods of encouragement for couples. *The Family Journal: Counseling and Therapy for couples and Families, 13,* 320–350.
Eckstein, D., & Kern, R. (2002). *Psychological fingerprints: Lifestyle assessment and interventions* (5th ed.). Dubuque, IW: Kendall/Hunt.
Edgar, T. E. (2006). The creative self in Adlerian psychology. In S. Slavik & J. Carlson (Eds.), *Readings in the theory of Individual Psychology* (pp. 107–110). New York: Routledge/Taylor & Francis Group.
Erikson, E. H. (1964). *Insight and responsibility.* New York: W. W. Norton.
Evans, P. D., & White, D. G. (1981). Towards an empirical definition of courage. *Behaviour Research and Therapy, 19,* 419–424.

Evans, T. D., & Milliren, A. P. (1999). Open-forum family counseling. In R. E. Watts & J. Carlson (Eds.), *Interventions and strategies in counseling and psychotherapy* (pp. 135–160). Levittown, PA: Accelerated Development.

Frankl, V. (1984). *Man's search for meaning.* New York: Washington Square Press. (Original work published 1946)

Fromm, E. (2006). *The art of loving.* New York: HarperCollins. (Original work published 1956)

Furtmuller, C. (1979). Alfred Adler: A biological essay. In H. L. Ansbacher & R. Ansbacher (Eds.), *Superiority and social interest* (pp. 309–423). New York: Norton & Company.

Gardiner Lord, H. (1918). *The psychology of courage.* Boston: John W. Luce & Company.

Gibran, K. (1923/2005). *The Prophet.* 2001. New York: Alfred A. Knopf.

Glasser, W. (2005). *Treating mental health as a public health problem. A new leadership role for the helping professions.* Chatsworth, CA: William Glasser, Inc.

Godfrey, J. J. (1987). *A philosophy of human hope.* Dordrecht, Germany: Martinus Nijhoff.

Gomes, P. J. (2000). Introduction. In P. Tillich, *The courage to be* (pp. xi–xxxiii). New Haven, CT: Yale University Press. (Original work published 1952)

Grunwald, B. B., & McAbee, H. V. (1985). *Guiding the family: Practical counseling techniques.* Muncie, IN: Accelerated Development Inc.

Hall, D. T. (1976). *Careers in organizations.* Glenview, IL: Scott Foresman.

Hall, D. T. (1986). Breaking career routines: Midcareer choice and identity development. In D. T. Hall & Associates (Eds.), *Career development in organizations* (pp. 120–159). San Francisco: Jossey-Bass.

Hall, D. T. (2002). *Careers in and out of organizations.* Thousand Oaks, CA: Sage Publications.

Hall, D. T., & Mirvis, P. H. (1996). The new protean career: Psychological success and the path with a heart. In D. T. Hall (Ed.), *The career is dead—long live the career: A relational approach to careers* (pp. 15–45). San Francisco: Jossey-Bass.

Hall, D. T., & Moss, J. E. (1998). The new protean career contract: Helping organizations and employees adapt. *Organizational Dynamics, 26*(3), 22–37.

Jobs, S. (2005, June 12). Commencement address given at Stanford University, CA. Retrieved May 10, 2007, from *Stanford Report,* http://news-service.stanford.edu/news/2005/june15/jobs-061505.html

Johansen, T. M. (2006). The four goals of misbehavior: Clarification of concepts and suggestions for future research. In S. Slavik & J. Carlson (Eds.), *Readings in the theory of Individual Psychology* (pp. 231–242). New York: Routledge/Taylor & Francis Group.

Kortman, K., & Eckstein, D. (2004). Winnie-the-Pooh: A "honey-jar" for me and for you. *The Family Journal, 12*(1), 67–77.

Krakauer, J. (1996). *Into the wild.* New York: Anchor Books.

Lewis, C. S. (1976). *A grief observed.* New York: Bantam. (Original work published 1961)

Lewis, C. S. (1988). *The four loves.* New York: Harcourt Brace & Company. (Original work published 1960)

Lewis, C. S. (1996). *Problems of pain.* New York: HarperCollins. (Original work published 1940)
Lin, Y. (1959). *From pagan to Christian.* Cleveland, OH: The World Publishing Company.
Lin, Y. (1996). *The importance of living.* New York: William Morrow. (Original work published 1937)
Lingg, M., & Wilborn, B. (1992). Adolescent discouragement: Development of an assessment instrument. *Individual Psychology, 48,* 65–78.
Lombard, D. N., Melchior, E. J., Murphy, J. G., & Brinkerhoff, A. L. (2006). The ubiquity of life style. In S. Slavik & J. Carlson (Eds.), *Readings in the theory of Individual Psychology* (pp. 207–216). New York: Routledge/Taylor & Francis Group.
Lopez, S. J., & Snyder, C. R. (Eds.). (2003). *Positive psychology assessment: A handbook of models and measures.* Washington, DC: American Psychological Association.
Losoncy, L. E. (2000). *Turning people on: How to be an encouraging person.* Sanford, FL: InSync Communications LLC and InSync Press.
Losoncy, L. E. (2004, June). *Building the encouraging school district, agency or corporation.* Preconference workshop presented at the North American Society of Adlerian Psychology 52nd Annual Conference, Myrtle Beach, SC.
Manaster, G., & Corsini, R. J. (1982). *Individual psychology: Theory and practice.* Itasca, IL: F.E. Peacock.
Mansager, E. (2003). Adlerian psychology and spirituality in critical collaboration. In A.M. Savage & S. W. Nicholl (Eds.), *Faith, hope and charity as character traits in Adler's individual psychology: With related essays in spirituality and phenomenology* (pp. 61–69). Lanham, MD: University Press of America.
Mansager, E. (2008). Affirming lesbian, gay, bisexual, and transgender individuals. *The Journal of Individual Psychology, 64,* 123–136.
May, G. G. (1988). *Addiction and grace: Love and spirituality in the healing of addictions.* San Francisco: Harper.
May, R. (1969). *Love and will.* New York: W. W. Norton & Company.
May, R. (1975). *The courage to create.* New York: W. W: Norton & Company.
May, R. (1977). *The meaning of anxiety* (Rev. ed.). New York: W. W. Norton & Company.
May, R. (1983). *The discovery of being.* New York: W. W. Norton & Company.
McBrien, R. J. (2004). Expanding social interest through forgiveness. *Journal of Individual Psychology 60,* 408–419.
McGee, R., Huber, J., & Carter, C. L. (1983). Similarities between Confucius and Adler. *Journal of Adlerian Theory, Research & Practice, 39,* 237–246.
Messer, M. (1995). *The components of our character.* Chicago: Anger Institute.
Messer, M. (2001). *Managing anger: A handbook of proven techniques.* Chicago: Anger Institute.
Miller, R. B. (2005). Suffering in psychology: The demoralization of psychotherapeutic practice. *Journal of Psychotherapy Integration, 15,* 299–336.
Miller, W. I. (2000). *The mystery of courage.* Cambridge, MA: Harvard University Press.
Miller, W. R. (1999). *Integrating spirituality into treatment: Resources for practitioners.* Washington, DC: American Psychological Association.

Miller, W. R. (2000). Rediscovering fire: Small interventions, large effects. *Psychology of Addictive Behaviors, 14,* 6–18.

Milliren, A. (in press). Relationships: Musings on the ups, downs, and the side-by-sides. In D. Eckstein (Ed.), *Relationship repair: Activities for counselors working with couples.* EI Cajon, CA: National Science Press.

Milliren, A. & Wingett, W. (2004). *Conversations in the style of Alfred Adler: RCI/TE.* Unpublished workshop handout. West Texas Institute for Adlerian Studies, Odessa, TX.

Milliren, A., & Clemmer, F. (2006). Introduction to Adlerian psychology: Basic principles and methodology. In S. Slavik & J. Carlson (Eds.), *Readings in the theory of Individual Psychology* (pp. 17–32). New York: Routledge/Taylor & Francis Group.

Milliren, A., Clemmer, F., Wingett, W., & Testerment, T. (2006). The movement from "felt minus" to "perceived plus": Understanding Adler's concept of inferiority. In S. Slavik & J. Carlson (Ed.), *Readings in the theory of Individual Psychology* (pp. 351–363). New York: Routledge/Taylor & Francis Group.

Milliren, A., Evans, T. D., & Newbauer, J. F. (2006). Adlerian counseling and psychotherapy. In D. Capuzzi & D. Gross (Eds.), *Counseling and psychotherapy* (pp. 91–132). Upper Saddle River, NJ: Pearson.

Milliren, A., & Harris, K. (2006). Work style assessment: A Socratic dialogue from the 100 Aker Wood. *Illinois Counseling Association Journal, 154*(1), 4–16.

Milliren, A., Messer, M. H., and Reeves, J. (n.d.). "Reflections" on character. Unpublished manuscript.

Milliren, A., & Wingett, W. (2004). *Conversations in the style of Alfred Adler: RCI/TE.* Unpublished workshop handout. West Texas Institute for Adlerian Studies, Odessa, TX.

Milliren, A., & Wingett, W. (2005, January). *Socratic questioning: The art of precision guess work.* Workshop presented at Chicago Adlerian Society, Chicago, IL.

Milliren, A., Yang, J., Wengett, W., & Boender, J. (2008). A place called home. *The Journal of Individual Psychology, 64*(1), 83–95.

Mitchell, K. E., Levin, A. S., & Krumboltz, J. D. (1999). Planned happenstance: Constructing unexpected career opportunities. *Journal of Counseling and Development, 77,* 115–124.

Moran, L. (1987). *The anatomy of courage.* Gordon City Park, NY: Avery Publishing Group Inc.

Mosak, H. H. (1977a). Life style assessment: A demonstration focused on family constellation. In H. H. Mosak (Ed.), *On purpose* (pp. 198–215). Chicago: Adler School of Professional Psychology Chicago.

Mosak, H. H. (1977b). The tasks of life I. Adler's three tasks. In H. H. Mosak (Ed.), *On purpose* (pp. 93–99). Chicago: Adler School of Professional Psychology Chicago.

Mosak, H. H. (with Dreikurs, R.). (1977c). The tasks of life II. The fourth life task. In H. H. Mosak (Ed.), *On purpose* (pp. 100–107). Chicago: Adler School of Professional Psychology Chicago.

Mosak, H. H. (with Dreikurs, R.). (1977d). The tasks of life III. The fifth life task. In H. H. Mosak (Ed.), *On purpose* (pp. 108–117). Chicago: Adler School of Professional Psychology Chicago.

Mosak, H. H., Brown, P. R., & Boldt, R. M. (1994). Various purposes of suffering. *The Journal of Adlerian Theory, Research & Practice, 50*, 142–148.

Nelson, J., Erwin, C., Brock, M. L., & Hughes, M. L. (2002). *Positive discipline in the Christian home: Using the bible to develop character and strengthen moral values.* Roseville, CA: Prima Publishing.

Oswald, R. F. (2008). The invisibility of lesbian and gay parents and their children within Adlerian parenting materials. *The Journal of Individual Psychology, 64*, 246–251.

Palmer, P. J. (1997). *The courage to teach: Exploring the inner landscape of a teacher's life.* San Francisco: Jossey-Bass.

Palmer, P. J. (1999). *Let your life speak: Listening for the voice of vocation.* San Francisco: Jossey-Bass.

Peterson, C., & Seligman, M. (2004). *Character strengths and virtues: A handbook and classification.* Oxford: Oxford University Press.

Phillips, C. (2004). *Six questions of Socrates: A modern-day journey to discovery through world philosophy.* New York: W. W. Norton & Company.

Prochaska, J. O., & DiClemente, C. C. (1982). Transtheoretical therapy: Toward a more integrative model of change. *Psychotherapy: Theory, Research, and Practice, 19*, 276–288.

Putnam, D. (1997). Psychological courage. *Philosophy, Psychiatry, & Psychology, 4*, 1–11.

Rachman, S. J. (1990). *Fear and courage* (2nd ed.). New York: W. H. Freeman and Company.

Rawls, J. (2005). *A theory of justice: Original edition.* Cambridge, MA: Harvard University Press.

Rollnick, S., & Miller, W. R. (1995). What is motivational interviewing? *Behavioral and Cognitive Psychotherapy, 23*, 325–334.

Sandberg, D., & Yang, J. (2006). Spirituality at work: Usefulness of analogy and questions [Special issue]. *Illinois Counseling Association Journal, 154*, 17–28.

Savage, A. M., & Nicholl, S. W. (2003). *Faith, hope and charity as character traits in Adler's individual psychology: With related essays in spirituality and phenomenology.* Lanham, MD: University Press of America.

Savickas, M. (2005, April). *Career construction theory.* Paper presented at American Counseling Association Annual Convention, Atlanta, GA.

Seligman, M. E. P. (2002). *Authentic happiness: Using the new positive psychology to realize your potential for lasting fulfillment.* New York: Free Press

Slagle, D. M., & Gary, M. J. (2007). The utility of motivational interviewing as an adjunct to exposure therapy in the treatment of anxiety disorders. *Professional Psychology: Research and Practice, 38*, 329–337.

Snyder, C. R. (1994). *The psychology of hope: You can get there from here.* New York: Free Press.

Snyder, C. R. (Ed.). (2000). *Handbook of hope: Theory, measurement, and applications.* San Diego, CA: Academic Press.

Snyder, C. R., & Lopez, S. J. (Eds.). (2000). Handbook *of positive psychology.* New York: Oxford University Press.

Sonstegard, M. A., & Bitter, J. R. (2004). *Adlerian group counseling and therapy: Step-by-step.* New York: Brunner-Routledge.

Sonstegard, M. A., Dreikurs, R., & Bitter, J. R. (1983). The teleoanalytic group counseling approach. In G. Gazda (Ed.), *Basic approaches to group psychotherapy and group counseling* (3rd ed., pp. 507–551). Springfield, IL: Charles Thomas.

Sori, C., & McKinney, L. (2005). Free at last! Using scriptural affirmation to replace self defeating thoughts. In K. B. Helmeke & C. F. Sori (Eds.), *The therapist's notebook for integrating spirituality in counseling: Homework, handouts, and activities for use in psychotherapy* (pp. 223–234). New York: Haworth Press.

Stein, H. T. (n.d.). *Classical Adlerian quotes: Overcoming difficulties.* Retrieved November 21, 2004, from Alfred Adler Institute of San Francisco, http://ourworld.compuserve.com/homepages/hstein/qu-over.htm

Stein, H. T. (1991). Adler and Socrates: Similarities and differences. *Individual Psychology, 47*(2), 241–246.

Stein, H. T., & Edwards, M. E. (n.d.). Classical Adlerian theory and practice. Retrieved November 21, 2004, from Alfred Adler Institute of San Francisco, http://ourworld.compuserve.com/homepages/hstein/theoprac.htm. (Reprinted from *Psychoanalytic Versions of the Human Condition: Philosophies of Life and Their Impact on Practice*, by P. Marcus & A. Rosenburg, Eds., 1998, New York University Press.)

Stoltz, K. (2006, March). *The work life task: Integrating Adlerian ideas into career development counseling.* Workshop presented at Illinois Career Development Association, Glen Ellyn, IL.

Stone, M. H. (2006). The creative self. In S. Slavik & J. Carlson (Eds.), *Readings in the theory of Individual Psychology* (pp. 93–105). New York: Routledge/Taylor & Francis Group.

Stone, M. H. (2008). Immanuel Kant's influence on the psychology of Alfred Adler. *The Journal or Individual Psychology, 64,* 21–36.

Suprina, J. S., & Lingle, J. A. (2008). Overcoming societal discouragement: Gay recovering alcoholics' perceptions of the Adlerian life tasks. *The Journal of Individual Psychology, 64*(2), 193–212.

Templeton, J. (1999). *Agape love: A tradition found in eight world religions.* West Conshohocken, PA: Templeton Foundation Press.

Terner, J. R., & Pew, W. L. (with Aird, R. A.). (1978). *The courage to be imperfect: The life and work of Rudolf Dreikurs.* New York: Hawthorn Books.

Tillich, P. (2000). *The courage to be.* New Haven, CT: Yale University Press. (Original work published 1952)

Virginia Tech Convocation [Producer]. (2007, April 17). [Video file]. Cassell Coliseum, Blacksburg, VA. Remarks partially transcribed by Yang, J. Video archived by the Virginia Tech Athletics Internet Services Web site: http://www.hokiesports.com/convocation.html

Walton, F. X. (1996a). *How to get along with oneself.* Paper presented at the annual meeting of the Florida Society of Adlerian Psychology.

Walton, F. X. (1996b). *An overview of a systematic approach to Adlerian family counseling.* Paper presented at University of Texas Permian Basin Spring Counseling Workshop, Odessa, TX.

Walton, F. X. (1996c). *Questions for brief life style analysis.* Paper presented at University of Texas Permian Basin Spring Counseling Workshop, Odessa, TX.

Walton, F. X. (1998). Use of the most memorable observation as a technique for understanding choice of parenting style. *The Journal of Individual Psychology, 54*(4), 487–494.

Watts, R. E. (1992). Biblical agape as a model of social interest. *Individual Psychology, 48,* 35–39.

Watts, R. E. (1996). Social interest and the core conditions: Could it be that Adler influenced Rogers? *Journal of Humanistic Education and Development, 34*(4), 165–170.

Watts, R. E. (2000). Biblically based Christian spirituality and Adlerian psychotherapy. *The Journal of Individual Psychology, 56,* 316–328.

Way, L. (1962). *Adler's place in psychology.* New York: Collier Books.

Wingett, W., & Milliren, A. (2004). Lost? Stuck? An Adlerian technique for understanding the individual's psychological movement. *Journal of Individual Psychology, 60,* 265–276.

Wolf, M. S. (2002). *Philosophical and spiritual implications of Adlerian psychology.* Retrieved November 21, 2004, from Alfred Adler Institute of San Francisco, http://ourworld.compuserve.com/homepages/hstein/theoprac.htm

Wolfe, W. B. (1957). *How to be happy though human.* London: Penguin Books. (Original work published 1932)

Yang, J. (1991). Career counseling of Chinese American women: Are they in limbo? *The Career Development Quarterly, 39,* 350–359.

Yang, J. (1992). *Chilly campus climate: A qualitative study on white racial identity development attitudes.* (ERIC Document Reproduction Service No. ED352576).

Yang, J. (1998). *Understanding worldviews in the 21st century: Global and postmodern perspectives.* Paper presented at the 7th International Counseling Conference: Relating in a Global Community, Sydney, Australia.

Yang, J. (2006, July). *The color of courage: Unlearning oppression in the work place.* Workshop presented at National Career Development Association, Chicago.

Yang, J. (in press). Inconsolable secret. In D. Eckstein (Ed.), *Relationship repair: Activities for counselors working with couples.* El Cajon, CA: National Science Press.

Yang, J., & Drabik, G. (2006, May). *The courage for harmony: On suffering and social interest.* Workshop presented at North American Society of Adlerian Psychology, Chicago.

Yang, J., & Milliren, A. P. (2004, October). *Yin, yang, and social interest: In search of laws of social living across cultures.* Paper presented at the North American Society of Adlerian Psychology 52nd Annual Conference, Myrtle Beach, SC.

Yang, J., & Waller, B. (2005). Transforming a work life into a life work [Special issue]. *Illinois Counseling Association Journal, 153,* 21–31.

Yearley, L. H. (1990). *Mencius and Aquinas: Theories of virtue and conceptions of courage.* Albany: State University of New York Press.

Zeig, L. B. (2009). For better and for worse or until the multicultural problems do us part: The challenges of multicultural adaptation to couples. In D. Eckstein (Ed.), *Relationship repair: Activities for counselors working with couples.* El Cajon, CA: National Science Press.

The Authors

Julia Yang, PhD, NCC, is a Professor of Psychology and Counseling at Governors State University, University Park, Illinois. She received her doctoral degree in counseling from Ohio State University. Yang was an elementary school art teacher and a vocational rehabilitation counselor prior to her career in counselor education. She has taught at Pennsylvania State University at Shippensburg, and California State University at Fresno. She was the founding chair for the counseling department at National Kaohsiung Normal University in Taiwan. She has published journal articles and book chapters about counseling at-risk youths, and spiritual and cultural aspects of work. She is a proud "Adlerian" single mother of two who share the value of education, music, friendship, family, social equality, and God.

Al Milliren, EdD, NCC, BCPC, is Associate Professor of Psychology and Counseling at Governors State University in University Park, Illinois. He also serves as an adjunct faculty member for the Adler School of Professional Psychology in Chicago. Milliren holds a doctorate degree from University of

Illinois, Champaign. He is a past president and holds the diplomate in the North American Society of Adlerian Psychology. He has been a junior high school counselor and teacher, an elementary school counselor, and a professor of counseling at Illinois State University and at the University of Texas of the Permian Basin. He is a national and international workshop presenter, and has authored or coauthored several books and numerous articles on Adlerian psychology and related topics. He is a proud father of three.

Mark T. Blagen, PhD, CAC, is an Assistant Professor in the Human Services Department at University of Illinois, Springfield, where he teaches and coordinates graduate courses in the Alcohol and Substance Abuse Counseling concentration. He received his PhD from Old Dominion University, Norfolk, Virginia. Blagen had a career in the Navy for 21 years. He is a Certified Addictions Counselor. He has been an assistant professor of psychology and counseling at Regent University, Virginia, and an associate professor of counseling at Adams State College, Colorado. His primary research interests include defining the spiritual dimensions of addiction recovery, understanding the therapeutic factors of 12-step recovery, understanding the nature of natural recovery, and investigating the relationship of purpose in life and the use of alcohol and other drugs. Blagen holds a special interest in working with the Taiwanese Aborigine population. He is a proud father of two children.

Author Index

A

Adler, A., xix, xv, xvii, xx, xxi, xxii, 4, 6, 8, 10, 11, 12, 13, 14, 15, 17, 18, 19, 20, 25, 26, 27, 28, 32, 37, 54, 55, 58, 59, 63, 67, 68, 71, 75, 89, 90, 91, 93, 94, 96, 97, 100, 101, 104, 115, 119, 120, 123, 125, 130, 139, 140, 147, 152, 166, 171, 175, 177, 192, 193, 216, 217, 218, 219, 220, 221, 222, 223, 224, 225, 227, 229, 231, 232, 233, 234, 235, 236, 237
Agenlian, M., 226
Aird, R.A., 244
Andreas, C., 224, 229
Andreas, S., 224, 237
Ansbacher, H.L., 18, 218, 224, 227, 237, 240
Ansbacher, R.R., 18, 218, 224, 227, 237, 240

B

Bass, M.L., 180, 238
Bazzano, M., 221, 232, 238
Becker, G.D., 218, 238
Beecher, M., 122, 227, 233, 234, 236, 238
Beecher, W., 122, 227, 233, 234, 236, 238
Beethoven, L.V., 9, 189, 224
Bellah, R., 217, 238

Bettner, B.L., 167, 238
Bitter, J.R., 29, 83, 223, 225, 228, 229, 234, 243, 244
Blagen, M.T., xvi, 218, 229, 233, 236, 238, 248
Bleurer, J., 237
Bloch, D.P., 226, 238
Blustein, D.L., 238
Bockern, S.V., 196, 198, 238
Boender, J., 165, 170, 242
Boldt, R.M., 232, 243
Brendtro, L., 196, 198, 238
Brett, C., 224
Brinkerhoff, A.L., 230, 241
Brock, M.L., 227, 243
Brokenleg, M., 196, 198, 238
Brown, P.R., 232, 243
Butler, L.H., 227, 238

C

Cacciapaglia, H.M., 238
Careles, R.A., 238
Carlson, J., xvi, xxiii, 77, 145, 154, 180, 193, 219, 227, 235, 236, 237, 238, 239, 240, 241, 242, 244
Carns, A.W., 235, 238
Carns, M.R., 235, 238
Carter, C.L., 220, 241

249

Chang, I., 84, 228, 238
Cheever, S., 229, 234, 239
Cheston, S.E., 235, 239
Cleary, T., 228, 239
Clemmer, F., 193, 219, 242
Confucius, xx, 11, 89, 90, 220, 222, 228
Cooke, P., 221, 239
Curlette, W.L., 180, 238

D

Dahlsgaard, K., 220, 239
Darby, L., 238
Dermer, S., 227
Dewey, E.A., 230, 239
DiClemente, C.C., 236, 243
Diller, J.V., 228, 239
Dinkmeyer, D., 77, 154, 164, 227, 235, 236, 239
Dinkmeyer, D. Jr., 77, 154, 164, 227, 235, 236, 239
Dixon, P.N., 219, 239
Drabik, G., 232, 245
Dreikurs, R., xvii, 27, 29, 68, 74, 76, 78, 92, 154, 166, 177, 192, 217, 219, 222, 223, 224, 227, 228, 229, 230, 234, 235, 236, 237, 239, 242, 244

E

Eckstein, D., 144, 164, 165, 195, 221, 235, 236, 239, 240, 242, 245
Edgar, T.E., 239
Edison, T.A., 9
Edwards, M.E., 229, 235, 244
Erikson, E.H., 239
Erwin, C., 227, 243
Evans, T.D., 218, 221, 230, 235, 239, 240, 242

F

Frankl, V., 218, 232, 240
Fromm, E., 227, 240
Furtmuller, C., 231, 240

G

Gardiner Lord, H., 12, 218, 240
Gary, M.J., 243
Gibran, K., xxiii, 226, 240

Glasser, W., 217, 240
Godfrey, J.J., 233, 240
Gomes, P.J., 230, 233, 240
Grunwald, B.B., 154, 167, 227, 236, 239, 240

H

Hall, D.T., 225, 226, 240
Harris, K., 165, 242
Helmeke, K.B., 214, 244
Holbrook, R., 93, 229
Huber, J., 220, 241
Hughes, M.L., 227, 243

J

Jobs, S., 225, 240
Johansen, T.M., 227, 240

K

Kant, I., 231
Keller, H., 9
Kern, R.M., 144, 180, 238, 239
Kortman, K., 165, 240
Krakauer, J., 230, 240
Krumboltz, J.D., 226, 242
Kurato, W.T., 145, 238

L

Lao Tzu, 53
Lawson, J., 85, 228
Levin, A.S., 226, 242
Lew, A, 167, 238
Lewis, C.S., 120, 226, 227, 232, 233, 234, 240, 241
Liebenau, G. L., 237
Lingg, M., 235, 241
Lingle, J.A., 225, 227, 228, 229, 244
Lombard, D.N., 230, 241
Lopez, S.J., 233, 241, 243
Losoncy, L.E., 47, 142, 164, 212, 226, 235, 236, 241

M

Madsen, R., 217, 238
Maniacci, M., 219, 235, 238
Mansager, E., 227, 231, 241

Maslow, A., 217, 218, 224
May, G.G., 110, 217, 218, 219, 225, 230, 241
McAbee, H.V., 154, 167, 240
McBrien, R.J., 232, 241
McCandless, C., 111, 230
McGee, R., 220, 241
McKinney, L., 214, 244
McWilliams, A.E., 180, 238
Melchior, E.J., 230, 241
Messer, M., 202, 209, 230, 241, 242
Miller, R.B., 236, 241
Miller, W.I., 218, 234, 241
Miller, W.R., 149, 229, 233, 235, 241, 242, 243
Milliren, A., xv, 7, 163, 165, 170, 175, 183, 193, 195, 209, 219, 221, 228, 230, 234, 235, 242, 247
Milliren, A.P., 189, 194, 240, 245
Mirvis, P.H., 225, 226, 240
Mitchell, K.E., 226, 242
Moran, L., 218, 242
Mosak, H.H., 29, 224, 225, 227, 230, 231, 232, 242, 243
Moss, J.E., 225, 240
Murphy, J.G., 230, 231, 241

N

Nelson, J., 227, 243
Newbauer, J.F., 221, 230, 235, 242
Ng, K., 145, 238
Nicholl, S.W., 233, 241, 243
Nietzsche, F., 12, 13, 119, 220, 231, 232
Nightingale, F., 47
NIV Topical Study Bible, 227, 234, 237

O

Obama, B., 215
Osipow, S., 225
Oswold, R.F., 243

P

Palmer, P.J., 225, 229, 235, 243
Pepper, F.C., 154, 236, 239
Peterson, C., 220, 239, 243
Pew, W.L., 228, 244
Phillips, C., 3, 218, 243

Prochaska, J.O., 236, 243
Putnam, D., 218, 243

R

Rachman, S.J., 243
Rawls, J., 228, 243
Reeves, J., 209, 242
Richmond, L., 226, 238
Rollnick, S., 149, 243
Ruiz, E., 145, 238

S

Sandberg, D., 226, 243
Savage, A.M., 233, 241, 243
Savickas, M., 226, 243
Schopenhauer, A., 119
Schweitzer, A., 47
Seligman, M.E.P., 220, 233, 239, 243
Slagle, D.M., 243
Slavik, S., 180, 193, 236, 237, 238, 239, 240, 241, 242, 244
Snyder, C.R., 233, 241, 243
Soltz, K., 76, 154, 227, 239
Sonstegard, M.A., 29, 83, 223, 225, 228, 229, 234, 243, 244
Sori, C.F., 214, 244
Spinoza, B., 219, 231, 232
Stein, H.T., 140, 217, 224, 229, 235, 237, 244
Stoltz, K., 226, 244
Stone, M.H., 231, 244
Strano, D.A., 219, 239
Sullivan. W.M., 217, 238
Suprina, J.S., 225, 227, 228, 229, 244
Swider, A., 217, 238

T

Templeton, J., 234, 244
Terner, J.R., 228, 244
Testerment, T., 193, 219, 242
Tillich, P., 119, 121, 231, 232, 233, 240, 244
Tipton, S.M., 217, 238

V

Vaihinger, H., 231

W

Waller, B., 226, 245
Waltz, G., 237
Watts, R.E., 124, 219, 234, 235, 238, 240, 245
Way, L., 28, 220, 224, 228, 245
Weatherhead, 233
White, D.G., 218, 239
Wilborn, D., 235, 241
Wilson, B., 93, 223, 234, 239
Wingett, W., 165, 170, 174, 175, 183, 189, 193, 194, 219, 234, 242, 245
Wolf, M.S., 245
Wolfe, W.B., 31, 106, 219, 225, 227, 229, 230, 245

Y

Yang, J., xv, 5, 30, 91, 145, 165, 170, 225, 226, 228, 229, 232, 233, 234, 236, 238, 242, 243, 244, 245, 247
Yearlry, L.H., 220, 245
Yep, R., 237

Z

Zeig, L.B., 83, 84, 228, 245

Subject Index

A

Abilities, xx, 18, 21, 28, 29, 100, 157, 205, 223
Academic failure, 77
Acceptance, 4, 10, 56, 57, 59, 65, 83, 90, 94, 107, 122, 124, 125, 130, 150, 196, 197, 198. *See also* What is, is
  defined, 121
  of unpleasant reality, 101, 203
Act as if, 47, 91, 93, 124, 125, 196
  hope, 124, 125
  live life as if, 93
  neurotic fiction, 106
  schizophrenia, 106
Action stage, 137
Addictions, 32, 92, 93, 105, 106, 108
Affection, 54, 65, 70
  and courage, 11
  and parental training, 76
  vs. love, 53
Affectional orientation, 60, 61
Affectlessness, xvii
Affirmation, 65, 119, 150. *See also* Harmony
  affirmation coupons, 160–161
  in agape marriage, 59, 124
  and ambivalence, 109–111
  and anxiety, 101, 199
  and being part of, 28, 33, 95
  constructive, 125, 164
  and freedom, 103
  and harmony with self, 4, 10, 14, 29, 95, 132
  self-, 10, 86, 110, 119, 121, 149, 231, 232
  spiritual, 174, 213–214
Affirmative action, 41
African Americans, 84, 98, 114, 215
Agape, xx, 8, 13, 53, 54, 56, 90, 130, 133, 222. *See also* Love
  and acting as if, 124, 125
  biblical roots, 124, 234
  as common denominator of Individual Psychology, Confucianism, and humanist psychology, 123
  as core value of world religions, 123
  and courage, 123–125
  defined, 11, 53
  effects on friendship, 70
  effects on love, 56
  as facilitator of change, 124, 135, 236
  in family context, 80, 81
  as gift love, 123

as love thy neighbor, 64
in marriage, 58, 59
as perfect love, 64–65
and same-sex love, 62
social interest as expression of, 65, 91, 124, 125, 135, 236
in social relationships, 124
training of, 124
vs. Eros, 57, 59, 70, 81, 104
Alcoholics Anonymous, xx, xxiv, 92, 93, 94, 105, 197, 229, 234
sayings, 93, 125
Alienation, 77
Ambiguity, xviii, 217
Ambivalence, xviii, 43, 62, 64, 84, 89, 95, 110, 111, 140, 217, 232
and affirmation, 189–191
and anxiety, 110
constructive, 138, 149, 150
and freedom, 110
Anger, 75, 102, 104, 199, 201, 202. *See also* Goal seeking behaviors
appropriate, 101, 203
and belonging, 85, 88
Annoyance. *See* Goal seeking behaviors
Anxiety, 5, 6, 44, 101, 149, 199, 202, 207, 213, 225, 235. *See also* Fear
and ambivalence, 110
as apprehension of social living, 6
in children, 73, 74, 76
existential, 117
function of, 5
and inferiority, 6, 219
as non-aggressive trait, 97
as weapon of aggression, 219
Apathy, 21, 23, 68, 86, 133, 215
cure of, xix–xx
as 20th-century problem, xvii
Aptitude, xix, 28, 29
for cooperation, 18
for social living, 21, 231
As if. *See* Act as if; Live life as if
Assessment
courage, 152–153
lifestyle, xxi, 135, 136, 138, 144, 180, 181
strength, 131, 138, 141, 173, 193
Assessment techniques, Adlerian, 136, 138
At-risk behaviors, 77

Attention seeking, 74, 75, 132, 166, 193, 235
Attitude modification, 138, 142–143
Attitudes, xvii
and belonging, 85, 91
better than/less than, 41, 85, 116
characteristic, 44, 143
constructive, 68
defined, 142
evaluative, 28, 29
fear-based, 32
and friendship, 70
life movement and, 133
and marriage, 56, 58
no, yes, yes/but, 95–101, 102, 112, 130, 133, 134, 194
oppositional, 68
relational, 124
replacing negative with positive, 199–202
replication of parental, 79
socially useful, xx, xxi, 10, 12, 67, 153, 236
spiritual, 116, 121–122, 125, 231
and temperament types, 78
toward life, 29, 31, 40, 46
toward social interest, 80, 196
toward work, 44, 165
useless, 68, 80, 133, 153, 164, 236
yang and yin, 146, 147
Authenticity, 12, 70, 96, 111, 124, 154, 189
Authority, defying, 9
Avoidance, 10, 32, 62, 152, 189. *See also* Inadequacies

B

Ba gua, 145, 146
Balance, 91, 111. *See also* Harmony
cooperation/contribution, 21
and direction of change, 147
and golden mean, 90
life tasks, 96
present needs/demands of evolution, 21
and social usefulness, 9
subjective power/social responsibility, 96
worksheet, 147
yin/yang, 146, 147

Be, courage to, xxi, 79, 95, 100, 108, 110, 111, 119, 163, 196, 233
Being
    as existential task, 28–29
    power of, 119 (*See also* Will to power)
Belonging, xviii, xix, 9, 10, 26, 32, 38, 43, 51, 54, 74, 83, 94, 152, 163, 164, 199
    and addiction, 92
    and Alcoholics Anonymous, 94
    and better than/less than attitudes, 7
    in children, 166
    in circle of courage, 197
    as component of character, 101, 204
    effect of fear on, 6
    and equality, xx, 4
    as existential task, 28–29, 31
    as foundation for self-worth, 196
    genesis of, 215
    and harmony with world, 132
    and individual inferiority, 77
    obstacles to social equality, 89
    and obstacles to social equality, 7
    prejudice, discrimination and, 85
    problems and opportunities, 198
    problems of, 83–86
    and self-transcendence, 125
    spiritual, 115, 132, 235
    task of, 95
    via contribution and cooperation, xix, 65
Birth order, 81, 138, 178
    and attitudes toward life, 70–71
    and career choice, 44
    and dethroned feeling, 71
    facilitation exercise, 143–145
    and family constellation, 70–73
    first born children, 71, 72, 144, 145, 188
    last born children, 71, 144
    middle children, 69, 71, 144
    only children, 71, 72, 144, 159, 178, 181, 182
    psychological, 44, 71, 73, 134, 136, 144
    as psychological investigation tool, 136
    and sibling competition, 71, 72, 144
    as socio-gram, 72
Bisexual orientation, 60. *See also* Same gender love; Transgender love

Bravery, 12
Brotherhood, 92, 221. *See also* Agape; Keen keeping; Social interest
Buddhism, 13, 220, 221. *See also* Zen Buddhism

C

Care, xviii, xix, 13, 37, 107, 133, 216
    in marriage, 63
Career construction theory, 44–46, 226
Century
    of apathy, xvii
    of fear, xviii
    of psychology, xviii
Change, 43, 51, 99, 112, 124
    behavior *vs.* attitude, 143
    childhood, 158, 159
    components of facilitating, 135
    conditions of, 4, 137
    courage for, 134
    creation of, 24
    decision to, 175
    direction of, 147
    eight directions of, 145, 146
    and encouragement, 163
    fear of, 5
    in harmony, 138, 145–147
    incessant, 43
    as learning process, 130
    positive personal, 173
    in St. Francis' prayer, 125
    stages of, 137, 138
Character, 100
    components, 101, 148, 203–209
CHARACTERistics, 101, 131, 138, 170
Chi, 13. *See also* Life force
Children at risk, 77
Children's goal seeking behaviors. *See* Goal seeking behaviors
Chinese, 13, 145–146
Christianity, xx, 92, 117, 123, 221, 231, 232, 234
Clumsiness, 104
Collective courage, 122
Collective inferiority, xx, 41–42, 85, 86, 91, 95
Collective wellness, 123
Common sense, xxii, 13, 25, 77, 89, 90, 133, 139, 221. *See also* Social interest

Subject Index

Common weal, 15, 26, 68, 90, 94, 220, 221, 222
Communication, 12 road blocks, 210–212
Community feeling, 135. *See also* Social interest
   A.A. as example, 92, 94, 197, 229
   and agape, xx, 54, 64, 123
   and communal value of suffering, 83, 88
   Confucius' concept, 11–12
   and courage, 25–26
   and courage to work, 46–47
   as cure of apathy, xix–xx, 215
   and mental health, 17
Comparison, 96, 103, 133
   and competition, 4, 32, 47, 87, 91, 102, 134, 145
   motivation by fear, 102
Compassion, 10, 11, 26, 89, 152, 209
   as co-requisite to courage, 26
   for justice, 13
Compensation, 5, 8–10, 38, 98, 152, 188
   bad, 9, 32, 152, 153
   good, 9, 10, 14, 133, 134, 152, 153
   for lack of intimacy, 57
   neurotic, 10
   over-, 9, 133, 152, 153, 188, 194
   under-, 9, 133, 152, 153, 194
Competition, 4, 32, 47, 87, 91, 102, 134, 145
   absence of equality with, 70, 87
Confidence, 11, 79, 83, 94, 149, 152, 153, 192, 200
   and belongingness, 86
   as component of character, 101, 204
   as conjunctive emotion, 103
   relationship to courage, 11
   role in agape family, 81
Conformity, 20, 56, 102, 133. *See also* Fear; Parenting
   in eros love, 70
Confucius of the West, 11, 220
Consequences, 210. *See also* Punishment
   in democratic parenting methods, 82
   instead of fear, 81
   in life movement/attitudes, 133
   in love and social relationships, 124, 130
   natural and logical, 47, 76, 79, 87, 137
   resulting from choices, 207
Constructive optimism, 125. *See also* Act as if
Consultation, with parents and teachers, 138, 154–156
Contemplation stage, 137
Contribution, 13, 14, 18, 19, 20–21, 22, 24, 26, 27, 38, 47, 65, 67, 68, 87, 91, 119, 133, 134, 145, 156, 223. *See also* Evolution
   belonging and, xix
   and Chinese world view, 147
   as conjunctive emotion, 103
   in Individual Psychology model of courage, 5
   and process of healing, 120
   and social interest, 21, 100
Cooperation, 13, 14, 18, 19–20, 22, 24, 26, 27, 38, 47, 65, 67, 68, 87, 91, 106, 119, 133, 134, 143, 145, 156, 208, 222, 223, 233
   in agape love, 70
   and character components, 101
   in Chinese world view, 147
   as conjunctive emotion, 103
   courage as precondition of, 10, 32, 152
   and courage to work, 38
   in family, 80
   in healing process, 120
   in Individual Psychology model of courage, 5
   and marriage, 55, 57, 227
   negative, 22, 23
   in relationship, 54
   and social equality, 87
   and social interest, 18, 21, 69, 100
   in social relationships, 124
   style of, 28, 165
Coping method, 4
Cosmic inferiority, 116
Cosmic social feeling, xxi, 94, 116
Courage
   of acceptance, 121, 122
   acts of, 4, 14
   to agape love, 123–125
   alllied characters, 10, 152
   art of facilitating, 129
   assessment, 152–153
   to be, 95–112
   to belong, 83–94
   Chinese character for, 13

co-requisites, 10, 32, 152
defined, 3–4
facilitation tools, xvi, 138–198
of facilitators, 129–130
of faith, 121
for family and friendship, 67–82
to heal, 118–121
to hope, 122
for imperfection, 4, 9, 87
in-spite-of, 5, 10, 111, 119, 120, 121, 122
as intrinsic life force, 4
to love, 53–65
meaning of, 14, 132, 163
as mental strength, 14
Native American circle of, 196, 197
as perseverance, 10, 12
as precondition of cooperation, 10, 32, 152
as psychological construct, 4, 14
as psychological muscle, xvi, 14, 133
psychology of, 3, 4
of recovery, 92–94, 218
and religion for democracy, 92
of self-affirmation, 10, 86, 110, 111, 119, 121, 149, 230, 231, 232
as social function, xvii, 25
to spiritual wellbeing, 113–125
as striving power, 121
Tillich on, 119, 121, 233
to transcend suffering, 120
as virtue, xx, 3, 4, 13, 14, 121, 218, 220, 236
to work, 37–51
Creative power, xx, 14, 231, 232, 235. *See also* Will to power
and agape, 91
and children's goal-seeking behaviors, 75, 235
to overcome inferior feelings, 71
and self-preservation, 7
as striving force, 8, 115, 119, 121
and urge to overcome, 13
and will to power, 119
Creativity, 21, 31, 111, 133, 157
chaos as precondition to, 132
Culture and experiences. *See also* Belonging; Social equality
African American, 84, 98, 114
Chinese American, 84
cross-cultural marriage, 83–84

cultural deprivation, 85
Hispanic, 41
Native American, 88, 196–197
racial violence, 84
Whiteness, 39, 41, 84, 98

D

Daydreams. *See* Dreams
Defeat, 6, 9, 22, 116, 121, 168, 198
fear of, 74
suffering and, 117
Democracy. *See also* Social equality
and equality, 87
at home, school, and work, 89
religion for, 92
Depression
and belonging, 85
as sideshow, 32
as socially acceptable anger, 104
Despair, xxiv, 109, 110, 117, 119, 173, 233
courage in spite of, 5, 10, 119
risking, 112
Determination stage, 137
Detours, 96, 97, 98, 107, 118
as evasion of life tasks, 31–33
as sideshows, 112, 143
Diagonal model, 100, 120. *See also* Social interest
Directed reflection, 138, 147–149, 155
examples, 203–209
Discouragement, 84, 131, 132, 163–164, 193, 235
as consequence of evading life tasks, 96, 97
as enabler of life movement, 134
and fictional beliefs, 40
and neuroses, 106, 135
replacing with courage, 200–201
and same-gender relationships, 62
Disney characters, strength and stress responses, 165–166
Displayed inadequacy, 74, 193
Dispositions, 29
Distance
from community feeling, 112
hesitation at, 107
and self-interest/social interest disparity, 96, 97
to world front, 69
Do the next right thing, 93

Dreams, 8, 112, 130, 142
  day and night, 134, 156, 158, 159
DSM-IV classification system, 230

E

E-5 group, 138, 156–163
Early recollection, xxi, 45, 46, 55, 136, 173, 174, 176, 189–192, 218, 226, 236. *See also* Psychological investigation
Emotional injury. *See* Suffering
Emotional strength, 12
Emotionally unemployed, 56
Emotions. *See also* Feeling
  anger, 75, 85, 88, 101, 102, 104, 199, 202, 203
  annoyance, 75, 104
  conjunctive feelings, 102, 103, 112, 152, 153, 174
  depression, 32, 85, 104
  disgust, 102, 104, 218
  disjunctive feelings, 102, 103, 112, 153, 174, 175, 213, 214, 228
  envy, 59, 97, 102, 124
  grief, 104, 120, 233
  hopelessness, 9, 75, 78, 85, 102, 104, 199
  hostility, xvii, 6, 56, 68, 74, 87, 97, 102, 104, 105, 133, 143, 215
  hurt, 64, 74, 75, 104, 167, 193, 201
  isolation, xviii, 9, 32, 54, 56, 102, 106, 117, 122
  joy, 92, 102, 103, 111, 122, 125
  loneliness, 56, 83, 102, 105, 133
Encouragement, 154, 156, 157, 164, 173, 179, 193, 235, 236
  in agape family, 81
  as attitude, 133, 235
  defined, 132–133, 163, 226
  in friendship, 69
  and life movement, 133, 134
  parental use of, 75–76, 81
  practical use of, 131–134
  as psychological concept, 133
  self-, 87, 174, 175
  as set of skills, 133, 235
  in social relationships, 124
  as spiritual concept, 221
  tactics of, 134, 163
  in the workplace, 47

Endurance, 4, 10, 147, 173
Energy, 12, 13, 14, 23, 110, 145, 146, 201. *See also* Creative power
  ba gua uses, 145, 146
  as Chi, 13
  of opposites, 145
Enthusiasm, 12
Equality (social), 89, 156, 157, 200, 205
  absence of, 87
  and affirmative action, 41
  approach in Individual Psychology, 228
  and belonging, xx, 83
  as component of character, 101
  as conjunctive emotion, 103
  courage of, 86–89, 87
  and democracy, 67, 87
  and equal opportunity fallacy, 41
  in family, 62
  in friendship, 70
  and gender, 57
  and life movement, 133
  obstacles to, 86
  in parenting, 82
  in social relationships, 124, 135
  Taoist principles of, 90–91
  training for, 87
  vs. competition and comparison, 87
  vs. dominance and control, 63
Eros, 55, 56. *See also* Love
  defined, 53
  disappointments in, 64
  effects on family, 81
  effects on friendship, 70
  effects on love, 57
  effects on marriage, 59
  motivation by fear, 54
  vs. agape love, 57
  vs. sexuality, 226
Eternal destiny, 115. *See also* Striving
Eternal recurrence, 13, 119. *See also* Will to power
Eternity, 24, 91, 222, 232
Evaluative attitude, 11, 18, 21, 28, 29, 153
Evasion, xxi, 5, 39, 106. *See also* Sideshows
  and addiction, 92
  and bad compensations, 32
  of friendship task, 68
  of life tasks, 4, 31–33
  of reality, 107, 230

Evolution, 26, 147, 231. *See also* Contribution
    social, 30, 147
Existential courage, 122, 221
Existential psychology, xx, 218
Existential tasks, xvii
    being and belonging, 28–29, 95
    and harmony with self/universe, 27, 113
    as life tasks, xxi, 4
    and will to power, 12, 119
Existentialism, 121, 231
    and will to power, 231, 236

F

Facilitation, xxi, 137
    of change, 135
    of courage, xvi
Facilitators, 134
    courage, 129–130, 136, 234
    psychological disclosure by, 136–137
    psychological investigation by, 135–136
    relationship considerations, 135
    reorientation tasks, 137–138
Faith, 122, 213, 221, 231, 233
    and agape love, 124
    in agape marriage, 59
    and courage, 13, 121–122
    C.S. Lewis on, 120
    and social usefulness, 114
    and suffering, 232
    Tillich on, 121, 233
Fake it till you make it, 93
Family
    agape family, 81
    courage for, 67–81
    encouragement in, 75–76
    eros family, 81
    and fitness for marriage, 63
    Greek meaning, 53, 70
    in Individual Psychology model, 5
    in life task map, 30
    and parental favoritism, 72
    parenting methods and mistakes, 76
    primary purpose, 80
    and sibling competition, 72, 80
Family constellation, 44
    birth order and, 70–73
    as socio-gram, 72

Fear, xvii, 5–6, 39
    as basic human emotion, 235
    behaviors motivated by, 32
    in children and family relationships, 74, 77
    Christian thoughts on, 213, 214
    of defeat, 104
    as disjunctive feeling, 102, 103, 153
    effect of agape love on, 64
    in eros friendship, 70
    and eros love, 54
    in eros marriage, 59
    of failure, 4, 5, 109, 112, 199
    and fictional goals, 9
    in Individual Psychology model, 5
    of inferiority, 85
    in life movement diagram, 133
    in marriage, 58
    of mistakes, 5, 8
    and neurotic traits, 107
    and "no" attitudes, 95–98
    of not being good enough, 9
    of not belonging, 74
    operating from, xvii, 6, 134
    and oppression, 88
    overcoming for democracy, 89
    in parenting, 80, 82
    as precondition to courage, 218
    and protean careers, 42–44
    and punishment, 79, 80
    of rejection, 4, 5, 9, 32
    relief from, 207
    as root of all neuroses, 105
    as safeguard, 10
    and same-gender love, 61
    and sideshow activities, 7
    of undeserved success, 199
    as unfounded anxiety, 5
    of unknown, 118
    usefulness of, 5, 6
    vs. agape love, 123
    vs. courage, xviii–xix
    workplace, 40, 41
Feeling. *See also* Emotions
    community feeling, xx, 17, 23, 25–26, 46–47, 54, 64, 92, 94, 197, 215, 229
    conjunctive feelings, 102, 103, 112, 152, 153, 174
    danger, 5, 136

disjunctive feelings, 102, 103, 112, 152, 153, 174, 175, 213–214, 228
goal of protection, 5
at home, xvii, 17, 19, 25, 26, 94
inferiority, 4, 5, 6–8, 9, 10, 12, 17, 39–40, 41–42, 75, 80, 87, 95–96, 107, 115, 116, 122, 201, 219
social feeling, 17, 18, 32, 80, 102, 116, 135, 235
Fictional beliefs/life goals, 8, 87. *See also* Act as if
compensation, 9
as compensation, 9
fictional finalism, 231
neurotic fiction, 106
perfection, 40
in schizophrenia, 106
superiority, 9
FLAVER model, 131, 170. *See also* Socratic questions
Forgetfulness, 104
Fortitude, 12
Friends, making, 69–70, 132
Friendship, 67
agape love as inspiration for, 70, 123
agape love in, 124
and attitudes toward society, 70
defined, 226
family as preparation for, 67
as Greek *philia*, 53, 67
as life task, 5, 27, 28, 30
making friends, 69–70
preparatory role of, 63
Socratic questions, 132

G

Gemeinschaftsgefühl, 17, 18, 25, 26, 31, 33
Getting even, 74, 104
Global humanity, xx–xxi, 89, 222
GLTB. *See* Marriage; Same gender love; Transgender love
Goal disclosure, 75, 136, 166–169. *See also* Guessing
hidden reason technique, 166
Goal seeking behaviors
in children, 73–77
in teens and adults, 77–78
God, as goal of perfection, 14
Golden mean, 90. *See also* Balance; Harmony

Grief Observed, A, 120
Guessing, 137, 169, 236. *See also* Goal disclosure

H

Happenstance, 47, 50, 51
Happiness, xviii, 191, 215, 230. *See also* Harmony
Adler on, 90
as goal, xx
health as construct of, xix
and meaning of life, xix
Harmony
balanced give and take in, 91
and becoming whole again, 119–120
change in, 145–149
Christian view, 13
with collective courage and self-courage, 122
with community, 89–92
of complementary opposites, 91, 145–146, 232
in Confucian thought, 90
and courage for community feeling, 89
as criteria of good compensation, 9
in Eastern philosophy, 13, 145–146
and healing process, 120, 125
with one's instrument, 22
with others and universe, 4, 5, 10, 14, 26, 27, 113
with self, 4, 5, 9, 10, 14, 27, 29, 95, 107–109, 132
social, 89, 91, 94
socratic questions, 132
and spiritual wellbeing, 113–114
and suffering, 119
in Taoist worldview, xx, 13, 90–91
and task of being, 29
and task of belonging, 29
Healing, 235
by acting as if, 125
attainment of, 120
courage for, 118–121
and education for ideal cooperation, 120
and *A Grief Observed*, 120–121
processes of, 120
Helplessness, 9, 106, 107, 198
Holy Spirit, 13
Home page, 169–172

Subject Index • 261

Homosexuality, 59. *See also* Intimacy; Same gender love; Transgender love
Honesty, 11, 12
Hope, 231
  AA example of, 93
  and agape love, 57, 64, 124
  as allied spiritual attitude to courage, 173
  as choice, 162, 173–175
  Christian perspective, 124, 213–214
  courage to, 122
  and living as if, 112, 125
  and self-transcendence, 122
  as way of coping, 233
  worksheet, 174, 213–214
Hopelessness, 9, 104. *See also* Goal seeking behaviors
  among Native Americans, 85
  and children's goal seeking behavior, 75
  and envy, 102
  as passive goal, 78
Hostility, xvii, 87, 215. *See also* Emotions; Neurotic traits
  defined, 104
  in Eros love, 56
  fear as hidden, 6
  and fictive perfection, 102
  neuroses as concealed, 105
  and "no" attitudes, 97, 133
  in parenting, 74
  as safeguarding strategy, 143
Hurt, 193, 201. *See also* Getting even
  and children's goal seeking behaviors, 74, 75
  in Eros love, 64
  and parenting, 76

I

Ichgebundenheit, 220. *See also* Self-boundedness
Identification, 26, 218
  capacity for, 19
  and cooperation, 19
Imperfection, 100
  courage for, xxiii, 4, 9, 87
  overcoming through creative power, 115
  worth despite, 147, 200, 208

In-spite-of, 100, 111, 119, 121, 122, 147, 200, 208
Inaction, 13, 91. *See also Wu-wei*
  action through, 122, 232
Inadequacies, 10
  overworking to compensate for, 40
  as safeguarding devices, 7
  as sideshow, 102
  in underworking individuals, 40
Individuation, 119. *See also* Self-affirmation
Industriousness, 12
Infantile attitudes, 102
  and Eros love, 56
InFEARiority, 5–6
Inferiority, 5, 6–8, 17
  and anxiety, 6
  collective, xx, 41–42, 85
  cosmic, 117
  courage as answer to, 10
  and creative power, 75
  and cult of personal greatness, 80
  in discouraged individuals, 4
  faith overcoming, 122
  feeling of, 116
  and goals of perfection, 96
  individual, xx, 39–40, 87
  neurotic traits due to, 107
  and norm of self-elevation, 95
  striving due to, 12
  and striving for superiority, 115
  vs. good enough, 201
Inferiority complex, 219
Insight, 49, 75, 121, 137, 176
  of happenstances, 50
  as means to end, 137
  through psychological disclosure, 135
  through Socratic questions, 130
Integrity, 12
Intimacy, 53, 55
  Adler on, 218
  agape love and, 123, 124
  contrasting effects of eros and agape love on, 104
  and demands of companionship, commitment, cooperation, 57
  and eros, 53
  as life task, xxi, 28
  as love task, 57
  poor candidates for, 63

in same-gender and transgender love, 59–62
and sex task, 58
and sexual roles, 54
as spiritual gift, 64
training for, 62–63

J

Joy
  as allied spiritual attitude to courage, 122, 125
  as expression of social feeling, 102
  God as source of, 111
Justice
  commitment to social, xvi
  to commonweal, 220
  Individual Psychology theory of, 228

K

Karma, 114, 225
Keen keeping, 223

L

Life force, 13, 14, 88, 91, 112, 116, 122, 147, 232. *See also* Creative power; Striving
  courage as, 4
Life movement. *See* Movement
Life style
  defined, 8
  in insecure children, 222
  mistaken beliefs or, 134
  mistaken sexual practices, 54
  translation to work style, 166
  as unity of action, emotion, thinking, 44
Life style interview, 138, 180–182
Life task map, 30
Life tasks, 174, 224. *See also* Unified personality
  Adler's, xxi
  assessment, 236
  bad compensation for, 9
  being and belonging, 29, 31, 95–112
  belonging, 83–94
  birth order and, 143–144
  and early recollections, 192
  evasion of, 31–33

existential, 29
friendship, 27
in Individual Psychology model, 5
keen keeping, 223
love, 28
map, 29, 30
psychological investigation tools, 136
self acceptance, 29
social relations, 28
Socratic questions, 132
spiritual wellbeing, 29, 113–125
work, 27
Lifestyle assessment, xxi, 180, 181. *See also* Assessment
Live life as if, 93
Live life as is, 93
Loss, 46, 112
  and courage to heal, 118–121
  fear of, 95
  and grief, 104
  A Grief Observed, 120–121
  and pain/suffering, 116
Love
  agape love, 11, 64–65
  as basic task, 27–28
  courage to, 53, 123–125
  defined, 53–54
  effects of eros and agape on, 57
  eros love and friendship, 53, 56, 70
  evasion of, 31–33
  Greek etymologies, 53–54
  infantile, 63
  as life task, 5
  in life task map, 30
  and marriage, 57–59
  and myth of romance, 55–57
  natural love, 53, 54, 65
  need love, 54, 64
  philia, 53
  and social interest, 58
  social relationships and agape, 124
  storge, 53
  training for, 62–64
  transgender and same-gender, 59–62
  vs. sex, 54

M

Main tent activities, 31, 33, 124, 133
  vs. sideshows, 7, 32
Maintenance stage, 137

Make-believe, 9. *See also* Fictional
    beliefs/life goals; Private logic
Marriage
    characteristics of agape love in, 124
    contracting out of fear *vs.* courage, 58
    and cooperation, 55, 56, 227
    cross-cultural, 83–84
    effects of eros and agape on, 59
    happiness in, 56, 57
    and myth of romance, 55–59, 63
    as partnership for the world, 55
    problems of love and, 57–59
    same gender and trans gender, 61, 62
    training for, 62–65
    trial marriage, 56
Me-centeredness, xviii
Meaninglessness, 6, 48, 96, 202
Medical model, *vs.* public health model, 217
Melancholia, 107
Mental health, xviii. *See also* Community feeling; Social interest
    Adler's theory of positive, 217, 224
    community feeling and, 17
    harmony as, 145
    horizontal and vertical axes, 22–25
    and life task map, 29–30
    measure of, 21–22
    social interest as measure of, 21, 65, 217
Misbehaviors
    autocratic responses to, 80
    goals of, 74–76, 167, 192–193
    hidden reasons for, 166
    as results of distorted as ifs, 231
Mistaken beliefs, 117, 134
Moods. *See* Emotions
Moral belief, 12
Most Memorable Moment tool, 187–188
Motivation scale, 194
Motivational interviewing, 149
Motives, 211
    intrinsic *vs.* extrinsic, 47
Movement. *See also* Striving; Will to power
    away from felt minus, 7, 102, 105, 156
    in courage, 4
    of creative power, 75
    destructive, 25
    development as, 145
    direction of, 15, 146
    encouraging, 103, 235
    forward, 6, 21, 102, 104, 121
    horizontal plane, 20
    life, 133, 134
        in children, 75
    life as, xx, 15, 115
    life attitudes and direction of, 134
    life movement, 133
    partaking in cosmic, 147
    psychology of, 183
    rejection, 102, 103
    in relation to social usefulness, 104
    from self-realization to self-actualization, 136
    as striving, 8
    Taoist view, 13
    towards life goals, 8, 96, 103, 132, 137, 230, 233
    towards perceived plus, 7, 105, 156
    trust only the, 192–194
    vertical plane, 20
    with yes attitudes, 120
Mutual respect, 47, 56, 57, 58, 59, 63, 68, 87, 102, 103, 104, 133, 135, 154, 164, 198, 208, 228
    as conjunctive emotion, 103
    cooperation and, 208
    and equality in relationship, 68
    in love inspired by agape, 56, 59
    in marriage, 57, 58
    in relationship, 135
    training for, 87

N

Native Americans, 88
    circle of courage, 196, 197
Natural love, 53
Nervous manifestations, 97
Neurosis. *See also* "No" attitudes; "Yes" attitudes
    characteristics, 106
    as concealed hostility, 105
    and discouragement, 106, 235
    evasion of life tasks through, 32
    as excuse for non-participation, 106
    fear as root of, 105
    and isolation, 106
    as subjective escape, 106
    as way of living, 230

Neurotic traits, 106, 107
"No" attitudes, 95–98, 102, 130, 133, 134
Normative ideal, 29–31

O

Open retreat, 107
Oppositional defiance, 77
Oppression, 61, 85, 215. *See also* Belonging
    collective superior attitudes as basis of, 116
    internalized, 61
    unlearning, 88
Organ inferiority, 107
Other directedness, 4, 37, 90, 131, 133
Overcoming, 3, 4, 15, 51, 98, 102, 105, 115, 136, 147, 231, 232
    goal of, 116
    natural desire for, 91
    striving as spiritual, 115
    as striving for perfection, 20, 220
    as striving for superiority, 8
Overcompensation, xx, 4, 9, 153, 188, 194, 225
Overeating, 22, 105

P

Pain. *See* Suffering
Pampering, 59, 74, 77, 80, 191
Paranoia, 107
Parenting, 78–81. *See also* Family
    autocratic, 82
    choice of style, 180
    common mistakes, 76
    democratic, 82
    efficient methods, 76
    modifying techniques, 188
    praise *vs.* encouragement in, 75
    private logic of, 187
    punishment in, 75, 76
    in same-gender and trans gender couples, 62
Participation, 109, 118, 119
    as characteristic of agape love, 124
    courage of, 10
    evading issues of social, 105
    making friends by, 69
    sexual choices away from social, 54
    in social relationships, 95
    vs. individuation, 233
    in work, 38
Passion, as aspect of courage, 11, 14, 121, 220
Perfection. *See also* Compensation; Striving
    goal of, xx, 9, 11, 13, 15, 91, 96, 115, 116, 118, 137, 235
Persevering, 4, 124
Phenomenological approach, 4
Plus gestures, 97
Positive psychology, xx, 218, 220, 233
Possessiveness, 57, 105
Postmodern ethics, 221
Power
    and children's goal seeking behaviors, 74
    as component of character, 101
    creative, xx, 7, 8, 9, 13, 14, 18, 44, 75, 91, 115, 116
    in eros marriage, 59
    fiction of, 97
    good compensation and sense of, 10
    in parenting, 76–77, 80
    quiet, 13
    relationships with higher, 62
    of silence, 24
    as socially useless goal, 78
    striving for, 104, 119
    transformative, in AA, 93
    unjust exercise of, 85
    will to, 12, 110, 119
Power differential, 42
Power struggle, 74, 104, 193
Pragmatic approach, 4, 222
Praise, 133. *See also* Punishment
    competition and desire for, 102
    encouragement *vs.*, 47, 75, 81, 164
    in eros family, 81
    work for, 107
Prayer, 50
    and participation in community/unity of life, 91, 92
    Serenity Prayer, 125, 234
Precontemplation, 137
Pregnancy, early, 77
Prejudice, 60, 85, 86, 88. *See also* Belonging
Private logic, 7, 8, 25, 87, 118, 136, 170, 171, 175. *See also* Most Memorable Moment tool

and children's goal seeking behaviors, 75, 77, 166
in parenting, 187
Problems, as opportunities, 47, 198
Processes of change, facilitating, 134–138
Progress not perfection, 93
Protean careers, 42–44
Psychological camouflage, 9
Psychological disclosure, 135, 136–137
Psychological investigation, xxi, 135–136, 137, 169
Psychological movement, 7, 26, 113, 175, 183, 231
Public health, xix
vs. medical model, 217
Punishment, 68, 75, 76, 102, 133, 136. *See also* Consequences; Praise
in autocratic parenting, 82
Biblical views of, 78–81
fear and, 64, 79, 80
vs. discipline, 77, 79
vs. natural/logical consequences, 47, 81, 87
Purposefulness, in children's goal seeking behaviors, 75

Q

Question, The, 130, 177, 234
Questions. *See* Socratic questions

R

Recognition reflex, 75, 166, 167. *See also* Children's goal seeking behaviors
Recollections. *See* Early recollection
Reconciliation, 53, 87
of opposites, 147
Record of Rites, The, 228
Recovery, courage of, 92–94
Relapse stage, 137
Relationship, 53
agape love in, 124
augmentative, 194, 195
cooperation in, 19, 22, 33
dependent individuals in, 56
eros love *vs.* agape love in, 54
facilitative, 129–139
manipulative/coercive, 194

parent-child, 53, 75–78
synergistic, 23, 195
Respect, 18, 47, 56, 57, 58, 59, 63, 68, 82, 86, 87, 102, 103, 104, 124, 133, 135, 154, 157, 164, 198, 208, 228
Respectful Curious Inquiry (RCI), 130, 170
Revenge, 74, 193
Rightness, 11
Roadmap, 114
Romance, myth of, 55–57

S

Safeguarding, 7, 8, 10, 12, 33, 39, 44, 77, 134, 142, 143, 164, 220, 235. *See also* Compensation; Fictional beliefs/life goals
Same gender love, 59–62, 67, 84, 218. *See also* Marriage
Schizophrenia, 107
as neurotic fiction, 106
Self-absorption, 116, 122
Self-affirmation, 10, 86, 110, 121, 149, 231, 232. *See also* In-spite-of
courage as, 119, 230
Self-boundedness, 220
Self-care, 29, 192
Self-destruction, 93, 205
and neurotic traits, 107
Self-elevation, 95, 143
Self-help, xx, 139
Self-ideal, 9, 12, 131, 232
Self-interest, 5, 51, 54
eros friendship and, 70
eros love and, 57
eros marriage and, 59
modifying to social interest, 4
Self-preservation, 4, 5, 7, 75, 116, 231
Self-psychology, xx
Self-regard, 13
Self-sabotage, 107
Self-sacrifice, 11
Self-will, 92
Self-worth, 20, 26, 37, 96, 129, 196
Selflessness, 4, 135
Serenity, 87, 101, 108, 208
Serenity prayer, 125, 234
Sex
conversion of, 54
eros love and, 57

266 • Subject Index

as expression of character, 54
as expression of isolation and timidity, 54
as intimacy, 54, 218
and masturbation, 54
uses and misuses, 54–55
Sexual competition, 58
Sexual orientation, 42, 60, 84, 88. *See also* Same gender love; Transgender love
Sideshows, xv, 7, 33, 80, 102, 112, 133, 143
as bad compensation, 32
as evasion of life tasks, 31
in marriage, 55
sexual, 54
Sin, 105, 125
Sleeplessness, 104, 107
Social adjustment, 115, 223. *See also* Overcoming
Social discouragement, 62, 84
Social equality, 156, 228
Adler's views on, xx
and belonging, 83
courage of, 86–89
obstacles to, 86
training for, 87
Social feeling, 12, 17, 18, 32, 80, 97, 102, 116, 129, 135, 235
Social ideal, xx, 14, 89
Social interest, xix, 17–19, 27, 28, 44, 217. *See also* Community feeling
AA approach and, 93
as ability, 18, 221
activating with encouragement, 134
agape family and, 81
and agape friendship, 70
agape love and, 57, 64, 65, 123, 236
agape marriage and, 59
as aptitude, 18, 221
assessing, 131, 170
and capacity for give and take, 21
career satisfaction and, 46
as character, 100
as community feeling, 25
and Confucian *ren*, 11, 89, 90
cosmic, xxi, 94
courage and, xx
as criterion for mental health, 217, 224
defined, xvi, 17–19

diagonal model, 100, 120
as evaluative attitude, 18
four types of activities, 79, 219
horizontal plane, 20
in Individual Psychology model, 5
as innate potential, 18
life task map and, 29, 30
mature love and, 58
as measure of mental health, 21
measuring by cooperation and contribution, 100
as movement, 26, 96
religious value of, 13, 221
replacing self-centeredness with, 202
and same gender love, 62
self interest *vs.*, 222
and sexual function, 55
as spiritual belonging, xxi
spiritual implications, 91
strategic model of, 124
teachability of, 130
training for, 18, 19
vertical plane, 20
vs. neuroses, 105
as what can be, 31
and willingness to contribute, 68
as willingness to contribute, 20
work in context of, 38
and "yes" attitudes, 122
Social masterfulness, 12
Social rejection, 62, 98
Social usefulness, 9, 26, 104, 108, 114, 116, 152
Socratic questions, xvi, xxi, xxiv, 72, 130–131, 132, 138, 139–142, 175, 181, 189, 194, 218, 226. *See also* FLAVER model; *Question, The*; Respectful Curious Inquiry (RCI)
Songs of Kabir, 113
Spirit, 13, 26, 213, 214
Spiritual attitudes, 116, 121–122, 125, 231
Spiritual belonging, xxi, 51, 65, 115, 132
Spirituality
Christianity, 117, 123, 221
Confucianism, xx, 11, 89, 90, 117, 220, 222
cosmic embeddedness, 29
as life task, 113–115

as the question, 49
subtasks, 113
Taoism, 90, 117
Zen Buddhism, xx
Stages of change, 137, 138
Strength assessment. *See* Assessment
Striving
 for agape love, 123
 for belonging, 83
 causes and elimination of, 117
 to collective wellness, 123
 and compensation, 9
 for cooperation, 222
 as courage to overcome, 115–116
 goal of, 115
 from incompletion to completion, 8
 inferiority as cause of, 115
 life movement as, 8
 for overcoming, 20
 for perfection, 12, 115, 220, 231
 for power and status, 25, 104, 119
 as spiritual overcoming, 115
 for superiority, 8, 12, 20, 115
 toward meaning and more life, 119
 toward perceived plus, 105
 towards eternal destiny, 115
 and will to power, 231
 for will to power, 12
Sub speice aegternitatis, 91, 222, 232
Substance abuse, 77
Success, criterion for, 17
Success formula, 44, 226
Suffering, 83, 116–118
 communal value of, 120
 courage to transcend, 120
 and divine grace, 232
 due to desire and attachment, 232
 in healing process, 120
 kinship in, 93
 as loss of meaning and purpose, 232
 and problems of being and belonging, 125
 and striving for more life, 119
Superiority. *See also* Striving
 fictional belief of, 87
 goal of, 6, 12, 20, 89, 104, 115, 164, 232
Symptoms
 children's selection of, 75
 neurotic, 104–107

T

Taoism, xx, 13, 90, 91, 117, 122, 145, 221, 232, 236
Teens at risk, 77
Temperament types, 78, 219
Training
 for community feeling, xix
 for courage, 218
 family, 87
 for love task, 62–64
 for parenting, 80
 parents' efficient and mistaken methods of, 76
 for social equality, 87
 for social interest, 18
Transgender love, 59–62, 218. *See also* Marriage
Trauma, 118

U

Undercompensation, xx, 4, 9, 152, 153, 194, 225
Unified personality, 115

V

Valor, 12
Venus, 226
Vigor, 12
Virginia Tech campus shooting, 123
Virtues, xx, 121
 Confucian, 220
 Plato's *Republic,* 220
 three, 220
Vitality, 12

W

What can be, 31
What is, is, 133, 221
Will to power, 12, 110, 119, 220, 231, 232, 233, 236
Will to seem, 220
Willfulness, 12, 13
Wisdom, xx, 11, 90, 121, 125, 147, 153, 216, 220, 221
Wishful thinking, 8, 54, 57, 102, 133
Wizard of Oz, 220

Work
- affirmative action issues, 41
- as basic task, 27–28
- best fit concept, 38
- career construction, 44–46
- and collective inferiority, 41–42
- and congruence, 44
- courage to, 37
- defined, 37–39
- encouraged workers, 46–48
- and equal opportunity fallacy, 85
- family constellation and, 44, 165–166
- and individual inferiority, 39–41
- and life style, 44
- and Protean career, 42–44
- sacredness of, 48–51

Wu-wei, 122

Y

Yang attitudes, 146, 147
"Yes" attitudes, 98–101, 120, 130, 133, 134, 194
Yin attitudes, 146, 147

Z

Zen Buddhism, xx, 221
Zest, 12

Lightning Source UK Ltd.
Milton Keynes UK
UKHW022027211119
354008UK00009B/249/P